WHEN STARS AND STRIPES MET HAMMER AND SICKLE

WHEN STARS AND STRIPES MET HAMMER AND SICKLE

The Chautauqua Conferences on
U.S.-Soviet Relations, 1985–1989

ROSS MACKENZIE

To Svétlanc and Marle
who by falling in love
united two great cultures.

Ross Mackenzie

06 - 25 - 06

UNIVERSITY OF SOUTH CAROLINA PRESS

© 2006 Ross Mackenzie

Published by the University of South Carolina Press
Columbia, South Carolina 29208

www.sc.edu/uscpress

Manufactured in the United States of America

15 14 13 12 11 10   09 08 07 06   10 9 8 7 6 5 4 3 2 1

Library of Congress Cataloging-in-Publication Data

Mackenzie, Ross, 1927–
   When stars and stripes met hammer and sickle : the Chautauqua Conferences on U.S.-Soviet
relations, 1985–1989 / Ross Mackenzie.
       p. cm.
   Includes bibliographical references and index.
   ISBN-13: 978-1-57003-635-4 (cloth : alk. paper)
   ISBN-10: 1-57003-635-7 (cloth : alk. paper)
   ISBN-13: 978-1-57003-636-1 (pbk : alk. paper)
   ISBN-10: 1-57003-636-5 (pbk : alk. paper)
   1. Chautauqua Institution/The Eisenhower Institute Conference on U.S.-Soviet Relations—
History. 2. United States—Relations—Soviet Union—Congresses—History. 3. Soviet
Union—Relations—United States—Congresses—History. I. Title.
   E183.8.S65M29 2006
   303.48'247073—dc22   2006004523

This book was printed on Glatfelter Natures Natural, a recycled paper with 50 percent post-
consumer waste content.

In memory of Daniel L. Bratton and John Wallach and in honor of the citizen and official delegates of the Soviet Union and the United States who, participating in these Chautauqua conferences, stood for the preservation of peace in the face of the threat of war

CONTENTS

ACKNOWLEDGMENTS

THE WORK THAT FOLLOWS has its origin in the commission I received in 2002 from Scott McVay, then president of the Chautauqua Institution, to write "a substantial, thorough and accurate narrative" of the Chautauqua conferences on U.S.-Soviet relations, held between 1985 and 1989. Two of the conferences were held on the grounds of the institution itself, two in the former Soviet Union, and the fifth at the University of Pittsburgh.

My grateful thanks go to the following for their willingness to be interviewed or for the materials they provided for research into the history of the conferences:

First, the citizen delegates and others: Rita Argen Auerbach; Mary Frances Bestor Cram; Alan D. and Carolyn (Bluie and Kitty) Greenberg; Thomas and Susan Hagen; Jane Hawthorne; Mace Levin; Meredith Lipke; Mary Ann McCabe; Elaine Navias; Manana Ninidze; Eva Rosenberg; Iris Rosenberg; Marvin and Joan Rosenthal; Thom E. Shagla; Howard A. Steindler; Carl Viehe; and Jo-An Webb. Also, the administrators and official delegates: Thomas M. Becker, president, Chautauqua Institution; Wanita Bratton; Carol Halter; Susan Eisenhower, president of the Eisenhower Group Inc., founder and chair of the Center for Political and Strategic Studies; Joan Fox, director of public information, Chautauqua Institution; Gregory Guroff, president of the Foundation for International Arts and Education; Joseph C. Johnson, vice president and treasurer, Chautauqua Institution; Ojars Kalnins, director of the Latvian Institute, Riga; Mary-Therese Mennino, executive director, Capitol Center for the Arts, Concord, New Hampshire; the Honorable Mark Palmer, vice president of the board of trustees of Freedom House and former U.S. ambassador to Hungary; Vladimir Pozner, Russian television commentator; S. Frederick Starr, chairman of the Central Asia–Caucasus Institute at the Paul H. Nitze School of Advanced International Studies of the Johns Hopkins University; Mark Sullivan; John Wallach, former senior editor with Hearst Newspapers and founder of Seeds of Peace; Carol M. White, formerly executive assistant to the president, Chautauqua Institution; and Paul Winter, Grammy Award–winning artist who founded the Paul Winter Consort in 1967.

I express my appreciation also to those who gave me access to the Chautauqua archives: Marilyn Mathews-Bendiksen, reference archivist; Joyce Brasted, assistant archivist; Jonathan Schmitz, archivist; Helene Yurth, librarian; and Justin Mando. Without the careful assembly of the conference records by the former historian of the Chautauqua Institution, Alfreda Irwin, this book could not have been written.

A special word of thanks is due to Peter W. Bumsted Jr., my research assistant. Then a student at Kenyon College, "PJ" checked every word, selected the photographs, compiled the index, and prepared the manuscript for publication with skill, a sharp eye, and a keenly critical mind.

The sources for the chapters that follow are the archival collections in the Smith Library of the Chautauqua Institution, specifically volumes of the *Chautauqua Assembly Herald* from 1876, its successor, the *Chautauquan Daily,* from 1906, and the *Chautauqua Weekly,* also from 1906. The standard histories of the Chautauqua Institution and the Chautauqua movement are Victoria Case and Robert Ormond Case, *We Called It Culture: The Story of Chautauqua* (New York: Doubleday, 1948); Joseph E. Gould, *The Chautauqua Movement* (Albany: State University of New York, 1961); Gay MacLaren, *Morally We Roll Along* (Boston: Little, Brown, 1938); Theodore Morrison, *Chautauqua: A Center for Education, Religion, and the Arts in America* (Chicago: University of Chicago Press, 1974); Rebecca Richmond, *Chautauqua: An American Place* (New York: Duell, Sloane, and Pearce, 1943); Alfreda L. Irwin, *Three Taps of the Gavel: Pledge to the Future,* 3rd ed. (Chautauqua: Chautauqua Institution, 1970); Jeffrey Simpson, *Chautauqua: An American Utopia* (New York: Harry N. Abrams in association with the Chautauqua Institution, 1999); John Heyl Vincent, *The Chautauqua Movement* (Boston: Chautauqua Press, 1886).

PREFACE

I express the hope that the dialogue between the official and citizen's delegations will not only continue the tradition which has been developed since the first Chautauqua meeting but will also add to it a new quality—more understanding and a deeper knowledge of each other.

Vladimir Petrovsky

THE FIVE CONFERENCES on U.S.-Soviet relations began in the era of the American struggle against "the evil empire." Few in this period had any doubt about President Reagan's detestation of the Soviet system or of his concern about the Soviet military buildup. A historian must also record, however, Reagan's stated determination to continue negotiating with the Soviet Union and, indeed, to achieve ultimately the total elimination of nuclear weapons from the face of the earth. To members of the British Parliament in 1982 he posed his sonorous rhetorical question, "Must civilization perish in a hail of fiery atoms?"

This was the era also of glasnost and perestroika, words that became part of the political vocabulary of the 1980s. Mikhail Gorbachev (born March 2, 1931) came to office as general secretary of the Central Committee of the Communist Party of the Soviet Union in the winter of 1985, advocating the need for drastic economic, political, and social reform. The goal was a profound renewal of all aspects of the nation's life. By the end of his term of office, there had been four summit meetings with President Reagan, the signing of the intermediate-range nuclear forces treaty (December 1987), and the completion of military withdrawal from Afghanistan. In 1988 Gorbachev sought to restructure the legislative and executive branches of government. A new bicameral parliament, the Congress of People's Deputies, came into being; Gorbachev was elected president.

In 1991, however, nearly two years after the final Chautauqua U.S.-Soviet conference, with the Soviet economy crumbling and unrest in the constituent republics of the union, a group of Communist hard-liners and some key military and KGB leaders attempted in a political coup to reintroduce autocratic central rule.[1] A massive force of tanks and military vehicles took up positions throughout Moscow. The short-lived stratagem failed, however. The army sided with the people, and the leaders of the coup were arrested and accused of treason. On September 3, a sobered Gorbachev, having resumed his duties as president, addressed a session of the Congress of People's Deputies. Admitting that he had learned "a very hard lesson," he nevertheless defended the years of perestroika and glasnost. The coup d'état, he insisted, had confirmed "that what we have been doing since 1985 made it possible to create new realities and a new basis for our country." Then, in a memorable phrase, he summarized his legacy: "We did not work in vain, you and I, in our new thinking."

On December 25, 1991, Gorbachev resigned the presidency of the Soviet Union. With his resignation, the dissolution of the USSR was final. The new government of Boris Yeltsin brought an end to the rule of the Communist Party and the political influence of the military-industrial complex. Yeltsin joined with heads of other republics in drawing together a loose, new Commonwealth of Independent States, an alliance of twelve of the fifteen former republics of the USSR.

The five Chautauqua conferences were held during most of the years of this complex history. They were, at a local level, differentiated contours of speech, music, confrontation, and conversation that accompanied the global realities of glasnost, perestroika, and the surge towards self-identity on the part of the republics of the USSR. Chapter 2 traces the origins of the conferences in the history of the Chautauqua Institution itself. According to its founders, the "Chautauqua idea" was to inform and enrich people's outlooks on what is going on in the world. To have neglected developments then taking place in the Soviet Union in the discussions of these years would have been a forsaking of that idea.

---

1. James Billington writes that the events of the period may be recognized in time to have been the most important single political happening during the second half of the twentieth century. See James H. Billington, *Russia Transformed: Breakthrough to Hope* (New York: Free Press, 1992), 3. Billington, as the librarian of Congress, had arrived in Moscow just before the storm of August 19–21 to attend meetings of the International Federation of Library Associations. See also Hedrick Smith, *The New Russians* (New York: Avon Books, 1991), 622–47.

In chapters 3 through 7, the records of the conferences from 1985 to 1989 make clear that the international political mood was perceptibly changing from confrontation and suspicion to qualified trust and increasing collaboration. What Chautauqua had to contribute to the larger developments in U.S.-Soviet relations was its insistence that the conferences should involve *citizen* diplomacy. It was of major importance for their audiences to hear Soviet and American diplomats, politicians, and military leaders speak formally and from prepared texts on a national platform. It was quite another thing for these Soviet and American audiences to hear appointed delegates debating one another and even being controverted by one another and by members of their audience, including some of their own citizens. It was important to learn of trends and statistics regarding arms control, regional issues, human rights, and the bilateral agenda. It was quite another thing for ordinary citizens who participated in a particular week's conference to find that the opportunity of being guests in local families transformed their experience of the week into the sudden awareness of the bystander at the 1987 conference who said, "They look just like us." Citizen diplomacy for Chautauquans meant discussing national and political concerns along with domestic and family issues over the breakfast table or on a stroll after supper.

The concluding chapter 8 offers a general assessment of the five conferences and the impact they may have made on Soviet and American politics of the period and on the lives of the Soviet and American citizens who participated. It is important to ask if the conferences played a part, minor though it may have been, in the political transformations of the 1980s and 1990s. It is essential to record, in the words of one of Chautauqua's founders, that for five years and in an international situation heavy with danger, "lovers of our great Republic, lovers of common humanity" made one common cause, recognized their situation, and raised themselves up to the magnitude of the occasion.[2]

2. "Introduction by Lewis Miller, Esq.," in John H. Vincent, *The Chautauqua Movement* (Boston: Chautauqua Press, 1886), vii.

WHEN STARS AND STRIPES
MET HAMMER AND SICKLE

CHAPTER ONE

Citizen Diplomacy

W INSTON S. CHURCHILL was invited to Fulton, Missouri, on March 6, 1946, to receive an honorary degree from Westminster College. He opened his speech accepting the honor by stating that he proposed to place before his audience "certain facts about the present position in Europe." With a phrase that came to define U.S.-Soviet relations for over a generation, he grimly summarized the political situation in Europe: "From Stettin in the Baltic to Trieste in the Adriatic, an iron curtain has descended across the Continent."[1]

The alliance between the Soviet Union and the United States and its allies during World War II had been more military necessity than partnership. New regional power struggles sprang up in Europe following the war. Josef Stalin warned early in 1946 that since the Second World War had stemmed from the contradictions of capitalism, the struggle for world resources would inevitably produce both conflict and war in the future. George F. Kennan, a career diplomat in Moscow, sent his famous "long telegram" that ultimately became the basis of U.S. policy in dealing with the Soviets for the following forty years. He warned that there could be no permanent, peaceful coexistence with the Soviet Union. The threat of Soviet expansion into areas and relationships that were vital to U.S. security became a central focus of U.S. foreign policymakers.

As early as 1955, however, Albert Einstein and Bertrand Russell had issued a manifesto warning of the dangers of thermonuclear war and calling on their fellow scientists to "find peaceful ways for the settlement of all matters between them."[2] Their appeal led to the creation of a series of

1. Robert Rhodes James, ed. *Winston S. Churchill: His Complete Speeches, 1897–1963*, vol. 7 (New York: Chelsea House, 1974), 7285–93.
2. From the "Russell-Einstein Manifesto," issued July 9, 1955, at a press conference held in Caxton Hall, London.

conferences on science and world affairs, first held at the village of Pugwash, Nova Scotia. At the first conference in July 1957, twenty-two scientists—seven from the United States, three from the Soviet Union, and others from Australia, Austria, China, France, and Poland—assembled at the estate of American philanthropist Cyrus Eaton to discuss ways of reducing the arms race. Subsequent Pugwash conferences were held in other countries, including the Soviet Union. During the early period of the cold war, the Pugwash conferences were among the few lines of communication open between the United States and the Soviet Union.

Even at the height of the cold war, delicate feelers came intermittently from both sides of the iron curtain, testing to see what response the overtures might evoke. Early in his second presidency, Dwight D. Eisenhower had indicated that he was willing to support exchanges between the United States and the USSR in the cultural, technical, and educational fields. On January 27, 1958, the first cultural agreement between the two governments was signed in Washington, D.C., by the Soviet ambassador and a representative of the State Department. It was a modest start in a renewed engagement between the two countries. However, when the Soviet Union brought down America's U-2 spy plane in 1960, the episode led to a breakdown in U.S.-Soviet relations. Eisenhower, troubled by the rupture, commented to Norman Cousins, then editor of *Saturday Review of Literature,* "I can't talk with the Soviets, but somebody better."[3]

The "somebody" was Cousins, a strong opponent of the testing of nuclear weapons and a self-described world citizen. In October 1960, Dartmouth College in New Hampshire, with the support of the Ford Foundation, invited him to lead the first of a series of conferences that brought together Soviet citizens and others from the United States. The intention was to create a nongovernmental channel to link the United States and the Soviet Union and to allow the thirty participants—historians, economists, lawyers, artists, and administrators—to engage one another in frank and open conversations about arms control, the economic development of the third world, the search for peace, and the part that ordinary citizens might play in foreign policy.

In the following May, the second Dartmouth conference took place over a ten-day period on Soviet territory, on the Crimean peninsula. The meeting was generally pacific in tone, not so much because any agreements had

---

3. Quoted in Carnegie Corporation of New York, *Carnegie Reporter* 3, no. 3 (Fall 2005).

been achieved, but because the participants had been able to clarify how and where they differed, how they interpreted conflicting positions, and how they could achieve peaceful relations beyond the conference table. In contrast, a third conference, held at Andover, Massachusetts, in October 1962, was highly charged, since the resolution of the Cuban missile crisis—war or peace—appeared to be hanging in the balance. Twenty-four scholars, lawyers, public officials, and administrators turned again under the shadow of war to discuss how it might be possible to maintain peaceable relations between the two nations and to suggest how lines of communication might be kept open.

The Dartmouth conferences did not simply help to keep open contacts between the Soviet Union and the United States at an acutely dangerous time. They also opened up a new level of dialogue between adversaries— citizen diplomacy.

Eisenhower himself was well aware that high-level diplomacy was frequently sterile or ineffective, and he had more confidence that what came to be called "track two" or citizen diplomacy—unofficial initiatives of private citizens and groups—could at times produce more creative solutions and build trust between those involved in international conflicts. If Eisenhower may be regarded as the father of citizen diplomacy, the most articulate advocate of the concept was Joseph V. Montville, a Foreign Service officer in the State Department (and later a platform speaker at the first Chautauqua conference). Montville distinguished "track one diplomacy," the official channel of government-to-government relations, and "track two diplomacy," the unofficial channel of people-to-people relations. This second track, he argued, was "a supplement to the understandable shortcomings of official relations." In track one diplomacy, the officials were obligated to assure their followers that they would defend them against the enemies who sought to conquer or destroy them. In track one, worst-case assumptions about the intentions of the adversary were the norm. In track two, altogether new types of relationships were possible: "Track two diplomacy . . . is open-minded, often altruistic, and . . . strategically optimistic, based on the best case analysis. Its underlying assumption is that actual or potential conflict can be resolved or eased by appealing to common human capabilities to respond to goodwill and reasonableness."[4]

---

4. See William D. Davidson and Joseph V. Montville, "Foreign Policy according to Freud," *Foreign Policy* 45 (Winter 1981–82): 145–57.

Even with track two diplomacy, however, there were difficulties. Almost all the Soviets who participated in exchanges in the United States, for example, had been screened by Soviet authorities to ensure that they were politically reliable. Also, the number of participants in the early years of the agreement was small, probably not more than a thousand in total in any one year. In the years just prior to the first Chautauqua conference, U.S.-Soviet relations had deteriorated, and the number of exchanges correspondingly declined. By 1984, for example, scientific exchanges were running at 20 to 25 percent of their 1978–79 level. Even so, according to U.S. State Department reports, a total of three hundred to five hundred U.S. scientists went to the Soviet Union in the 1983–84 academic year, and around 250 of their Soviet colleagues came to the United States.

Ordinary tourists from the United States also had their part to play, though in number these had declined. In 1976, for example, the Soviet Union granted over sixty-five thousand visas to visitors; by 1980, however, the number had fallen to under thirteen thousand, though it rose again by the end of 1983 to thirty-eight thousand. In contrast, the United States granted visas to nearly twelve thousand Soviets in 1976, and this number also declined to about eight thousand in 1976. By 1984, however, the number was returning to its 1976 level. Already by this time the International Research and Exchanges Board, a private organization supported in part by the American Council of Learned Societies and the National Endowment for the Humanities, had been administering exchanges with the Soviet Union. The Carnegie Corporation had also supported a joint U.S.-Soviet study of the problem of dealing with crisis between the two countries.

American scholars and students were generally assigned to universities in Moscow and Leningrad and forbidden to travel further than forty kilometers from their place of study. In response to this latter requirement, the State Department imposed its own limit of twenty-five miles on Soviet students in the United States. Troubles with the Soviet bureaucracy and secrecy were constant. Even as late as the 1980s, Mikhail Gorbachev complained that all his initiatives quickly became lost in the byzantine channels of Soviet bureaucracy, where they "gradually suffocate, as if in layers of cotton wool."[5]

The five Chautauqua conferences on U.S.-Soviet relations took place in what W. W. Rostow called the third of three distinct cold war cycles, from

5. Quoted in Fred Weir, "Putin's Duel with Bureaucrats," *Christian Science Monitor,* February 22, 2002.

1973 to 1987.[6] Within this third period, the Soviet Union was displaying aggressive military and political activism in the Caribbean, Central America, Angola, Ethiopia, Yemen, and Indochina. In 1979 it invaded Afghanistan. The presence of six hundred thousand Soviet troops in Europe was a constant reminder that the Soviet Union had become, by 1985, a dominant superpower. It was, however, a one-dimensional superpower. The concerns of the armed forces had taken priority over any other national interests. In consequence, the rate of Soviet economic growth was in serious decline.

Any history of the Soviet Union during this period will inevitably, therefore, focus on the series of proposals for reform that Mikhail Gorbachev, one of the giants of the twentieth century, began to outline late in 1986. He had come to office in 1985, advocating the drastic need for economic, political, and social restructuring and seeking to ensure that the Soviet Union would enter the twenty-first century, in his own words, "in a manner befitting a great power."[7] He stated repeatedly that neither the Soviet Union nor any other major power could emerge victorious from a nuclear war. Gorbachev and his colleagues understood that the key to their ambitious new strategy was to establish a period of peace and to allow a massive political and economic change to occur. To that end, it was essential that both the allies and enemies of the Soviet Union recognize, welcome, and adapt to the new Soviet policies. Preventing nuclear war required more than discarding outdated ideological doctrines. It called for a wholly new way of thinking.

In one or more of the Chautauqua conferences and with a mixture of suspicion, curiosity, and hope, hundreds of Soviet and American citizens, diplomats, and citizen delegates came together on one another's territories. They became involved personally in the new thinking, seeking ways of solving what seemed otherwise to be intractable problems. The Chautauqua conferences on U.S.-Soviet relations were in many ways a continuation of the search, through a particular nongovernmental channel, for rational ways to address and peaceful ways to resolve actual or potential conflicts. The difference between the Chautauqua conferences and their predecessors lay mostly in the large numbers of citizen delegates who took part. Moreover,

---

6. See W. W. Rostow, "Containment: 40 Years Later; On Ending the Cold War," *Foreign Affairs* 65, no. 4 (Spring 1987): 831–51. The first cycle, according to Rostow, was the time of the Truman-Stalin duel (1945–55); the second (1955–75) included Khrushchev's nuclear threat.

7. Quoted in Coit D. Blacker, The Collapse of Soviet Power in Europe," *Foreign Affairs, American, and the World* 70, no. 1 (1990/92).

these later conferences provided an unprecedented opportunity for ordinary American and Soviet citizens to meet one another now in one another's homes. How significant the Chautauqua exercise in citizen diplomacy was we shall consider in the final chapter. In the meantime, we shall first review the history and ethos of the place and movement named Chautauqua and then outline more fully the intensely threatening situation to which a small educational institution in the far reaches of New York State responded with remarkable courage and foresight.

CHAPTER TWO

1874: "We Are Going to Do This"

Those who read these pages will attribute to sanguine temperament and Chautauqua enthusiasm what their more sober judgment pronounces chimerical and impossible.

John Heyl Vincent

ANY HISTORY OF THE CHAUTAUQUA INSTITUTION will inevitably focus on its distinguished lecture platform and particularly on the five conferences on U.S.-Soviet relations that were held from 1985 to 1989: two on the grounds of the institution, two in the Soviet Union, and the fifth and final one at the University of Pittsburgh. Chautauqua was an ideal setting for the series by reason of its history and the politics of the age.

Chautauqua County is a hilly and rolling region in the western part of New York State. Chautauqua Lake, described in an 1860 gazetteer as "a beautiful sheet of water," is the westernmost of the Finger Lakes, occupying a deep valley in the highland region. On the southern shore of the lake and on the site of a disused Methodist camp meeting ground, two friends, Lewis Miller and John Heyl Vincent, founded in August 1874 the Chautauqua Lake Sunday School Assembly. In the heart of a primeval forest, Fair Point, where the land projects far into the water, was to be the place of origin of what came to be known as the Chautauqua idea and the Chautauqua movement.

For the holding of the summer assembly, Vincent had urged on Miller his strong preference for an urban setting. Miller prevailed, however, sensing that the isolated, wooded spot on the lake would be a better place for the participants—four thousand of them—who were eventually to converge on the eighty-acre site. Miller himself was a successful inventor and manufacturer of farm equipment. His chief avocation outside his professional work was education. He was a member of the Akron School Board and the Sunday school superintendent of Akron's First Methodist Church. Vincent was a Methodist minister and a leader in the Sunday school movement.

The assembly was to be an educational experiment in summer and vacation learning. The two principles that Vincent and Miller brought to the development of the Chautauqua idea were organization and serious group study. They had no desire to offer anything of the primitive and unsophisticated "shouting Methodism" of the old camp meetings but rather intended to provide innovative education and the serious and organized study of what Vincent himself fulsomely called "larger views of the world and worthier views of life."[1]

In the first assembly, there were sermons and lectures on the Bible and Sunday school work, healthful recreation, music, and entertainment suitable to the prevailing evangelical piety. From the second year, however, the sheer vitality of the place made the demand for a wider program irresistible. With the visit of Ulysses S. Grant in 1875, the first of the nine U.S. presidents who came to the grounds, the assembly moved from mainly offering courses for Sunday school teachers to providing educational, cultural, religious, and political programs for adults and children alike.

The original two-week assembly had expanded to forty-three days by 1879. Twenty years later it lengthened to sixty days. Platform speakers were carefully chosen to help advance "the Chautauqua idea"—what Vincent sums up in his history, *The Chautauqua Movement,* as universal popular education with high standards of attainment; broad and comprehensive study of "the rich world of literature, the royal world of art"; a better understanding among the classes of society; and the proposition that "life is one and that religion belongs everywhere." George E. Vincent, who was president of the institution in 1913, called for a more deliberate focus on particular questions. The enormous increase of knowledge, he insisted, forced upon modern men and women the need "of fixing on certain interests and organizing their minds and lives about these." Chautauqua, for this reason, he said, stood as a protest against a "desultory, haphazard attitude toward life" through a well-balanced program that helped people select certain unified and significant groups—histories, literatures, sciences, philosophies—and to fix attention for a time on these.

Almost from the beginning, a distinction was increasingly to be seen in the programs of the assembly between plenary public lectures and more formal study in smaller groups. The Chautauqua Literary and Scientific Circle (CLSC), founded in 1878, began to enroll the first of hundreds, then

1. John H. Vincent, *The Chautauqua Movement* (Boston: Chautauqua Press, 1886), 74.

thousands, of readers who sought to secure "the college student's outlook upon the world of thought." The CLSC was a four-year course of directed home reading, leading to a diploma and graduation. An essential element in the directed reading plan was the local circle, in which readers throughout the country and abroad met to discuss the required books or to read papers on related topics. By 1891, Chautauqua reported that 181,000 had enrolled in the home reading circles. By 1918, the figure had reached more than 300,000. A handbook published in 1918 estimated that "more than half a million" had read the Chautauqua course. Lifelong learning became not only the core of the Chautauqua idea but also its major contribution to American education. The CLSC prepared the way in 1883 for what became Chautauqua University (later the College of Liberal Arts), a degree-granting institution that pioneered in summer school courses, directed reading, extension education, correspondence courses, and nontraditional ways of learning. With a charter from the New York State Legislature, the various educational programs were drawn together under the designation Chautauqua University. A gifted young scholar, William Rainey Harper, came from the faculty of the Baptist School of Theology in Morgan Park, Illinois, to offer instruction in Hebrew at Chautauqua. Something of an intellectual genius as well as a gifted administrator, Harper was later made principal of the College of Liberal Arts. In 1892 he became first president of the University of Chicago, a testimony to the increasing influence of the Chautauqua Institution on American intellectual life.

The performing arts came to occupy a central role in the summer programs. A symphony concert series began in 1920, and in 1929, on the eve of the stock market crash, Albert Stoessel organized Chautauqua's own symphony orchestra. Internationally renowned artists such as Jessye Norman and Yehudi Menuhin came to perform. George Gershwin composed his *Concerto in F* in a practice shack on the grounds. Also in 1929, the Chautauqua Opera Company was launched under Stoessel. The Chautauqua Repertory Company began its own season in the following year with Oscar Wilde's *The Importance of Being Earnest*.

The mixture of programs in Chautauqua's summer seasons—it describes itself at its main entrance as "a center for the arts, education, religion, and recreation"—has been rich and diverse from the start. A school of languages in the early years offered courses in Latin, German, French, and Anglo-Saxon. Other schools of education, fine arts, physical education, and music were quickly started. Ida M. Tarbell, sometimes identified as the leader of the "muckraking journalists," spent much of her childhood with her family on the grounds and drew from Chautauqua's programs at least some of her inspiration to focus national attention on the shadowy side of John D. Rockefeller's Standard Oil Company in her well-researched account of a "robber-baron" business monopoly and its unfair practices. The impulse to social reform, strengthening throughout the country in the 1890s, brought Jane Addams to Chautauqua to speak about settlement houses that offered facilities in industrial cities for recreation, protection for female workers, education, and a place to advance the cause of women's suffrage. Rudyard Kipling came to see what Chautauqua was like, said he admired the scores of pretty girls with books under their arms and "a pretty air of seriousness on their faces," but complained that something was wrong with Chautauqua, even if he did not quite know what.[2]

Within a generation of its founding, the Chautauqua Institution had given an impetus to the establishment of more than a hundred similar assemblies throughout the United States. During the peak years of the early 1920s, it has been estimated that close to thirty million Americans sooner or later sat in the tents of the traveling or "tent" chautauquas that spanned the continent. The Chautauqua Institution today is a 750-acre center of the arts, education, religion, and recreation with around seventy-five hundred in residence on any day during its nine-week season.

Glasnost and Perestroika

In June 1984, the Kennan Institute for Advanced Russian Studies of the Woodrow Wilson International Center for Scholars conducted a Conference on U.S.-Soviet Exchanges to review and evaluate the major reciprocal exchange programs involving American and Soviet academic and other specialist individuals and groups. President Ronald Reagan met with participants in the conference in the East Room of the White House. After listing several of the proposals that he had made to improve the U.S.-Soviet dialogue, he indicated that he was disturbed by recent reports that the Soviet government was taking repressive actions in an attempt to seal themselves off from the outside world.

> Civilized people everywhere have a stake in keeping contacts, communication, and creativity as broad, deep, and free as possible. The Soviet insistence on sealing their people off and on filtering and controlling

---

2. Quoted in Theodore Morrison, *Chautauqua: A Center for Education, Religion, and Arts in America* (Chicago: University of Chicago Press, 1974), 234.

contacts and the flow of information remains the central problem.
... That is why I feel that we should broaden opportunities for
Americans and Soviet citizens to get to know each other better.[3]

After his reelection in that year, Reagan appeared to be softening his earlier
rigid position on arms control. It seemed, especially in the light of events
taking place in the Soviet Union, that winds were coming in a different
direction from Moscow and that the Soviet administration might be ame-
nable to some kind of agreement. Relations between the United States and
the Soviet Union began to improve from 1985, and from late that year Reagan and Gorbachev met one another in a series of annual summit meetings.
In November 1985 the two leaders, meeting in Geneva, agreed in principle
to reduce armaments. Discussions were initiated to reduce both conventional forces and nuclear stockpiles. In a speech given in Santa Barbara, California, on August 19, 1985, Robert C. McFarlane, assistant to the president
for national security affairs, said:

> The real sources of conflict are things that can—and do—change. If
> there is a military rivalry between two great countries, it's caused less
> by the arms themselves than by the way the two sides think about mili-
> tary security. If there is a geopolitical rivalry, it's not caused by the facts
> of geography but by the way the two sides define their political security
> and their other interests. If there is a clash of ideas—well, not even ide-
> ologies are permanent.[4]

Although the terms glasnost and perestroika are usually associated with
Gorbachev, the need for such changes had been acknowledged years earlier
by a predecessor, Yuri Andropov, who took office in 1982. Andropov, the
former head of the KGB, was a cautious reformer who gave encouragement
to others who shared his views, notably to Gorbachev. Andropov died in
February 1984 and was replaced by rival Konstantin Chernenko. On coming to power in March 1985 after the death of Chernenko, Gorbachev took
as his main task a program of moderate and controlled reform through an

---

3. *U.S.-Soviet Exchanges: A Conference Report* (Washington, D.C.: Kennan Institute for Advanced Russian Studies of the Woodrow Wilson International Center
for Scholars, 1985), 50.
    4. "U.S.-Soviet Relations in the Late 20th Century," in U.S. Department of State
Current Policy Paper 733 (Washington, D.C.: U.S. Department of State).

expansion, first, of glasnost, openness. Soviet society was to be open to criticism from its creative thinkers—artists, scientists, poets, and others. Intellectuals were encouraged to reexamine history with a greater fidelity to facts and to discuss in the open ideological issues that previously had been off limits. Unlike Secretary of Defense Caspar Weinberger, Secretary of State George Shultz thought Gorbachev not just a "new face" but an entirely different kind of leader. Shultz first met Gorbachev in March 1985 at Spaso House, the residence of the U.S. ambassador in Moscow, and later reported to Vice President George Bush that Gorbachev was "quicker, fresher, more engaging, and more wide ranging in his interests and knowledge. . . . I came away genuinely impressed with the quality of the thought, the intensity and the intellectual energy of this new man on the scene."[5]

Concurrently with glasnost, Gorbachev's second main task was to achieve a restructuring of the Soviet political and economic system. Even prior to assuming office, he had spoken of the need for "deep transformations," not to undermine the Soviet system but rather to increase its efficiency. Consequently, in February 1986 he presented a program of economic, political, and social restructuring—perestroika. Gorbachev himself admitted that "the next two to three years will be the most difficult," for if fulfilled, the proposal would lead to the dismantling of a state system that had dominated for nearly seventy years.[6]

Time to Show the Chautauqua Temperament

In the seventy years between Roosevelt's first address at the institution and Reagan's presidency, the Chautauqua Institution had heard little, if anything, about Russia or the Soviet Union. In 1929, Ivy L. Lee, described as a New York publicist who had made several trips to Russia, argued that the United States should be ready to negotiate with the present Russian government, even though it was not willing to recognize that government. "My attitude," he said, "is that there is nothing to be lost by sitting around a table and seeing what the other fellow has to say." A few years later, in July 1933, a representative of the Foreign Policy Association spoke on the theme of whether the U.S. government should recognize the Soviet Union and noted that the United States had already, prior to that year, taken steps to reestablish diplomatic relations. Toward the end of August, Norman Thomas, who

5. George P. Shultz, *Turmoil and Triumph: My Years as Secretary of State* (New York: Charles Scribner's Sons, 1993), 532.
6. Speech to the 27th Congress of the Communist Party of the Soviet Union.

had been the Socialist candidate in the 1932 election, also urged recognition of Russia in the interest of peace. Answering a question on how sincere the Russian proposal was for complete disarmament, Thomas asserted that Russia really wanted peace so that it could stabilize its domestic program. "This is hopeful," he said. "For once people get the habit of peace, it is hard to break the habit for any theory."

A survey of the first fifty years of nineteenth-century CLSC readings discloses likewise only minimal attention to Russia. A recommended text from 1894—*Europe in the Nineteenth Century*—gives only 10 out of 336 pages to the subject, the chapter ending peremptorily, "The nineteenth century has not yet dawned in Russia."[7] References thereafter to Russia in the CLSC selections were few and minor until the end of World War II and the years immediately following. For example, in his 1943 book, also a CLSC selection, *U.S. Foreign Policy: Shield of the Republic,* Walter Lippmann wrote, "The crucial question of the epoch that we are now entering is the relationship between Russia and that Atlantic community in which Britain and the United States are the leading military powers."[8] A dozen years later, Chester Bowles, in another selection, asserted that the greatest challenge to the individual American of the period was "to play an explicit and conscious role in the conduct of our foreign policy." He continued, "What the Kremlin itself must fear most is that we will break loose from the hypnotic grip that Communism has upon us, cease to think largely in terms of negative response to it, realize the broad dimensions of our own great strength, and rally to the support of positive policies keyed to needs and objectives of mankind."[9] From that period the CLSC book selections only occasionally dealt with the Soviet Union, nuclear warfare, disarmament, and U.S.-Soviet relations.

The summer seasons prior to the first Chautauqua conference on U.S.-Soviet relations increasingly focused attention at the main lecture hour on the Soviet Union. In 1975, for example, John G. Stoessinger, who later served as acting director of the United Nations Political Affairs Division, lectured on the U.S.-Soviet détente. From 1982 the attention became constant.

7. Henry Pratt Judson, *Europe in the Nineteenth Century* (New York: Chautauqua Century Press, 1894), 254.

8. Walter Lippmann, *U.S. Foreign Policy: Shield of the Republic* (Boston: Little, Brown, 1943), 146.

9. Chester Bowles, *The New Dimensions of Peace* (New York: Harper & Brothers, 1955), 385.

A dominant figure at Chautauqua in the early 1980s, widely regarded as one of the top foreign correspondents of the period, was John P. Wallach, foreign affairs editor for Hearst Publications. Wallach had been president of the State Department Correspondents Association and was a frequent guest on NBC's *Meet the Press,* for CBS on *Face the Nation,* and for PBS on *Washington Week in Review.* In August 1982, speaking at Chautauqua, Wallach took as his theme "The Reagan Administration: A Foreign Policy Report Card." In August 1983, he moderated a lecture given by Malcolm Toon, former U.S. ambassador to the USSR, titled "Our Relations with Soviet Russia." In August 1984, Dimitri Simes, senior executive for Soviet foreign policy in the Carnegie Endowment for Peace and a former adviser to the Communist Party, lectured on "The Anatomy of the Soviet Challenge." The following day, Kathleen Troia, who was principal assistant secretary of defense, and Oleg M. Sokolov, who was to be the leader of the Soviet delegation in 1985, shared the platform in a discussion on the nuclear threat. A pattern, however shadowy, had been set.

Before becoming the fifteenth president of the Chautauqua Institution, Daniel L. Bratton had spent his whole career in educational administration. From 1973 to 1984 he was president of Kansas Wesleyan University in Salina, Kansas. The move from Kansas to Chautauqua brought Bratton a sense of homecoming, for western New York State and Chautauqua had been part of his early years. On Saturday, July 21, 1984, he was selected by the board of trustees as president of the Chautauqua Institution. The institution, over which Bratton was to preside for a quarter of his own life and sixteen years of Chautauqua's history, called for a president who would be far more than the leader of an arts festival. He was to supervise an educational system, serve as mayor of a village, be a prominent public relations figure, subscribe to a religious program, be curator of a cultural heritage, and act as steward of a long and beloved tradition. The tasks before him in 1984—administrative and programmatic—were daunting.

Bratton looked, therefore, for a strong and courageous board that would define its expectations clearly. Let it give support when the administration made tough decisions and help to advance the changes that would show greater responsiveness to the community it served. Aware that Chautauquans were fearful of change, he sought to convince his constituency that customary summer programs would continue. Yet he also wanted the board to respond affirmatively to the themes around which the Chautauqua audiences in the previous three seasons had shown deep interest—specifically international relations.[10] In this, he could undoubtedly claim support from John Heyl Vincent, who wrote in his history of the Chautauqua movement, "Chautauquans who read these pages will attribute to sanguine temperament and Chautauqua enthusiasm what their more sober judgment pronounces chimerical and impossible."

Words like "wildly impractical" and "impossible" were widely heard in 1984 and early 1985 when Bratton proposed to organize and assemble at Chautauqua a general conference on U.S.-Soviet relations. High-level U.S. and USSR political and diplomatic figures would enter into candid debate with one another. Critics on the institution's board of trustees reported to Bratton and to David Faust, chair of the board, their own and others' fears and worries—"We are being dupes. We are playing into the hands of the evil empire." Faust recognized and welcomed the wisdom and commitment of the new president. Putting his hands on the table at a board meeting, he declared straightforwardly, as if expecting no dissent, "We are going to do this." For Bratton, it was a great national opportunity. With Gorbachev expressing a readiness to end the cold war by arms reduction and political reform, Reagan's own anti-Soviet talk seemed to be switching to more conciliatory rhetoric. Chautauquans, Bratton knew, were bright and discerning, and in many ways were weary of the rhetoric of the cold war. It was time to show the Chautauqua temperament and enthusiasm. It was a bold proposal for a president in his first year of appointment.

Bratton's proposed initiative had at least three immediate sources. First, for all the anxiety about nuclear armaments and the Star Wars missile defense system, there was also much conversation in the country about the possibilities of negotiating with the Soviet Union. Second, in the summer of 1983, Wallach himself had commented after a lecture that Chautauqua Institution was uniquely located to provide a meeting place for Soviet and American citizens. Its tradition of civil dialogue on issues affecting the human family would surely, he insisted, allow intelligent debate between political leaders and citizens from both countries. Finally, in the summer of 1984, Karl Menninger, then in his nineties, addressed an audience in the Hall of Philosophy. He commented on the contrast between the Reagan attitude toward the evil empire and his own approach as a psychiatrist. Would

10. Daniel L. Bratton, remarks to the Chautauqua Institution Board of Trustees, February 16, 1985.

it not be good, he inquired, if Soviet citizens might be seen sometime walking about the Chautauqua grounds, talking with Chautauquans, and finding out from one another more about their beliefs and understandings? It was a time, it seemed, for many voices to be heard on both sides.

The fixed and unchanging idea for Bratton was that the U.S.-Soviet conferences that he envisioned should be not only a journey in open diplomacy but also a form of citizen-to-citizen diplomacy. Citizens and diplomats of both countries would intersect with one another in a "crossroads" experience at Chautauqua. True, neither the Soviet nor the United States government might regard nonspecialist or leadership conferences (such as the Dartmouth conference in 1960) as capable of yielding the results that could come from bilateral government-to-government exchanges. Both governments regarded these as complementary to official contacts, or, in the absence of such high-level contacts, at least a form of dialogue. The Chautauqua conferences would certainly involve government speakers at as high a level as possible—the third in the series eventually involved the president of the United States himself. But the originality of the Bratton proposal was to include both government speakers and citizen-to-citizen contacts.

Chautauqua has always been a "crossroads" experience for those who have come to it. In the United States, crossroads were historically places where general stores would be built and became meeting places for the news and gossip of the day. For more than a century, people had been coming to Chautauqua to give their attention to new ideas, to enjoy the broadening experience of meeting strangers, and to become part of an organic whole, not merely to form a temporary association of unrelated individuals. "The Chautauqua life is a veritable 'mixing,'" a nineteenth-century visitor reported, "effected by grouping people from all parts of the country on lines of common interest." Writing in the *Independent* in 1914, the second president of the institution, George E. Vincent, said, "Chautauqua will be in the future as in the past a center from which new knowledge, skill, and idealism will be distributed to all parts of the land. It will stand for social unity, mutual confidence, democracy. And in doing this Chautauqua will not be departing from its original purpose but only realizing in a larger way and under new conditions the ideal which lured the early Chautauquans to the grove beside the lake."[11]

11. George E. Vincent, "What Is Chautauqua?" *Independent,* July 6, 1914, 17.

The series of five U.S.-Soviet conferences that emerged from this conflu-
ence of ideas and mixing of peoples was a notable expression of the Chautauqua vision. It was the right moment for a sanguine temperament and
a Chautauqua enthusiasm to find a possible larger way to contribute to the
cause of peace.

CHAPTER THREE

1985: "A Significant Week at Chautauqua"

The essence of this conference may be in bringing together with the full approval of both governments Soviet citizens, entertainers, leaders, with a group of people called Chautauquans, and watching an interchange develop that has not been hostile at all, but, rather, has been both open and friendly.

Joseph V. Montville

I N HIS REMARKS to the participants in the Kennan Institute Conference on U.S.-Soviet Exchanges in the East Room of the White House, June 27, 1984, President Ronald Reagan had concluded by saying:

> It may seem an impossible dream to think that there could be a time when Americans and Soviet citizens of all walks of life can travel freely back and forth, visit each other's homes, look up friends and professional colleagues, work together in all sorts of problems, and, if they feel like it, sit up all night talking about the meaning of life and the different ways to look at the world.[1]

Reagan's words evoked the earlier conviction of Chautauqua's cofounder, John Heyl Vincent, that the Chautauqua idea (as he called it) was a belief "in the brotherhood of the race and its high destiny" and that Chautauquans were "proud to account themselves a part of it."[2] For Reagan, the dream was that, despite all evidence and opposition to the contrary, it could be possible for both the United States and the Soviet Union to seek a new attitude towards the nuclear arms race. The United States government would discuss openly with representatives of the "evil empire" rational and peaceful ways of settling disputes. Further, it would address common

1. *U.S.-Soviet Exchanges: A Conference Report,* 51.
2. Vincent, *The Chautauqua Movement,* 1.

human questions—the elements that bind communities together; health and human services; economic issues; family life; justice—indeed, and again to use a phrase of Vincent's, "all that makes for a rounded human life."

The institution had invited John Wallach to serve as director of its international affairs programs for the three seasons of 1982–84. He was the obvious choice to lead the first conference and to schedule meetings with leaders in government and higher education who could offer their views on the topic. By December 1984, Wallach had obtained an appointment for Bratton and himself to meet with Ambassador Anatoly Dobrynin at the Soviet embassy in Washington, D.C. The two extended an invitation to representatives of the Soviet Union to participate in a weeklong conference on international affairs at Chautauqua in the summer of 1985.

In the following February, Wallach sent a letter to the deputy chairman of the Soviet Presidium, Gennadi Yanaev, inviting a delegation of Soviet officials to participate in the conference. Making reference to the Chautauqua Institution as "one of the most historic sites in America," for here Franklin Delano Roosevelt had made his "I hate war" speech in August 1936, Wallach expressed hope that the conference would reach millions of Americans through the facilities of public broadcasting. The letter ended: "While we understand that it is extremely unlikely, we hope that His Excellency Mikhail Gorbachev, whose recent visit to Great Britain was such an unqualified success, will consider leading the Soviet delegation."[3]

In a memo dated February 21, members of the board of trustees learned that under Wallach's guidance Chautauqua had developed a very strong week of speakers to address the theme, now called "The Chautauqua Conference on Soviet-American Relations." The Soviet embassy had officially informed Wallach that there would be a seven-member delegation at Chautauqua the entire week. Furthermore, the embassy had invited Wallach and Bratton to go to Moscow in April to confer with representatives of the Soviet government, the Union of Soviet Friendship Societies, and the USSR-USA Society in an attempt to get the highest possible level of Russian involvement in that delegation. "It is clear," the memo to the board continued, "that this will be a significant week at Chautauqua."

> This clearly is not a casual act by the Soviet Union. It is very evident that they have decided that a presence with American officials in a

3. Copy of letter in Daniel L. Bratton Papers, Chautauqua archives.

non-political setting would be very timely at this point in history. The tactical dimensions of this are staggering to consider—security, publicity, which should be enormous, housing, funding, etc., are all of considerable dimensions. . . . There are clear risks involved. The Soviets could cancel at the last moment. Something could happen (e.g., the shooting down of the Korean airplane) which could create angry Chautauquans. Strong conservative organizations could make their presence and objections known. However great these risks, the possibilities are greater.

Preparations for the forthcoming conference went forward. Meetings were held with representatives of the Foreign Affairs Institute, the Department of State, the Public Broadcasting System, and with Vladimir Parastaeyev, first secretary in the Soviet embassy and the official in charge of arrangements for the institution. At Chautauqua, Mary-Therese Mennino, program director, proposed that there should be evening entertainment reflective of the week's theme. These would include an evening with leaders of the American theater offering Russian drama and readings; the Paul Winter Consort, recently returned from the Soviet Union, with Yevgeny Yevtushenko, Russia's leading living poet; the Louisiana Repertory Jazz Ensemble, which had recently completed a Soviet tour; and Eugene Fodor, an American pianist who had won the Tchaikovsky Competition in Moscow.

In a letter addressed to Chautauquans in March, Bratton suggested what the proposed conference would mean. It would, he said, mean that at an absolutely crucial stage in U.S.-Soviet relations, Russian and American delegations would be interacting at Chautauqua with each other and with American citizens. Soviet citizens and officials would see democracy at its best in a free and open atmosphere of dialogue and exchange. Where better could this happen if not at Chautauqua? The opportunity of having the very people who influenced the policy and goals of the world's greatest superpowers come together for conversation was one that Chautauqua was ideally located to provide in a movement towards the peace and understanding that were crucial to the future of the world. "Let us hope," he concluded, "that the conference does occur. It could be a great moment for our country, our world, and our children. Chautauqua is a place where history has been written. This would again be the case."[4]

4. Ibid.

Interviewed on the opening day, Bratton laid out in broad terms the purpose of the 1985 conference:

> The theme of the conference can't be summarized in a catchy little sentence. What makes this a unique conference is basically twofold. First, we are looking at U.S.-Soviet relations from all points of view— political, historical, psychological, and cultural. Most of these conferences are cultural exchanges and just come at it from one angle. The special quality of this conference is that it's going at it from all points of view. The other unique quality of this conference is the openness that characterizes Chautauqua. This is not a conference being held behind closed doors. It is not a conference being held with an invited guest. It's being held for anyone who wants to come, and not just listen but talk.

The amphitheater was filled on Monday, June 24, 1985, for the opening of the conference. In typical Chautauqua style, each of the public lectures and seminars included written or oral questions from members of the audience. Evening performances of music, poetry, and dance linked Soviet and American performers. Along the many paths and on the cottage porches of the institution, many conversations took place that linked strangers in the kind of crossroads experience that is typical of every Chautauqua summer season.

In general, three questions dominated the week as it proceeded. Whether in the dialogue at the amphitheater podium or in the interchange among poets, musicians, and entertainers, the nature of the relationship between Soviet and American citizens was at the core of the experience. Who are we as peoples, and where are we in that relationship? A second question continuously raised in the discussions was the possibility of improving that relationship. What do the Soviet and American governments need to do to move towards eventual nuclear disarmament? The final question was the cogent issue of Star Wars. What was the Strategic Defense Initiative, why was it such a barrier in conversations between the governments, and what could be done to lessen the tensions raised by it?

The Debate Begins: Palmer, Sokolov, and Abrahamson

In introducing the first presentation, and to rousing applause from the audience on completing his statement, Wallach welcomed the Chautauqua conference on U.S.-Soviet relations for four significant reasons. First, he began, it was rare, in view of present relations between the United States and the Soviet Union, to have a high-ranking Soviet and a high-ranking American official appear on the same stage. Second, to have Soviet and American performers on the stage together was also something of a feat. Third, most conferences on U.S.-Soviet relations around the country took place behind closed doors. This conference was open and showed democracy at its finest. Fourth, this conference had the support of both the United States and Soviet governments.

Wallach then introduced the opening speaker, R. Mark Palmer. A graduate of Yale University, where he majored in Soviet studies, Palmer (who later became U.S. ambassador to Hungary) began his political career serving at U.S. embassies in India and the Soviet Union. He later came to serve as deputy assistant secretary of state in charge of U.S. relations with the Soviet Union and East Central Europe. As director of the State Department's office of strategic nuclear and conventional arms control, he was particularly familiar with issues relating to the Soviet Union.

Palmer opened his statement with encouraging words of praise for the Russian people. "In so many ways we are the same," he said. "Russians are courageous, fun to be with, warm, and talented in the arts and in many fields. They are our adversaries, but they are also human beings." He noted that there had never been war between the United States and Russia. He recognized, however, that there were immense dangers before the world in the present impasse, for it was a totally new era. "In twenty or thirty minutes we could destroy civilization. This fact imposes an element of fear and concern. There is no more important problem for humanity."

The need, Palmer suggested, was to get to what the British call "bottom" in dealing with the Soviets. The nations today confronted two temptations. One was the argument of preemption. Some in this country had asserted that if only the United States could cut the USSR off, the Soviet Union would come apart. The argument was unrealistic. It failed to deal with the facts. The USSR, the major power in the Asian land mass—indeed in the world—spanned eleven time zones. It had more oil and gas than Saudi Arabia, a fantastic nuclear arsenal, and 4.5 million men under arms, a number far exceeding the United States with its 2 million.

The other temptation, Palmer continued, was one of naiveté. If only there were enough goodwill, the argument went, we could reach agreement with them. But this was an equally incorrect approach, for there were enduring and profound differences between the Soviets and ourselves. The question was one of differing ideologies and values. Both were crusading, even imperial nations, with dreams and visions.

Palmer went on to list what Shultz regarded as the four key issues in any U.S.-Soviet engagement: arms control, regional issues, human rights, and the bilateral agenda. These were the issues around which the four subsequent Chautauqua conferences were organized.

On arms control, Palmer said, it was of utmost importance to gain a reduction in intercontinental ballistic missiles and medium-range missiles. Unfortunately, he had little to report on this, mainly because the USSR was not willing to engage in substantial reductions. Reagan, in contrast, was looking for a reduction in the area of 50 percent. On the question of verification, the major impediment was that the USSR placed such a high value on secrecy. Opening up a society as closed as the Soviet Union would be hard to do.

Regional issues—consistently the flashpoints in international relations—had received insufficient attention. Palmer pointed again to Reagan and his recent proposal to initiate discussions about regional problems by getting experts together and seeing what each side was trying to achieve or trying to avoid.

In contrast to the position of the United States, the USSR did not believe that human rights formed a legitimate part of the bilateral relationship. Palmer expressed his particular discouragement at the situation of Jews in the USSR who sought to emigrate. He noted that, in this regard, he was echoing what had frequently been stated in official circles for some time. For example, at the leadership assembly of the National Conference on Soviet Jewry, held the previous October, Shultz had commented that he wished he could have brought the assembly encouraging news but the situation remained "very grim." Hebrew teachers were being arrested, Soviet authorities were threatening "refuseniks," anti-Semitic propaganda was widespread, and emigration had come to a standstill.[5]

In regard to the bilateral agenda, Palmer noted that in his speech at the Smithsonian Institution, Reagan had outlined eighteen or nineteen areas in which cooperation could be achieved: space rescue, for example, or cultural exchanges and grain sales. It would also be important to get the militaries together.

Palmer ended his speech with a mixture of pessimism and guarded optimism. "We are in a period where the overall relationship is bad," he admitted. "We should not look for much transformation before the end of the century. No sudden breakthrough is likely." Nevertheless, he concluded, he could find reasons for making headway in some areas. Shultz and Foreign

5. Quoted in "Soviet Jewry and U.S.-Soviet Relations," in U.S. Department of State Current Policy Paper 628, October 22, 1984 (Washington, D.C.: U.S. Department of State).

Minister Andrei A. Gromyko had had six meetings in the previous year; Reagan had also invited Gorbachev to come to Washington, D.C., for a summit meeting.

Oleg Sokolov, a graduate of the Moscow State Institute of International Relations, had served in the foreign ministry of the Soviet Union from 1960 and later as deputy director of the American division. He had had three tours of duty at the Soviet embassy in Washington in the late 1960s, 1970s, and 1980s, had participated in the summit meetings of 1973, 1974, and 1979, and in 1982 was appointed minister counselor or chargé d'affaires of the Soviet embassy in Washington, D.C.

Sokolov began his response to the Palmer address by emphasizing that Soviet-American relations affected the entire course of international developments. Both nations had a special responsibility, therefore, for the future of human civilization. Both had to decide which road humankind would take—toward genuine reductions in nuclear and conventional arsenals and the nonmilitarization of outer space, or towards a further incessant arms race, making even the heavens an area for competition in weaponry. Should the latter happen, the risk of all-out nuclear war would increase.

The danger in the present period, Sokolov insisted, was a clear change in the American approach towards the Soviet Union. Previously, it had been recognized that there could be no peaceful international order without a constructive relationship between the two nations. Today, it was like the cold war mentality all over again. Americans, he said, argue that the struggle against communism was the moral imperative of the present time. No question, the moral values were profoundly different. "In a nuclear age," Sokolov affirmed with emphasis, "the true moral imperative, despite these difficulties and differences, is the preservation of peace and the struggle against the threat of war." A loud burst of applause from the audience followed the remarks.

Sokolov then turned to what would be a recurrent theme in the week's discussions, indeed throughout the whole series of conferences—the Strategic Defense Initiative (SDI), or Star Wars. He listed the Soviet objections to the deployment of such weaponry.

First, the Stars Wars project opened up outer space for weapons. This would mean that hundreds of lasers, weapons, and high-velocity guns would be an ever-present threat impending the whole world. The Soviet position, in contrast, was to urge that outer space should not be turned into a source of mortal danger, that this last frontier should remain instead a venue of peaceful collaboration. With this comment, the Chautauqua audience again offered its approval in the form of loud applause.

Second, even a purely defensive shield, if it were possible, would para-doxically be dangerous and destabilizing. It would not offer real protection. It could not sustain a counterstrike from the other side. But it could give some hotheads the idea that they could attack first, in the hope that the few remaining missiles of the opponents would not be able to penetrate that shield.

In sum, the development of such a system would put the world on the brink of war. The Soviet Union, in response to this threat, would be forced to beef up its offensive forces. Developing the SDI was bound to generate an unprecedented arms race of unpredictable consequences. Sokolov pressed his main point: "There is only one reasonable way, we feel, to coexist peace-fully—to preserve the arms control regime, or whatever remains of it, and to work on further measures of arms limitation and reduction."

The minister drew his speech to a close with a strong appeal to the United States. From the Soviet viewpoint, he maintained, the overriding issue was whether the American side would seriously seek ways to prevent the militarization of outer space or would choose instead to proceed with its Strategic Defense Initiative.

In the typical Chautauqua manner, written questions from the audience were then presented to the morning speakers. Two of the key questions addressed the issue of equal security and defense against ballistic missile attacks.

> QUESTION: Mr. Sokolov cites equality and equal security as the basic principle of arms control. Does the U.S. government endorse this prin-ciple and has it ever said so?
>
> PALMER: We certainly accept the principle of equality. We do not accept that Soviet definition of equal security. Their definition of equal security is that they should have as many nuclear weapons as all the other nuclear powers in the world have together. The effect of that would be that the United States would have fewer weapons than the Soviet Union. That is not a basis for arms control agreement.
>
> SOKOLOV: This is the core of the argument. In the basic principles agreed on in 1972 there is the principle of equal security. It was fixed and made the basis of our relationship at that time. You are saying now that this principle is no longer applicable. We feel that this princi-ple of equal security is the basis of our relationship, especially in the area of strategic arms. If this interpretation of your attitude is exhibited in Geneva it would not enhance the prospects of agreement. You must take into account, for example, the huge geographic differences

between us. We face, for example, the NATO alliance on our borders, the forward base systems of the United States. If on that basis and on those conditions we were to accept equality in numbers, we would be acting against the best interests of the USSR. We cannot and will not do that.

PALMER: SALT I and SALT II were based on equal numbers.

SOKOLOV: Yes, on the limited scope to which the treaties were devoted. But once we deal with another phenomenon—the introduction of medium-range nuclear missiles into the European soil, which are within reach of the European parts of the USSR—we are within six minutes of attack by the United States.

PALMER: The United States has been in your situation in the last twenty years, with Soviet submarines off our coasts that can hit our cities within six minutes or less.

SOKOLOV: The overriding factor is that you have military bases surrounding the USSR. You have military alliances where nuclear weapons are deployed, surrounding the USSR. All this has to be considered when we talk about equality.

The second question related to defense against a ballistic missile attack:

QUESTION: The Soviets, regardless of any American exaggerations in the past, do have a significant advantage in first-strike weapons, ballistic missiles that are capable of knocking out missiles on the other side. Would a possible way out of this impasse be to allow a limited deployment of ballistic missile defenses on each side to reduce the danger of a first strike?

SOKOLOV: To answer the latter part of your question, I think no. We cannot enhance anybody's security by going by way of perfecting or increasing the weaponry itself. We do not subscribe to what you say, that the USSR has significant advantage. This is a classic example of how the arms race started and proceeded. There was a bomber gap, a missile gap, many other gaps. That ultimately proved to be false. We are witnessing the advent of that selfsame phenomenon for the third or fourth time. That is very regrettable.

PALMER: I find what Oleg just said quite astounding. It is simply a fact that the Soviet Union has the only functioning antiballistic missile system in the world. They are upgrading it even as we are sitting here. They also have the only functioning antisatellite weapon in the world today. If there is any question about who is out ahead in the race and in the development and modernization of ABM systems and of space systems, it is the Soviet Union.

In the afternoon lecture that followed, Gen. James Abrahamson spoke vigorously on the Strategic Defense Initiative to a packed audience in the smaller Smith-Wilkes Hall. In the three years prior to the Chautauqua conference, Abrahamson had been appointed NASA associate administrator for space transportation systems, later serving as head of the Strategic Defense Initiative Organization. The Soviet delegates, however, chose to boycott his speech. Asked to explain their absence, Vladimir Parastaeyev said, "We don't approve of Star Wars. We don't want to hear about it." The view was echoed by Pavel Podlesny, head of the Department of Foreign Policy Studies at the USA and Canada Institute in Moscow, who said that the relations between the two countries were at their lowest level in the past fifteen years. The American position on nuclear arms reduction, he said bitterly, was irresponsible.

Abrahamson began the speech by saying that he was delighted to explain Reagan's position. It was, in a phrase, to abolish all nuclear weapons. The plan, formally designated as the Strategic Defense Initiative, should really be called Star Peace, because it had the potential to make nuclear missiles impotent and obsolete. The objective of the SDI was to make the system so complex that if a conflict broke out, the Soviets could not defend against a barrage of fake and real missiles all at once. The idea was to create a "defense in depth" that would create a more stabilizing situation between the two powers. Abrahamson pointed out that the Soviet Union had three times as many warheads and megatons of explosive materials as the United States. The proposed policy would change the two countries' weapon strategy from offensive to defensive.

The Anti-Ballistic Missile (ABM) Treaty of October 1972 had made it illegal to build certain antiweapons systems, because having such a system made it possible for one country to attack the other without worrying about retaliation. "I think we sincerely gave it a try," Abrahamson said, "exposing ourselves to attack without a defense, in hopes of getting a peace agreement." But in the meantime, he went on, "the Soviets had been developing an antisatellite system and an antimissile system." The present program was entirely legal under the ABM Treaty, still only in the planning phase, and development decisions would not be made until the 1990s.

The proposed system would operate in three phases. In the first phase, missiles would be sensed while they were rising in the atmosphere. In this phase they moved very slowly and were therefore easiest to knock out. A second phase would deal with those missiles that reached outer space. Missiles with multiple warheads would sit in space and fire warheads as well as dummies intended to deceive radar and antiweapons systems. Satellites would seek out such missiles. The third phase would strike at weapons on their way back into the atmosphere, headed for U.S. defense sites or cities.

Following Abrahamson's address, many Chautauquans voiced their serious concerns about the militarization of space. Questions of cost, safety, and reliability were raised. Abrahamson continued to argue that the real issue was the safety and security of the peoples of the world. He admitted that the ABM Treaty would have to be modified or abandoned in order to carry out the program. "Two and a half billion dollars is being discussed in Congress," he said, in an estimation of the cost.

One member of the audience, obviously in resistance to the comment by Abrahamson, bluntly declared: "Nuclear war is insanity. We should not make peace through rearmament but through disarmament." Abrahamson agreed that nuclear war was an insanity. "But," he said, "consider that a very large-scale conflict may be arising. What is the best means to avoid that war?"

Sonnenfeldt and Podlesny on the Origins of the Crisis

The question of how it might be possible for the United States and the Soviet Union to avoid large-scale conflict and improve relations with one another came before the audience on the following day.

Helmut Sonnenfeldt had served in the U.S. government since 1947. From 1952 to 1969 he was research and intelligence specialist in the Department of State, dealing with Soviet and East European and international Communist affairs. He began his lecture by noting that the causes of the present crisis could be found in the history of the cold war.

At the end of World War II, he began, the United States was prepared to withdraw from Europe and to do so as soon as possible. It was prepared, with some reservations, to rely on the United Nations and to seek ways of collaborating with the Soviet Union and other countries in shaping the postwar order. In the late 1940s, a series of moves on the part of the Soviet Union led to a fundamental redefinition of American interests and commitments: Soviet actions in Eastern Europe, the incorporation of one East European country after the other into the Soviet empire, the imposition there of Stalinist regimes, the protracted presence in Iran of Soviet forces, and Soviet claims on Turkey and on parts of the Mediterranean region. The freedom and security of Western Europe—at least the parts that had not been over-run by the Red Army—and of other rim lands around the Soviet periphery became a major American concern, interest, and commitment.

Sonnenfeldt pressed his argument. This redefinition of American interests and commitments, brought about by the disillusionment and disenchantment with what happened immediately after the war, was such that the Soviets themselves began to see the United States as threatening them. For the United States, the Soviet threat was not only one of expansion in the geopolitical sense. It related also to the potential spread of the totalitarian form of oppression that prevailed in the Soviet Union and was reestablished with full force after the war. Sonnenfeldt noted that there had been vigorous debates in this country about how the United States should deal with these conditions. Polls indicated general approval of arms control and of working with the USSR for a better world. Yet large majorities also expressed suspicion and concern about whether the USSR could be trusted to keep agreements.

The détente of the 1970s, sometimes now viewed with nostalgia, was never unchallenged in the United States. As in the late 1940s, however, the Soviets contributed greatly to suspicions about détente. Reviewing the developments of the previous twenty-five years or so, Sonnenfeldt listed the reasons for such suspicion. First, the Soviets continued in this period the massive arms buildup that they had projected in the 1960s. Secondly, despite the better atmosphere of the détente period, the Soviets continued to treat the third world as an arena for geopolitical aggrandizement and maneuver. Yet they did little or nothing to further the social and economic progress of these often disadvantaged and poor countries. Thirdly, they contributed to the disenchantment about détente by maintaining the essentially repressive nature of their regime at home and demonstrating the basic injustice and unnaturalness of their empire in Western Europe. In the meantime, East Germans, Hungarians, Poles, and others rebelled against the repression and tried to break out of their straitjackets. All that had its impact on the American consciousness and on any notion of improving relations between the United States and the USSR.

Noting that there had been fewer severe crises between the Soviet Union and the United States in the past five years than in any earlier five-year period, Sonnenfeldt went on to ask how the United States could address the present crisis. No real peace had come, yet there were reasons for hope. If the two countries could only strive for greater steadiness with fewer promises of dramatic change, if they could define their mutual interests and pursue them with restraint, they might be spared the constant sequence of open conflict and crisis.

Pavel Podlesny, head of foreign policy research at the USA and Canada Institute in Moscow, began his response to Sonnenfeldt with an immediate rebuttal. "I disagree with Dr. Sonnenfeldt in many ways, because he has given us a simplistic picture of the beginning of the Cold War. It was quite evident that relations between our countries after the Second World War would be difficult." According to Sonnenfeldt, the cold war did not start after the war but during the war. That was true. The two countries knew very well that, irrespective of their cooperation during the Second World War, there were serious difficulties in their relations. He continued:

> Let me remind you that we reached agreement to open the second front in 1942, but the United States and Great Britain decided to postpone it for two years. These two years were a heavy burden for the Soviet Union to wage decisive battles on its own and to try to defend our country and our children. Dr. Sonnenfeldt has failed to tell about this. The second front was opened only after it was clear that the Soviet Union would be able to end the war by itself, even without the second front.

Podlesny ended his rebuttal of Sonnenfeldt's statement with a comment on how easy it was for the Soviet Union and the United States to fight each other over various issues. Each would have a long list, but that would not help: "Instead of accusing each other, we should draw the lessons from the seventies. We should try to see what is possible in our relationship and what is not, how we can and how we cannot cooperate."

In the question-and-answer period that followed, the issue of the Strategic Defense Initiative was immediately raised, evoking the following interchange.

> Sonnenfeldt: The problem is that the Soviet side has changed the agreement made by Secretary Shultz and Soviet Foreign Minister Gromyko concerning the relationship between the space weapons, offensive strategic weapons, and intermediate-range nuclear weapons. Instead of insisting on an interrelationship, they have insisted *as a precondition* for talking that the United States must first agree to the prohibition of research. That was not the agreement reached by Secretary Shultz and Foreign Minister Gromyko. So in this case the fault does not lie with an American refusal to talk about the interrelationship.

The Americans are quite prepared to do that, and I hope that the Soviet side will also be.

PODLESNY: Maybe Dr. Sonnenfeldt has demonstrated how difficult it is for us to deal with the Americans and to understand the agreements that have been reached. In regard to the negotiations in Geneva, according to my understanding we put no preconditions to this subject. What we are suggesting is simple: that we should reach agreement for the two countries to undertake two tasks, one being space strike weapons. Without agreement on this subject it would be impossible to reach agreement on the radical reduction of other strategic weapons. Any effort on the American side to isolate one of the two tasks—trying to reach agreement on the medium range, for example—is not acceptable for us. It violates the principle of interrelationship on which we agreed at the meeting between the two ministers of foreign affairs.

SONNENFELDT: I hope you listen carefully to what our Soviet guest said to you just now. It is one thing for the Soviet Union to make a proposal. They can make any proposal they want, including one to prohibit space strike weapons. What is not constructive is to say that unless this proposal is accepted we cannot talk about anything else. That, it seems to me, defeats the whole purpose of give-and-take negotiations. Our negotiators are willing to talk about all three sets of issues simultaneously or in sequence, but with no preconditions.

Nitze and Malkov on Eliminating Nuclear Weapons

On the fifth day of the conference, June 28, 1985, Wallach introduced the opening speaker, Paul Nitze, in warm terms. For over forty years, Nitze had been one of the chief architects of U.S. policy toward the Soviet Union. He was Reagan's chief negotiator of the Intermediate-Range Nuclear Forces (INF) treaty from 1981 to 1984 and in that latter year named special adviser to the president and secretary of state on arms control. The speech that Nitze gave, however, was so tough that at its conclusion Wallach felt compelled to remind the audience of Nitze's reputation as a hard-liner but not "an unreasoning zealot."

Nitze began with a refutation of the Soviet accusation that the United States had expanded the arms race into a new area by initiating what they called the militarization of space. "One might conclude from this Soviet commentary," he said, "that the Soviet Union has no program comparable to our SDI. Such a conclusion would be far from correct." According to

Nitze, the Soviets were heavily involved in strategic defense with programs that went far beyond research. The Soviet Union had spent roughly as much on strategic defense as it had on its massive offensive nuclear forces. They had deployed around Moscow the world's only operational antiballistic missile system. They also had an in-depth national air defense force, a vast political leadership survival program, and a nationwide civil defense force and programs.

Nitze went on to list Soviet advanced technologies for strategic defense: high-energy lasers, particle-beam weapons, radio-frequency weapons, and kinetic-energy weapons, the same type of technologies being researched in the SDI program of the United States. They had over ten thousand scientists and engineers associated with the development of lasers for weapons and had probably achieved the capability to develop the necessary optical systems for laser weapons and prototype laser weapons. Since the early 1970s, the Soviets had had a research program designed to explore the technical feasibility of a particle-beam weapon in space. One designed to destroy satellites could be tested by the year 2000. Early in the next century, the Soviets could have a prototype space-based ballistic missile defense system ready for testing.

Nitze vigorously called "preposterous" Soviet criticism of the United States's SDI program. "Space has been militarized for many years, primarily by Soviet systems and programs. The Soviet disingenuousness is all too evident." At a minimum, the Soviets seemed to want to keep the United States from outstripping them in such technologies. The Soviet propaganda line against SDI was as predictable as it was hypocritical. Obviously the Soviets hoped to foster a situation in which the United States would unilaterally restrain its research effort, even though it was fully consistent with existing treaties. This would leave the Soviets with a virtual monopoly in advanced strategic defense research. It was important, he concluded, to recognize this propaganda for what it was, the key element of an overall strategy to divide the United States from its allies and elicit from us unilateral concessions.

The response to Nitze was given by Dr. Viktor Malkov, a professor at Moscow University specializing in contemporary American history. He began by congratulating the organizers of the conference, "a step in the right direction that is bringing us, the citizens of our two countries, face to face with real people." The political dialogue, he continued, is useful "if we want to reduce political tension and the risk of confrontation between our two countries." For Malkov, the elimination of nuclear weapons was absolutely imperative. It was the pivotal question in contemporary international relations. "There is no doubt," he said, "that a removal of the nuclear threat would lead to a fundamental improvement in the global situation, strengthen confidence between states, and give an impetus to broad and mutually advantageous cooperation between peoples." Malkov then listed the measures necessary as a first step: to stop the development, production, and deployment of nuclear weapons; to freeze nuclear arsenals and embark on their reduction; and to conclude a treaty banning all nuclear tests.

Malkov then turned to the "so-called Soviet military superiority." He quoted a recent interview by former United States Secretary of Defense Robert McNamara who had said that for a long time there had been a strong tendency in the United States to overestimate Soviet strength and underestimate Western strength. "That is not good for either of us," Malkov said, "because by overstating the size of Soviet forces and fearing that the USSR may become stronger, NATO countries are increasing their own strengths, and that, in turn, causes the Soviet Union and the Warsaw Pact countries to fear NATO strengths and to increase their own armed forces."

The Soviet Union had already suggested, according to Malkov, that both sides should reduce strategic offensive arms by one quarter and would have no objections to deeper reductions. All this would be possible, but only if space did not become the new arena of the arms race. No matter how the United States might justify its plans for militarizing outer space, the intent of the plans was clear: to gain the opportunity to deliver a first nuclear strike with impunity. "The Star Wars initiative leads to the de-stabilization of the entire system of international relations and to even stronger political and military confrontation than now." If preparations for Star Wars were to continue, the Soviet Union would have no other option than to take countermeasures, including the strengthening and improvement of offensive nuclear weapons. What was needed most of all was to keep open every possible avenue for continuing the dialogue on many levels. "And we believe," he concluded, "the Chautauqua conference contributed to this noble goal."

In the debate between Nitze and Malkov that followed, Nitze responded that the Soviets had approximately four hundred SS-20 missiles, each of which had three warheads. The United States, in contrast, had deployed about one hundred warheads in Europe, so the ratio was twelve hundred to one hundred. "The freeze at that level would freeze a very unequal situation." At this point, Wallach interrupted with a direct question: "Is Mr. Nitze making up these facts or are the Soviets hiding them? Where does the truth lie?" Podlesny quickly responded with a categorical denial: "We have," he said, "no research that is directed to the creation of what Dr. Nitze said, space weapons, and that is the crucial matter. We are absolutely against this."

Nitze retorted that the audience would now see what the problem was. Malkov had simply repeated what the Soviets had been saying, namely, that their systems were designed for good purposes and the American systems for bad purposes. This had been a consistent problem in negotiations from the beginning. Nitze pressed his attack on the Soviet position: would it be desirable, he inquired, to get to the point of totally eliminating nuclear weapons from the world? That objective the Americans surely shared with the Soviet Union. But the question at issue was how one was to get there. It was the American view that it would be easier to achieve that goal by developing good defenses against ballistic missiles. The United States, through its commitment to the United Nations charter, had declared that it would not be the first to use force against another side. Its leaders intended to honor that commitment. They had also indicated to the Soviets that they were prepared to discuss a joint declaration on the non-use of force. So it was the use of force and not just of nuclear weapons that the United States wanted to prohibit.

Wallach, seeking to draw the morning's lecture and discussion to a close, had one last question for Podlesny: "If the USSR really wants to begin reducing arms, why does it refuse to permit on-site inspection?" Podlesny replied that when the two countries were involved in the strategic arms limitation talks—of which Dr. Nitze was one of the architects—there was a provision for the verification of the treaty. So the general position of the USSR was that both countries should adhere to the essence of the agreements. "We are," he concluded, "for verification."

Conflict Analysis and Resolution

For several years the U.S. State Department had become involved in looking at conflict analysis and resolution, for example in U.S. relations with the Muslim Middle East. Joseph V. Montville, who held faculty appointments at Harvard and the University of Virginia medical schools, specialized in the relatively young discipline of political psychology, specifically the psychology of conflict. He had also worked in the State Department's Bureaus of Near Eastern and South Asian Affairs and Intelligence and Research, where he was chief of the Near East Division and director of the Office of Global Issues.

In the course of the week he explained his understanding of conflict analysis. It involved tracing the history of a conflict and gaining an idea of the psychological tasks involved in dealing with it. The new discipline of political psychology was based on the concept that the fundamental craving of all human beings is a need for security, whether in the form of respect or self-worth. If that security is not provided, there are consequences: narcissistic rage, depression, alcoholism, and aggression. Dehumanization can exist even in international relations, he said, and is therefore dangerous. It feeds suspicion. It filters out possibilities of resolving conflicts. It implies, for example, that all the good is on one side, all the bad on the other.

Turning to deal with the significance of the week's conference at Chautauqua, Montville offered praise for the design of the program, which was to stress aspects of the common humanity of both sides in the international conflict. "If you have lunch with a Russian, it is a little hard to demonize him. If you hear a poet talking about pain, yearning, love, it is hard to say that the people who produce this poetry are not human." He then quoted at length from a speech given by Reagan at the thirty-ninth session of the U.N. General Assembly the previous fall. In the speech Reagan had proposed a new approach to "the great end of lifting the dread of nuclear war from the peoples of the earth." Reagan invited the leaders of the world to join in a new beginning. "We need a fresh approach to reducing international tension," he said. Toward this end he proposed to the Soviet Union that the two countries institutionalize regular ministerial or cabinet-level meetings on the whole agenda of issues before them, including the problem of needless obstacles to understanding. "I believe that we should move rapidly to developing a new climate of policy understanding, one that is essential if crises are to be avoided and real arms control to be negotiated."

"This speech," Montville said, "offers a number of suggestions that implement the rehumanization process. The very fact that meetings would be held by responsible officials in the military and political levels would, we hope, extend the kind of process that we have been having at the breakfast and lunch table here at Chautauqua with our Soviet counterparts."

A Harvard professor of psychiatry, John E. Mack,[6] complemented Montville's address by introducing what he called ideologies of enmity. He posed the question: Why would psychiatrists be involved in the nuclear arms race or in the matter of Soviet-American relations? They would say initially that they were concerned about the effect the arms race was having on young

---

6. Mack gained some notoriety later by arguing in his book *Passport to the Cosmos* (New York: Crown Publishers, 1999) that "alien abductions" are not rare phenomena but signs that extraterrestrials have arrived on earth.

people growing up. He had recently learned of an exercise that a third-grade teacher in Menlo Park, California, had done with a group of twenty-three eight-year-olds. She asked them, first, to write the name of the most important person they knew in the world and, second, to say what was important to them that they wanted to communicate to that person. Most of the children chose to write to President Reagan. Fifteen out of the twenty-three, with no prompting with regard to the arms race or to Russia, referred either to the Russians or to the Russian-American relationship or to nuclear missiles or to World War III. One went, "Dear President Reagan. I don't want a war with the Russians. I want to make friends with other countries. I want the wars to stop. I hate when people kill whales. I hate when people are dead."

Mack then went on to spend some time on what he called the ideologies of enmity. By this he meant a way of looking at the world and structuring complex realities in simple terms that allowed it to be understandable and manageable psychologically. In the case of the Soviet-American relationship, he said, the ideologies of enmity were a set of perceptions and a system of thought, ways of looking at the enemy or adversary that protected the individual from a sense of trouble and responsibility. Ideologies of enmity had dual origins. They were found deep in the psyche of a child who tried to discover who is "me" and who is "not me," or what is friendly, what is hostile. The other root was the history of the nation and its cultural experience in relation to other nations. "You thus have," he said, "a complex interaction between that personal psychology and the way in which that psychology becomes organized in groups and is played out in the relations between nations. In extreme forms the ideologies of enmity become demonization and dehumanization."

Mack ended his statement with a pointed reference to Chautauqua: "The nuclear arms problem is going to be stopped by people like you—people in the towns and villages, the country and the cities of America, people steeped in our deepest traditions, who will petition our leaders to end this thing, so that their time and devotion will be towards ending this thing and establishing a relationship with our adversaries."

In another of the afternoon seminars Edward Keenan, professor of history, Russian Research Center, Harvard University, raised the historical question of what shaped Russian attitudes towards the United States.

First, he said, it was important to remember that for Russians the United States was an extension of the Europe with which they had such a complex relationship. Second, the formative critical experience of the Russians took form in the cultural web of communal subsistence agriculture. This was the womb of Russian culture. The structures and habits of thought of Russia were shaped in this matrix. As Russian society developed, there developed also the culture of the court, a delicately balanced system of collegial rule whereby members of warring clans traded off a number of goals in order to strive for the single most important goal, which was the suppression of violence among themselves. Third, the Muscovite bureaucracy was a wonderful invention because, against colossal odds in seemingly unmanageable territory and without previous training, it devised techniques to control a stable social order.

All three factors, he argued, form something of how the Russians see us. First, there was the avoidance of risk. The communal agriculturalist was not an innovator. Innovation that failed could mean extinction. The innovator who tried to change the balance among the warring clans was likely to create catastrophe. Politicians thought of political order as the result of a successful conspiracy against the natural condition of their class, which was chaos. They were willing to pay a high cost to avoid the risk of what might happen. Second, there was a lower expectation of human beings, when left to their own devices, about their ability and potential. Third, there was also the fear of chaos. "Russians think of us to be too much inclined to risk and unpredictable behavior. . . . They can't understand why we don't see that capitalism leads to an inevitable series of crises. They think it is lunatic that we rely on something as out of control as the electoral process, changing course every four years." Could the two cultures collaborate and find a common ground, to reduce tensions, to end the arms race? Yes, Keenan concluded, but if it happened, it would come through understanding what the other side made sense of in its own terms.

Marcus Cunliffe, professor of history at George Washington University, had agreed to take part in the conference and to describe a larger background against which the ideological conflict could be set. He proposed to do so by taking a fresh look at the question of empires. English by birth, he was well familiar with the British imperialist history.

Empires, he argued, come and go; all have features in common. They all tend to have a sense of mission. They often convey to others a sense of their own moral superiority, entitlement to acquire and annex. They all tend to be arrogant and hypocritical and to rationalize their exercise of power as peacekeeping. The nature of empires is that they are nationalistic with a sense of right and wrong. They also tend to have intense rivalries, commonly with one other power—Rome with Carthage, the British with the

Americans in the nineteenth century, and in the twentieth century, the United States with the USSR.

The "evil Soviet empire" for Americans was an empire of radical, subversive, and antireligious forces. In the American view of the world and of Russia in particular after 1917, there were two rival ideologies. These ideologies constituted a struggle that was fundamental and could never be brought to an end without the victory of one power over the other. This could mean only that the world was in terrible peril. Cunliffe, however, drew his observations to a more optimistic conclusion: "If we take a cynical view of human nature and history, then we would conclude that all attempts at social reform were doomed or pointless. The American Revolution should not have taken place, the Russian Revolution should not have taken place. But to say that left no room for purposeful action, only for cynical despair. What was needed was the word benevolence, a good word."

Music and Poetry

For well over a century, Chautauqua Institution has been a center of the arts, education, religion, and recreation—what one of its founders called "all the elements of a well-ordered life." The first conference on U.S.-Soviet relations involved most of these elements in various configurations as the experiences of the day moved, one by one, in the words of a participant, "from nuclear arms to bluegrass, from détente to Dixieland, from the historical to the psychological, from politics to poetry, from Moscow to Chautauqua." For four nights in a row Soviet and American artists performed on the same stage.

During the course of the week—significantly in a building known to Chautauquans as the "Amp," or the Amphitheater—Soviet poet Andréi Voznesénsky joined Tom Paxton and the Kingston Trio in an evening of folksinging, storytelling, and poetry reading. Voznesénsky, wearing a white suit, blueberry shirt, and a wide smile that evening, was known as one of the brightest stars in the new generation of poets who came to prominence in the more liberal years of the Khrushchev era. Many put him in the same cluster as Pushkin. He listened as his poems were read first in English, after which he delivered them with a percussive use of his native language as he rocked back on his heels and hammered the air with his forearm. At the end of his recital he read a poem in Russian, without a previous translation, that drew its imagery and sound from the life and liturgy of the old Russian Orthodox Church. In his rotund voice he seemed to echo the bells of St. Basil's Cathedral in Moscow.

The next evening, fellow poet Yevgeny Yevtushenko made his appearance, accompanied on this occasion by the Paul Winter Consort, in a many-colored celebration of poetry and music. Yevtushenko, with a host of others, had opened the door to a new kind of literature following the death of Stalin. Winter himself opened the evening with his captivating tribute to the world of whales. He read a news story on the rescue by a Russian icebreaker of one thousand to three thousand Beluga or white whales that had been trapped in a strait of shrinking waters. With whale sounds reverberating in the amphitheater and with drums and cello backing, Winter offered an ode of thanks on behalf of the Belugas. In a lighter vein he invited the audience to join him in the "howl-la-luyah" chorus tribute to the wolf population.

Then Yevtushenko, wearing a white peasant shirt and khaki pants, recited some of his poems about the Grand Canyon and birch trees. A tender work, "Lament for a Brother," described the interaction between two geese, one—"my dove-grey brother"—shot and killed, and the other recounting his own loves and conflicts, and ending poignantly with the words from another of his poems, "I Would Like": "I would like happiness, but not at the expense of the unhappy. And I would like freedom, but not at the expense of the unfree." Later in the program the poet read his poem "Babi Yar," a dramatic and touching testimonial to the victims of that massacre of Russian citizens by German soldiers during the occupation of Kiev. In the Soviet Union the poem had uncovered the issue of anti-Semitism, neglected totally by party leaders:

> Wild grasses rustle over Babi Yar,
> The trees look sternly, as if passing judgement.
> Here, silently, all screams, and, hat in hand,
> I feel my hair changing shade to gray.
> And I myself, like one long soundless scream
> Above the thousands of thousands interred,
> I'm every old man executed here,
> As I am every child murdered here.
> No fiber of my body will forget this.[7]

7. The poem sought to expose both the inhumanity of the notorious concentration camp and the injustice of the Soviet government after the war in refusing to raise a monument to the thousands of Jews (at least thirty-four thousand) and some others (gypsies, for example, and Soviet prisoners of war) who had been executed

Winter and Yevtushenko brought the evening to a close with a farewell tribute, "In a Circle of Friends."

Yevtushenko made a further appearance the following day, giving answers to questions from the Hall of Philosophy audience. He began by responding to an inquiry about his novel, *Wild Berries,* which dealt with the land and people of Siberia, where he grew up. His best poetry, he said, was written about Siberia. "A writer must embrace all branches and all the air of humanity," he said. "But he can do it only if he is deeply rooted in his own earth." He went on to describe how he wrote his poetry and what inspired him. "I can't write poetry in a room," he said. "I can work only when I'm walking. I write poetry in my mind. When I want to write something, I go walking for several hours, speeding. And that is why I spend a lot of time in the fresh air, even when it is cold."

Another member of the audience was curious to know about a trip that Yevtushenko had made to a Buffalo steel factory and a steelworker's home twenty years previously. Through his translator, Bert Todd, he explained that he and Todd had decided to read some of his poetry during a lunch break at a Buffalo steel factory. "In the Soviet Union," he explained, "poetry is read everywhere—in schools, auditoriums, and factories. I decided I would like to read poetry in America to the working people."

On another evening in the week, Soviet classical pianist Ekaterina Sarantseva met violinist Eugene Fodor—himself no stranger to the Soviet Union—on the stage of the Amphitheater. Sarantseva, at age twenty-two, was one of the leading pianists in the Soviet Union. In the year previous to her arrival at Chautauqua she had won the Montreal International Music Competition. Fodor, winner of the 1972 International Paganini Competition, had won, two years later, the highest prize awarded to an American violinist in Moscow's Tchaikovsky Competition. They agreed to play, among other pieces, Mozart's Sonata no. 4 in E Minor for piano and violin. The program also included Ysaye's "Ballad," Paganini's 24th Caprice, and pieces by Bach and Rachmaninoff.

For the audience it was a revelation of how music could transcend barriers of language or culture. The two musicians had met earlier that day

---

there by the Nazi troops. The lines selected are from a translation by Benjamin Okopnik. Both poems referred to are in the CD by Yevgeny Yevtushenko with the Paul Winter Consort, *The City of No—The City of Yes* (New York: Van Winkle Clef, 2000).

for the first time. Musically, Fodor later reported, "it's as though we had been living next door to each other all our lives." Wallach himself had been present earlier at a rehearsal by the musicians. He reported that although Sarantseva did not speak very much English, about three minutes after they met, and despite the fact that she had never seen two of the works that were going to be performed, she and Fodor were conversing easily with each other, talking the universal language of music. "And," Wallach said, "I mean, not only playing music but also talking with each other, with Gene Fodor speaking English and Ms. Sarantseva speaking Russian, and both of them completely unaware of the fact that while they could not understand one another's language, they were understanding each other." On another occasion, adding another dimension to Wallach's comment, Georgi Garanyan, a full-time Soviet composer and saxophonist, commented, "To be a musician is not a profession. It is a nationality. Musicians are the same throughout the world. Russian musicians as a people are the same as Americans. It's true!"

Attitudes and Values in the Soviet Union

Towards the close of the week, S. Frederick Starr, president of Oberlin College and former director of the Kennan Institute for Advanced Russian Studies, gave a lecture on public values and popular culture in the Soviet Union. Starr had written about the importance of jazz in Soviet culture as a way of understanding Soviet ideology. He began by making four general statements about attitudes and values in the Soviet Union.

First, most citizens of the USSR were loyal to their country. They might criticize the bureaucracy, but by and large they believed their system was right, fair, and on the correct course. Second, while they might make jokes about everything imaginable, even at their most critical they identified wholly with their nation. Third, universally Soviet citizens would profess a genuine, deep, and abiding interest in the cause of peace. Fourth, to a degree quite different from Americans, they were disengaged from politics. It was a reading population and a well-informed one but not, as in the United States, a population dominated by politics.

Earlier in the week Vladimir Parastaeyev had announced to the audience that members of both governments and representatives from Chautauqua would be invited to continue the dialogue at a similar conference, to be held in the Soviet Union before or after the following season. On the final day of the week, Wallach announced that all Chautauquans were invited to sign a resolution drafted by delegates from both countries to be sent to each nation. The resolution, which was unanimously endorsed by the audience at Thursday's morning lecture, read as follows:

> We, the Chautauqua Conference, both the undersigned respective members of the Soviet and American delegations and the audience, jointly recommend that the governments of the United States of America and of the Union of Soviet Socialist Republics take all the necessary steps to conclude a new cultural exchange agreement in the nearest future.

The resolution was placed in the Colonnade Building for any who wanted to sign it. Several hundred did indeed do so.

It was time to say farewell to the citizens and the diplomats who had made the long journey to Chautauqua. It fell to Montville to express in words something of the feelings of achievement, discovery, and hope formed slowly during the week:

> Today concludes this conference, perhaps in the minds of some with a sense of sadness, perhaps in the minds of others with a shred of relief, but hopefully, and most of all, with a feeling of hope. The essence of this conference may not necessarily be in the quality of the information and entertainment that you've heard, although that has been superb. It may not be in the incredibly stimulating full plate of activities, although these have been vital components of this week's success. The essence of this conference may be in bringing together, with the full approval of both governments, Soviet citizens, entertainers, leaders, with a group of people called Chautauquans, and watching an interchange develop that has not been hostile at all, but, rather, has been both open and friendly. Many here, myself included, feel that we have several new friends who call Russia home. To our guests behind me I think I can safely say on your behalf that you have hundreds of new friends who call America home. That alone makes this week incredibly successful. That alone offers hope.

In a speech to the General Assembly of the United Nations on October 24, 1985, a few months after the Chautauqua conference, President Reagan proposed an initiative by which it might be possible to achieve peace and reconciliation, end foreign military involvement, and foster economic reconstruction in areas of regional conflict. The proposal involved action at three levels. The first level was a process of negotiation. This was essential, Reagan said, to achieving an end to violence, the withdrawal of foreign troops, and national reconciliation. The second level involved continuing conversations aimed at eliminating foreign military presence and restraining the flow of outside arms. At the third level, efforts would be undertaken to welcome these countries into the world economy and the family of free nations. The main burden of the plan would be laid on the parties in conflict with one another in these regions. Neither the United States nor the Soviet Union should impose a solution.

Negotiation, conversation, and welcome—what Reagan called for at a global level, Chautauqua had already experienced and expressed at a local level. The discussions of the week, the experience of seeing the "enemy" up close, and the final resolution of the 1985 delegates were impetus enough to encourage the Chautauqua staff to set about the planning of a second conference. It would involve this time not seven but hundreds, even thousands, of Soviet delegates. Chautauquans would be present in their own hundreds to continue the work of citizen diplomacy. The Stars and Stripes were about to meet the Hammer and Sickle on the latter's home ground.

CHAPTER FOUR

1986: "A Vital Condition of Success"

The Riga meeting was dominated by tough talk on both sides rather than toasts to mir i druzhba (peace and friendship).

Time, September 29, 1986

THE 1985 CONFERENCE on U.S.-Soviet relations had been successful beyond the hopes of its planners for several reasons. One of the aims had been to open up the process of U.S.-Soviet negotiations to a section of the American public—to bring it out from behind the closed doors of diplomats and the specialized meetings of academics. The task was to learn something of the complexities of a very difficult relationship. That had been done at Chautauqua and with real understanding. To use the words of Wallach at the close of the 1985 conference, "We have a bit more sympathy for negotiators on both sides of this difficult question." Furthermore, artists, poets, and performers had shown that music and poetry constitute a language that could transcend differences of culture, history, or policy.

In the course of the 1985 week, there had been much discussion about the possibility of a follow-up conference on the Black Sea the following summer. If such an arrangement were possible, Wallach expressed the hope that the conference would be available on Russian television. Perhaps some of the participants who had appeared on the platform in 1985 might also take part. Certainly, many Chautauquans who had followed the discussions at Chautauqua with close attention would want to make the journey to the Soviet Union.

It was a bold proposal but one eagerly adopted after the summer season by Chautauqua's president and his senior staff. The nine-week summer season was the core of Chautauqua's life. No program with the distinctive Chautauqua "mix" (of education, recreation, religion, and the arts) had ever been proposed, let alone presented, beyond the season or beyond the gates. The complexity of such a venture seemed daunting, even impossible. Moscow was 4,694 miles away. Funding was a large and imponderable issue. It might be that the Soviets would be unwilling to collaborate. The Black Sea had been suggested, but geographical, political, and nationalistic difficulties could close that opportunity. The Soviet government might not be open. No suitable Soviet partner in the conference might be ready to collaborate. Once advanced, however, the very idea of a second conference was hard to put aside.

Relationships between the two nations remained unsettled and fractious. In November 1985, however, the United States and the Soviet Union signed in Geneva a new General Exchanges Agreement. This marked the resumption of official academic, cultural, and performing-artist exchanges between the two countries for the first time since 1979. The agreement had been signed by Shultz and Soviet Foreign Minister Eduard Shevardnadze. It included projects in the performing arts and citizen exchange. In addition, Reagan and Gorbachev endorsed a new and broad-based initiative to expand contacts between citizens of both countries. Reagan himself had earlier called for a series of new initiatives "in order to find as yet undiscovered avenues where American and Soviet citizens can cooperate fruitfully for the benefit of mankind."[1]

Gorbachev himself, however, seemed pessimistic about the quality of U.S.-Soviet relations. "The situation today," he said, "is highly complex, very tense. I would even go so far as to say it is explosive." According to Gorbachev, in the roughly two months since his November summit meeting with Reagan, the United States had rejected every overture from the Soviet Union, such as its proposals for moratoriums on tests of nuclear and antisatellite weapons. These were being dismissed as one more propaganda exercise by Moscow.

In a speech in April, Gorbachev rounded on the United States for putting its Star Wars program into full gear: "If, contrary to common sense, the U.S.A. persists in purveying this policy, we shall find a convincing response."[2]

Despite the tension in the relationship between the two countries, it was also becoming clearer that a desire to move beyond constraints of the polemical past was increasingly being felt both in the Soviet Union and in the United States. Earlier in February 1986, for example, Gorbachev presented his political report to the Twenty-seventh Congress of the Communist Party

1. Radio and television address to the nation on the upcoming Soviet–United States summit meeting in Geneva, November 14, 1985.
2. Excerpt from a speech to the auto workers at Togliatti, USSR, April 8, 1986.

of the Soviet Union. He advocated an "interaction of advanced ideas."[3] (The words would certainly have sounded congenial to the planners in the institution.) Ideas alone, he said, did not give shape automatically to a coherent and active worldview of the masses. Socialist ideology drew its energy and effectiveness from the interaction of advanced ideas with the practice of building the new society.

In the United States, former president Richard M. Nixon had been calling for "a new realism" in dealing with the Soviet Union, a realism based not on friendship but on respect. The older American policies of containment and détente were inadequate, according to Nixon, for dealing with the Soviet Union. American foreign policy toward the Soviet Union should be built on "the hard reality of mutual respect," not "the soft illusion of mutual affection."[4] He called on Reagan and Gorbachev to avoid an "insane" continuation of the nuclear arms race. Later in the year Foreign Minister Eduard Shevardnadze was to meet with his American counterpart, Secretary of State George Shultz. Schultz proposed that human rights, a topic shunned by his predecessors, should be given higher priority.

An Open, Chautauqua-type Meeting in Latvia

In May, Wallach met with Susan Eisenhower and the board chairman of the Eisenhower World Affairs Institute, Gen. Andrew Goodpaster. The subject of discussion was the institute's interest in the possibility of a U.S.-Soviet conference to take place in the Soviet Union the following fall. Eisenhower readily agreed that the institute would cosponsor the Chautauqua visit as partner. She also arranged to make a visit with Wallach to the Soviet Union to observe and assist with the negotiations to ensure a successful program.

One obstacle in the discussions at this time, which also involved Wallach and Palmer, was the Soviet proposal to hold the Chautauqua meeting at a conference site near Riga in Latvia. Unlike an earlier proposal to meet in the Black Sea area, this presented a major difficulty. Latvia had become independent at the end of World War I, November 11, 1918. In 1939, Stalin and Hitler signed the Molotov-Ribbentrop Pact, which, among other things, secretly divided the Baltic States into Nazi and Soviet spheres of influence. The pact paved the way for the Nazi invasion of Poland and the beginning of World War II. By August 1940, the Red Army had annexed Latvia and

3. Speech to the 27th Congress of the Communist Party of the Soviet Union.
4. Speech at the World Affairs Council, New York, March 5, 1986.

the other Baltic republics. The Latvian government was dissolved and re-placed by a puppet Soviet government. An ensuing reign of terror led to the arrest, execution, or deportation of thousands of Latvians. The Jewish pop-ulation of around ninety thousand was largely wiped out.

Many Latvians did welcome the Nazis as liberators and enlisted in Ger-man military units, but a large number fled to the West in 1944 and 1945 to avoid the Red Army's reconquest of their country. For Hitler, the 1939 non-aggression pact was a temporary and tactical maneuver. His decision to invade the Soviet Union in June 1941 was inspired by a desire to acquire the lebensraum that he had been seeking for Germany since 1925 and by a detestation of the Soviet system. By the fall of 1942, Latvia once again lay under domination, now that of Nazi Germany. The battle of Stalingrad ended a string of German victories, and by the summer of 1944 the Soviets had taken possession once again of the Baltic States and reoccupied Latvia. Latvians were subjected to arrests and executions, deportations to Siberia, and a systematic effort to make Latvians a minority in their own country. The Latvian language and culture were systematically suppressed. Latvia's total losses during World War II were around 450,000. Under Stalin, another 175,000 Latvians were killed or deported between 1945 and 1949. Between 1959 and 1979 the population increase consisted of 13.1 percent native Latvians and 63.5 percent Russians. Since the Soviet occupation in 1940, more than 600,000 non-Latvians had been brought into Latvia.

The policy of the U.S. government was not to recognize the 1940 annex-ation of Latvia, Estonia, and Lithuania by the Soviet Union. The difficulties in planning a conference in Latvia were eventually resolved when the American team was assured that the Friendship Society of the Soviet Union would be host of the conference. The conference would in no way involve official representatives of the Latvian Republic or party organization. Sup-port by the American side would in fact be conditional on continuing Soviet adherence to this position. Attempts to embarrass U.S. speakers by intro-ducing into the conference official representatives of the Latvian Republic would simply cause the Americans to withdraw their support.

For these very reasons, the Latvian-American community in the United States was initially opposed to the conference. In the United States, one of the strongest voices calling for freedom after forty years of subjugation was the American Latvian Association, founded in 1951. Ojars Kalnins, direc-tor of the American Latvian Association (ALA), worked with Aristids Lambergs, then president of the association, and with Palmer and Ambas-sador Jack Matlock, the head of the American delegation, former special assistant to President Reagan and then U.S. ambassador to the USSR, in seeking to assure the association that its interests would not be compromised as a result of the conference. (Matlock and Palmer were pivotal figures, because they served in the administration.) The association eventually came to recognize that the conference was worth the risk for several reasons. First, it would have high-level U.S. government involvement. Second, it would affirm the main goals of the association—to protect the nonrecognition policy of the U.S. government; to help increase public awareness of the Baltic people; and to bring a message of support to the Latvian people in their occupied homeland. Ten Latvian-Americans—mostly in their twenties —had originally agreed to join the Chautauqua delegation; three dropped out for various reasons.

On the positive side, more factors favored the choice of Latvia than militated against it. Along with Lithuania and Estonia, Latvia was geographically closer to the West and more attuned to the culture and politics of the West than any of the republics farther east. It also would be the first time U.S. and Soviet officials would debate in public in the Soviet Union in front of an audience comparable to the typical Chautauqua summer audience. Members of the public would be able to question policymakers from both sides. American citizens and their policymakers would have opportunity to compare and discuss the hopes, lifestyles, and aspirations of typical Soviet citizens. Each side would choose delegations of public and private citizens. The sending side was to be responsible for the cost of international transportation (which proved to be close to half a million dollars). The agenda was to be set by mutual agreement. The conference would be judged successful to the extent that citizens of the two countries became aware of the existence of the conference. To accomplish this end, the media of both countries were to be given access on an equal basis for the purpose of reporting.

Latvia was accordingly selected and Jurmala, near Riga, approved as the site. Agreement was reached about financial arrangements and the numbers to serve in the official delegation—a total of twenty, made up of eight in the political group, six in the cultural group, and six support and administrative personnel, including translators. Two hundred private delegates would make up the total. Each of the citizen delegates would pay the costs of the journey. Most would be housed in hotels.

On June 9, Chautauqua issued a bulletin announcing that the following September a group of 220 American citizens, officials, and performers would travel to the Soviet Union for "an open Chautauqua-type meeting with Soviet citizens and officials." According to Bratton, speaking that morning at a Washington press conference, "This will be the first time in history that there will be public and uncensored discussion and exchange of ideas in the Soviet Union between American and Soviet officials." The meetings had been officially designated as "The Chautauqua Institution-The Eisenhower Institute Conference on U.S.-Soviet Relations: A Journey in Open Diplomacy." The trip had been endorsed by the U.S. government and was to follow the pattern established by the previous summer's conference. Emphasizing part of Bratton's statement, Wallach insisted that the open debate was a crucial element, "because officials of the two countries are not in ordinary contact and they do not debate each other in public." The participation by citizens of both nations was another key element, he continued: "It is our hope that the conference will provide many opportunities for American citizens to ask questions of presenters, enjoy joint evening cultural programs, and meet informally with Soviet and U.S. participants." A week later Bratton extended an invitation to Chautauquans to participate as delegates to the Chautauqua conference in the Soviet Union on September 15–19, 1986.

The format of the September conference would emulate and even enlarge on the June 1985 experience: morning lectures with written questions from the audience, afternoon informal discussion with microphones open to the audience, no prior censorship, and evening entertainment by U.S. and Soviet performers. The conference would create a means through which Soviet and American citizens could directly question policymakers from either country. It would acquaint the Soviet and American people with each other's cultural heritage. It would demonstrate through joint performances by artists how the two sides could cooperate. It would provide an informal opportunity for the citizens and policymakers of each nation to discuss their hopes, lifestyles, and aspirations and to disseminate this process broadly through media coverage. The entire five-day conference would be open to the press of both countries.

By July, Wallach had secured agreements with both Pan Am and Aeroflot for the 220 Americans to travel from Washington, D.C., on Friday, September 12, to Leningrad and thence to Riga, with arrival at Riga in time for a good night's sleep before the start of the conference on Monday morning. The return journey at the close of the conference would be by way of Moscow. At the close of the conference, the better part of two days was to be spent seeing what Wallach called "the magnificent sights of that city."

At the end of the month Wallach received a letter from Reagan applauding "the first uncensored public debate of its kind covering major issues between articulate representatives of the United States and Soviet Union." "This," Reagan continued, "is precisely the kind of people-to-people initiative I envisaged when I proposed to General Secretary Gorbachev that we expand people-to-people contacts and exchanges." The private sector was one of the best ways to bring home to the Soviet people the spirit and creativity of the American people and their commitment to peace. "The Chautauqua Town Meeting is an excellent example of this," Reagan wrote. "It is a valuable American tradition that brings together outstanding individuals in wide-ranging and thoughtful discussions."

Early in August those Chautauquans who had applied to go to Jurmala as delegates received a letter from Aristids Lambergs confirming his support of the Latvian conference. He took pains, however, to point out that Latvia, along with its Baltic neighbors, had been forcibly annexed to the Soviet Union in 1940. "It is," he wrote, "an occupied country." At their earlier meeting with him, Palmer and Wallach had seemingly overcome the controversial aspects of the plan, specifically the decision to hold the conference in Latvia. Stephen H. Rhinesmith, coordinator of the President's U.S.-Soviet Exchange Initiative, had added his own support, indicating that he saw no difficulty in supporting the proposed conference and calling it "one of the most significant people-to-people projects conceived of since the Geneva summit."

Lambergs expressed the hope that it would give Chautauquans a rare opportunity to meet and get to know the Latvian people and their tragic plight under Soviet occupation. He particularly requested that, in accordance with Soviet regulations, some might feel willing to bring—provided free of charge by the Latvian association—a copy of a Latvian-language Bible. "Were you to leave this Bible behind after your stay in Latvia, there is always a chance that it would fall into appreciative hands." Although most of the Chautauqua delegation was initially interested in the U.S.-Soviet aspect of the conference, many in the course of the discussions became especially sensitive to the concerns of American Latvians. Kalnins briefed the group, presenting them with information packets about Latvia. The briefing was important, since it could be assumed that Soviet officials in Riga would regard the Latvians as potential troublemakers, raising politically uncomfortable issues.

On August 30 the news broke with the impact of a thunderbolt that Nicholas S. Daniloff, a *U.S. News and World Report* journalist, had been arrested in Moscow on charges of spying. The arrest came after a Soviet acquaintance handed him a packet later found to contain photographs and some maps marked as secret. Immediately the whole Chautauqua conference in Jurmala was in jeopardy. The explanation, it seemed, was that the Soviets had taken an American to trade for Gennadi F. Zakharov, a thirty-nine-year-old Soviet attaché employed at the United Nations Center for Science and Technology in New York. Zakharov had been arrested a week earlier after exchanging money for classified documents.

The matter was instantly debated at the Chautauqua Institution, even as preparations were being made to leave for the capital city. Bratton had been continually in touch with Thomas Becker (then Chautauqua's vice president for development). Wallach held strongly that the conference should not take place. To do so would be to disregard the political significance of Daniloff's arrest. Becker and Bratton no less strongly held that the conference should occur. At eight in the morning of the day of departure from western New York, Bratton came to Becker's front door to hear one side of a very loud conversation in which Becker (to use his own word) "screamed" at Wallach: "You can speak on your own, John, but you cannot represent this institution with the line you are taking. It is not our line."

According to the original plan, the two hundred Chautauqua delegates arrived in Washington on Wednesday, September 10. On the same day, Ambassador Dobrynin at the Soviet embassy confirmed an offer that Wallach had received from the KGB that Daniloff and Zakharov should both be remanded to their embassies. Shultz was aware of the difficulty that lay in such a bilateral action, and the delicate matter was compounded by the arrival of the Chautauqua delegation in Washington. As he later wrote: "The Chautauqua Institution, devoted to improving U.S.-Soviet relations in citizen-to-citizen dialogue through meetings alternatively in the United States and the Soviet Union, had scheduled a 'town meeting' in a Soviet city, Riga, Latvia, for mid-September."[5]

Shultz, speaking at Harvard University September 5, said that the arrest proved the dark side of a society prepared to resort to hostage-taking as an instrument of policy. Yet Shultz was not clear that the case was one of swapping a real spy for a reporter and wondered if the Soviets had been setting Daniloff up for years. At any rate, the case was building up to a major confrontation with the Soviets. "We had to be tough," Shultz wrote, "but we should not cancel important meetings." The proposed conference in Latvia had been hotly debated in the Reagan administration. Caspar Weinberger was opposed to permitting the conference to take place on the grounds that

5. Shultz, *Turmoil and Triumph,* 736.

for the delegates to go to Riga would appear to be cooperating with the Soviet government at a time when they had imprisoned an American journalist. The holding of the conference would also be interpreted as U.S. approval of the Soviet incorporation of Latvia. Shultz's view was that it was all the more important to have the conference, since it would permit American officials to have the unprecedented opportunity of denouncing the arrest on Soviet soil as well as denouncing the occupation of Latvia on Latvian soil. It was Shultz's judgment that prevailed. The U.S. government would not oppose the holding of the conference.

The Chautauqua delegation was meanwhile housed as guests in three local hotels in Washington. Dante Fascell, chairman of the House Foreign Relations Committee, spoke at the briefing at which representatives of the American Latvian Association, the World Federation of Free Latvians, and the National Conference on Soviet Jewry met Wednesday afternoon. For the latter group, the key issue was the situation of Soviet refuseniks. A refusenik (in Russian, *otkaznik*) was a Soviet Jew who had applied for an exit visa and had been denied permission. The official Soviet census of 1979 indicated that fewer than two million Jews lived in the Soviet Union, mainly in urban areas such as Moscow, Leningrad, and Kiev, with a large number in Latvia. Emigration was not a general right guaranteed to citizens. To receive an exit visa could take as long as months or years. The authorities gave various reasons for the refusal—for example, that emigration posed a "security risk" for the Soviet Union. In 1985 there were about fifteen thousand known cases of refuseniks, some of whom had waited as long as fifteen years. Refuseniks frequently faced repeated questioning by authorities, being fired, being forced into menial jobs, or expulsion from universities and professional societies.

The three days from Wednesday to Friday were tense in the extreme. Everything, it seemed, hung on the possibility of Daniloff's release. There was a question, too, of whether the chartered jet would wait. Saturday morning was the deadline. Six thousand dollars' worth of food had already been wasted. It was a question whether the Washington hotels would continue to offer their generous welcome. Reagan had sent Gorbachev a personal message almost a week before in which he assured Gorbachev of Daniloff's innocence.

At the appointed hour on September 11, the director of the U.S. Information Agency, Charles Z. Wick, welcomed the delegates to the day-long meeting. It was to be a quick introduction to what were to be the main themes of the Jurmala conference. Gregory Guroff, president of the Foundation for

International Arts and Education, began with a perspective on Soviet history and culture. Two of the American delegates who were to take prominent positions in the Jurmala conference also addressed the group—Jack Matlock, special assistant to the president for national security, and Palmer, at the time ambassador designate to the Hungarian People's Republic. Both spoke about the nonrecognition policy of the U.S. government toward Soviet rule in Latvia. Matlock gave a detailed background description of the Soviet occupation of Latvia, describing the 1940 elections there as "a farce." "This is not a conference in the USSR," he insisted. "This is a conference in Latvia among Americans, Soviets, and Latvians." Further comments were made by Ambassador Stephen Smith, coordinator of the Geneva Exchanges Initiative, that outlined what had been going on in U.S.-Soviet exchanges in the previous decade.

To the delight of the group in attendance, Shultz, accompanied by Marvin Kalb, put in a brief appearance. He honored the Chautauqua Institution for its long and distinguished record of free and open debate but posed the political difficulty presented by the Daniloff arrest in no uncertain terms: "It is ironic that an effort so motivated is put in jeopardy by the very kind of act that demonstrates so clearly the differences between our two societies. The seizure as a hostage of Nick Daniloff is an unacceptable act to which we will not become reconciled. He is a hostage. He is not an agent." He informed the delegates that they would be traveling without diplomatic immunity and that they would be talking to Soviet citizens and asking them questions. "Is that spying? You have to ask yourself: Are you going to be a potential hostage because you talked to a Soviet citizen? Are you going to be a potential hostage if somebody deposits something in your mailbox?"[6]

An invitation had been issued to the delegates to be received at the Soviet embassy Friday morning. In a fleet of taxis they arrived at the embassy, there to receive a warm greeting from Ambassador Dobrynin. "In a few days," he said to the delegates, "at a special conference that will open in Jurmala with representatives of the two countries for an open discussion of Soviet-American relations which, I hope, will be a positive contribution to the development of cooperation between the USSR and the USA." Soviet-American relations, he said, had known ups and downs and also dangerous crises. But in every instance when the leadership of the two countries demonstrated a responsible approach and political will, ways were found to

6. Ibid., 736. See pp. 728–39 for Shultz's discussion of the Daniloff case.

defuse the crises. The delegates listened carefully to the ambassador's words. "I tend to be optimistic about the future of our relations," the ambassador continued. "That optimism is not unfounded: the proof is that your group is going to the Soviet Union." Sustained applause followed. Then a question came: Was that polite, optimistic diplomatic rhetoric? It was certainly not an official announcement. Dobrynin moved towards an answer: "I have no doubt that in the Soviet Union you will receive a warm welcome. Your meetings with your Soviet counterparts—ordinary people—will contribute to better knowledge of the way of life, aspirations, and personalities of one another. It will lay to rest misconceptions and occasional negative stereotypes. I wish you all a pleasant and fruitful journey to my country."

Bratton guessed at that moment that whether the trip would in fact occur was a moment-by-moment issue. Oleg Sokolov, chargé d'affaires at the embassy and in 1985 a speaker at Chautauqua, spoke privately to a reporter from the *Washington Post*. He said that things would be taken care of. The reporter asked, "Does that mean an agreement has been reached about Nick?" Sokolov replied, "You will be going. Yes, you will go." With this word, to be reported the next day to the delegates, it was clear that Daniloff's release to the U.S. Embassy in Moscow was imminent, the only surprise being that the Soviet ambassador had not made the announcement himself. Daniloff was released from prison Friday, September 13, into the custody of the American embassy in Moscow.[7]

The delegates assembled again later. Tension was still high, for the news of the release was not yet public. Bratton came to the battery of microphones and announced simply, "The journey will occur." Long and loud applause followed his words. According to Mary Frances Cram, daughter of a former president of Chautauqua Institution, "we cheered and shouted and shook one another's hands with the same abandon that we were to display twelve days later *en route* home." Wallach spoke briefly. It was the intention of the conference to raise all outstanding issues between the Soviet Union and the United States—from human rights to Afghanistan and every other issue that divided the two nations. "We go there with one aim," he said, "to involve the Soviet public in an uncensored, five-day conference. Any subject

---

7. Daniloff was exchanged for Yuri F. Orlov, a prominent Soviet dissident who was freed from a labor camp in Siberia after ten years of imprisonment, stripped of his citizenship, and deported to the United States. He later became a senior scientist in the physics department at Cornell University.

is to be open to discussion. We hope that what happens next week will be seen throughout the Soviet Union and indeed the world." The retiring ambassador to the USSR, Arthur A. Harriman, addressed the group and repeated the official position on the nonrecognition of Latvia as a legal part of the Soviet Union.

The Flight to Riga

Saturday, September 14, the Chautauqua delegation finally left Washington, D.C., for Leningrad. Meeting in the ballroom of the Grand Hotel, the group heard its religious leader, William Jackson, pray, "As we depart now, we pray for safety in our travel and openness to each other as we share this event. And we pray for those whom we will meet that together we may strive for understanding and growth." The flight itself, two days delayed, was uneventful, with all passengers traveling first class. It was a stellar group of official delegates, headed by the two cochairmen, Bratton and Eisenhower, granddaughter of the postwar president, and including Stephen Rhinesmith; Edward Djerejian, special assistant to the president for public affairs and deputy press secretary; Guroff; Jack F. Matlock; R. Mark Palmer; Helmut Sonnenfeldt, a senior member of the National Security Council; S. Frederick Starr;[8] Strobe Talbott, Washington bureau chief of *Time;* and Ben Wattenberg, editor of *Public Opinion.* Reasons of state and more particularly the Daniloff question prevented other officials from agreeing to be part of the delegation, notably, Sen. William Bradley; Alan L. Keyes, assistant secretary of state for international organization affairs; Richard Perle, assistant secretary of defense for national security; Jeane J. Kirkpatrick, former ambassador of the United States to the United Nations; and McFarlane, director of the National Security Council.

Also on the plane were the performers who were to be featured in the course of the week's conference. Several of these had earlier expressed reservations about a visit to the Soviet Union. This was not a State Department operation. They had been asked to give their services to a comparatively unknown institution. Yet with remarkable generosity each of the performers had foregone the remuneration appropriate to their talents. These included

---

8. While the group was being delayed in Washington, D.C., Starr and a Chautauquan delegate, Richard Bechtolt, realized that there was no information available in Russian for their hosts that described the institution. Obtaining the services of a professional translator at short notice, they were able to accomplish the necessary task and brought the quickly translated and printed pamphlets to Riga.

Karen Akers, Tony Award–winning star of the Broadway musical *Nine* and a cabaret performer in the style of Edith Piaf; Ron Richardson, also a Tony Award–winner for his part in the musical *Big River;* the two-time Grammy Award–winning tenor and bass saxophone jazz artist Grover Washington Jr.; Patrick Bissell and Susan Jaffe, lead dancer and ballerina with the American Ballet Theater; Paul Connally, music director at the American Ballet Theater; Christian Holder, former lead dancer with the Joffrey Ballet; Henry Butler, jazz pianist; Mark Hummed, pianist; Tommy Cecil, jazz bass player; Michael Balance, coordinator and director of the coming week's musical program; and Fodor, who had already performed four times at the White House. Fodor had been a member of the American delegation for the groundbreaking Chautauqua conference a year earlier.

Mary-Therese Mennino, then program director for the institution, later recalled some of the difficulties she had faced in gathering her corps of performers. One of the performers had a serious drug problem but reputedly was then clean. Mennino warned the performer that there would be serious difficulties in the Soviet Union if anyone was found in possession of drugs. Her warning was sufficient, and the performer caused Mennino no further difficulties. She had wanted a particular jazz pianist who had agreed to come, but a day before he was due to leave, he had declined. "I don't blame him at all," Mennino later recollected. "Who were we to ask this star performer to go out into the wilds of the Soviet Union with us?" Many other players would have seized the opportunity to play with Washington. But Mennino had only twenty-four hours to find one. She and Washington finally made contact with Henry Butler in California. He agreed to go, but he needed a visa and a passport. Just as the first hint was being given at the Soviet embassy that the visit was to take place, Mennino was in a cab in Washington, collecting the necessary forms. She dashed into the Soviet embassy and triumphantly (if breathlessly) showed the necessary documents. Butler, in the meantime, was on a flight from California, ready to meet the party at Dulles Airport two hours before departure.

The delayed departure from Washington meant that the Pan Am jet did not arrive at Leningrad until two thirty in the morning. "Leningrad," one of the Chautauqua participants recorded, "was a beautiful, high-speed blur." The passengers, "somewhat numb and robot-like," according to Mary Frances Cram, cleared customs and immigration and made their way to the Pribaltijskaya Hotel or the Astoria Hotel for a brief sleep and breakfast at seven o'clock in the morning. However, the inspection did not go without adventure. A woman delegate who agreed to bring over a Latvian Bible was subjected to questioning. The Soviet customs agent asked if she spoke Latvian. She did not, she said. The agent queried, "Then why do you have this Bible?" She was taken aside and interrogated and had a special stamp put on her passport. Some around her wondered fearfully if this was to be the nature of their own reception. The unfortunate episode had a marked effect when the woman, visibly shaken, arrived at the hotel.

Under grey skies, a sightseeing tour began at eight o'clock in the morning. Most took advantage of the abbreviated bus tour, led by police escort, to the Hermitage Museum and St. Isaac's Cathedral. A visit was also made to the Piskaryevskoye Memorial Cemetery, burial place of more than five hundred thousand of the nine hundred thousand victims of the nine hundred-day siege of Leningrad in World War II. Bratton and Eisenhower placed a wreath beneath a large statue symbolizing the motherland. One of the delegation, Alfreda Irwin, recollected walking behind the high-stepping guards, taking notice of the stones and flowers marking the different mass burial sites. "I thought of those fearsome war days and how brave and luckless many Soviet citizens had been. They could not have known that we cared for them and that we prayed for their fortitude to be sustained." By early afternoon the group was ready to board a specially chartered airliner for the forty-five-minute flight to Riga.

A choir of young singers in native Latvian costume greeted the jet-lagged Americans, who seemed somewhat bewildered as they filed down the staircase from the plane. Some of the Latvian-speaking Americans requested that the young people sing a Latvian folk song, "Put Vejin." The travelers paused after they disembarked from the plane to accept bunches of wildflowers from the singers. They glanced briefly at the pine-lined scenery and walked to the seven waiting buses to reach the Latviya Hotel. After some initial confusion—one traveler called it "a mob scene"—most were settled in their rooms by late afternoon. At dinner, young Latvian players and dancers performed in native dress for the visitors. After dinner, a concert of classical and religious music was presented at the Dom Cathedral, now transformed to a concert hall. After a recital on one of the great European organs, Ron Richardson, to the accompaniment of the Riga Boys' Choir, sang gospel songs such as "Deep River," "Swing Low, Sweet Chariot," and "Were You There When They Crucified My Lord?" One of the moving moments for the audience was his singing of the words quoted by Martin Luther King Jr., "Free at Last." According to an American participant, the concert was "a unifying and moving beginning for the next day's confrontations."

The American Latvians in the group became politically active almost from the moment of arrival. They talked to as many local Latvians as they could and passed out U.S.-Latvian flag pins. Since the maroon and white Latvian flag had been banned in Latvia since 1940, such an action was regarded by the local Soviet authorities as subversive.

Jurmala, a twenty-minute bus ride from Riga, was the summer resort of choice for Soviet citizens who aspired to a taste of Western comfort. The region had been incorporated into the Soviet Union after the 1939 non-aggression pact the Soviets had signed with Nazi Germany, but it was an ideal spot for the conference. With nearby white sand beaches set among stands of pine and birch, mineral springs, therapeutic mud-bath clinics, and quaint turn-of-the-century country houses, Jurmala had a restful atmosphere, reputed to get creative juices flowing. Its main street had been closed to traffic and turned into a pedestrian mall. The shops and restaurants were bright and pleasant places to shop and dine.

The convoy of buses, passing through red lights, evoked considerable attention from passersby. To the chagrin of the Americans, the site of the conference was a chilly amphitheater-type of auditorium, set in a grove of trees already showing tints of fall color. Invited to sit anywhere, they found that the two thousand Riga citizens who had been invited to attend occupied the rear seats, leaving the front rows for the visitors. The Americans, although happy to receive the honor, sought to mingle with the Latvian citizens. All participants were given small receivers with earphones so that they could listen to the speeches in English, Latvian, and Russian. The signs of welcome on the stage were in the same three languages.

In an atmosphere of tense but eager anticipation, Bratton and Eisenhower offered words of welcome to all assembled on behalf of peace-loving people around the planet. The 220 who had come from America had brought, Bratton said, not only their personal greetings but also their desire that accord and not division might characterize the relationship between the two nations. "Chautauqua," he continued, "believes that the issues of life and living need open and serious consideration and discussion."

Eisenhower picked up on the theme: "Against the background of our present tensions," she said, "our presence here means all the more." It indicated a deep-seated desire on both sides to come together to participate in a very important dialogue. "It seems very fitting that we do so," she said, "as my grandfather stood for many of the ideals in which we are partaking today." She noted that it was the thirtieth anniversary of the signing by her grandfather of the U.S.-Soviet Exchange Agreement.

In the course of the following days at Jurmala, certain themes continued to recur in the frequently emotional and at times acute exchanges of views by representatives of the two sides: first, the need for better communication, in the sense of learning more of one another's character or of gaining an understanding of those who thought quite differently from one another; second, the need for collaboration—for working together to find whether it could be possible for two quite different peoples to achieve at least a partial elimination of nuclear and conventional weapons; third, the unresolved issue of "the hand of Moscow" in regional conflicts and Soviet objections to the global intrusion of "American imperialism"; and fourth, the need to examine and correct misinformation and cold war–hardened stereotypes of one another.

The Need for Better Communication

In a large variety of ways, speaker after speaker emphasized the need for better communication. Palmer and Vitaly Zhurkin were among the first. Speaking in Russian during the opening part of his address, Palmer noted that even in the worst of times, when there were no diplomatic relations between the two countries, it had still been possible to achieve better understandings of one another. It was, he said, a vital condition of success in matters of controversy to set up institutes of communication. The leaders of the two countries should hold annual meetings to lay down general guidelines and to map out priority political decisions. Foreign ministers should meet at least twice a year and specialists should concentrate on urgent problems such as agriculture or the rescue of ships in distress. "Reciprocity," Palmer asserted, "is one of the fundamental principles of bilateral cooperation." He noted in criticism that this was not the choice of the Soviet side. Broadcasts by the Voice of America, the BBC, Radio Free Europe, and others were often jammed. Moscow Radio, in contrast, could be heard without hindrance in the United States. Newspapers such as the *Washington Post* and the *New York Times* and magazines such as *Newsweek* were inaccessible to ordinary Soviet citizens, while Americans could subscribe to *Izvestia* and *Literaturnaya Gazeta*. The lack of reciprocity and the mania for secrecy were obstacles in the way of genuine, large-scale, bilateral cooperation.

The response to Palmer was given by Zhurkin, first deputy head of the Institute of USA and Canada Studies in the USSR Academy of Sciences. Palmer's statements about the need for better communication were destructive, he began. They expressed the spirit of the cold war and were based on a number of distortions. He disagreed that the *New York Times* was not available in the Soviet Union. Copies were easily accessible in libraries. He felt there were no reasons for it not to be sold on the streets in Moscow. Nodding his head as if recounting in his mind the misstatements, Zhurkin commented: "I personally counted twenty-one major distortions of historical facts and several dozen small ones, although I am not going to enumerate them." Nevertheless, despite all the difficulties and differences, the two countries had indeed managed to create a system of international treaties and agreements. For example, in October 1972, they signed and ratified the interim SALT I agreement. The first article of that agreement stated that neither the Soviet Union nor the United States should build new silos for intercontinental ballistic missiles. Since that time neither side had built a single silo. Pausing between each phrase, Zhurkin commented almost in awe, "Had it not been for that reciprocal agreement, God knows how many intercontinental missiles each side would now have on its territory."

Collaborating to End Conflict

Recalling the tense atmosphere of the Jurmala conference many years later, Bratton noted particularly the antagonism and mistrust that characterized the early debates. "We were still talking at one another," he said. "But like it or lump it, we gained a clearer picture of each other's stands—be they gloomy or hopeful—on various aspects of our troubled international relationships."

In their discussion of the issue of nuclear conflict early in the week, all the speakers agreed only that the prognosis was gloomy, even ominous. "The present state of our relations cannot be described as satisfactory, " Vladimir Petrovsky began. "We sense keenly the lack of trust in Soviet-American relations. Trust is needed in our relations. The nuclear era requires it." Petrovsky, deputy minister of foreign affairs of the USSR, went on to define what he saw as the two criteria for limiting and ending the arms race. The first was the principle of equal security, which had acquired new meaning in the nuclear and space age. The diminished security of one side simply led to unpredictable actions and instability in international relations. The second criterion, a vital one, was the prevention of an arms race in space and the end of the arms race on the planet. "Our aim is to create a nuclear-free world, a world free from nuclear and any other weapons of mass destruction."

He then outlined the concrete program of action the Soviet side had put forward at the Geneva summit the previous November, specifically the proposal that the antisatellite systems already in existence be eliminated. The

Soviet Union had also expressed its readiness to agree to limiting work in the field of the Strategic Defense Initiative to laboratory research, that is, to the threshold the United Stated had actually reached. "The time has come to stop associating this or any other country with the image of the enemy," Petrovsky concluded. "We have a concrete and real enemy—the nuclear threat to our planet." The present time demanded that political arbitrariness give way to dialogue, realism, and responsibility.

Jack Matlock, speaking initially in fluent Latvian—to enthusiastic applause from Latvians in the audience—expressed warm thanks for the wonderful hospitality already shown by their hosts. It was, he said, an extraordinary moment. Then, switching to Russian, he noted how the United States had openly declared its willingness to collaborate with its wartime partner. The United States had ended the war with a monopoly of a new and immensely destructive technology—the atomic bomb. Had it chosen to do so, it could have flexed its muscle and made demands that none could resist. It chose not to do so. Instead, the United States proposed that all nuclear weapons and technology be turned over to an international authority that would destroy existing weapons and maintain an inspection and control of all countries to ensure that they could not be created again. Stalin, however, rejected this plan and the inspection and control that would make it feasible.

In a rebuttal to Matlock, Petrovsky spoke wryly and with a measure of cynicism. "You say you stand for limiting the use of force. This is very good. I am happy to hear it at last from the American side. It is a great revelation to me. However, when the issue of the non-use of force is raised at the United Nations, who votes against it? But excuse me, Mr. Matlock, we can never agree to living in conditions when Soviet-American relations would develop while the question of war and peace would be put aside. Nobody is capable of living on a nuclear powder keg."

Matlock replied that no one was more interested in moving towards a radical reduction of nuclear weapons than the United States. "It is not the United States that is pushing for an arms race in space," he argued. "Space began to be used when the first ballistic missiles were developed to deliver nuclear weapons through space. We are trying to see and research if we can develop means of strategic defense that would protect people from nuclear weapons."

The adversarial positions of both Petrovsky and Matlock were often criticized by the American citizen delegates in private conversation and on one major occasion in public. At one point during the day, the huge audience applauded loudly when Florence Ross of Tamarac, Florida, a foreign-policy teacher at Broward Community College, told the Soviet and U.S. officials that she was tired of the continual bickering. "I am taking the prerogative of my age by saying that all of you sound like little boys playing 'one upmanship.' Maybe the leaders of both countries should dismiss all of you. We are less secure now than when all of you became leaders."

Expressed with a Soviet slant, but limited to two minutes on each day's events, an hour-long evening news program on Soviet television, *Vremya,* covered some of the major events of the day. The reports were highly critical of the U.S. side, blaming it for the start of a "confrontation," one calling Matlock's talk "typical of the Reagan administration in discussing Soviet-American relations with a declining level of calmness." It objected to Matlock's insistence on making the question of Daniloff practically the main subject. The Soviet news program, however, also commended the participants for making "a good beginning" and praised them for a "frankness" that would "improve understanding."[9]

A keynote address of the week was to have been given by Richard Perle, assistant secretary of defense for national security. Perle, however, had chosen not to travel to attend the conference because of the Daniloff case. His place was taken by Strobe Talbott. The theme was still the search for ways of resolving the nuclear conflict.

Strobe Talbott began his remarks by saying that at any other time in history, two great powers so embittered against one another would almost certainly have gone to war. The all-transforming difference between the Soviet-American rivalry in the last third of the twentieth century and all other great political rivalries of history was, he said, the existence of nuclear weapons. "There are simply too many weapons in the Soviet arsenal," Talbott argued, "and it seems suitable only for a first strike." Those in the United States who had raised questions about the wisdom of Reagan's Strategic Defense Initiative needed to recognize that SDI had its appeal in large measure because of precisely that excess in Soviet ICBM warheads. "I am convinced," Talbott concluded, "that Ronald Reagan would very much like to leave office having concluded a meaningful agreement in those talks, an agreement that would not only substantially reduce the numerical level of weapons on both sides, but that would also enhance strategic stability as well."

9. Vremya (Time), a state-run channel, provided an English digest of the day's events.

In his reply to Talbott, Colonel-General Nikolai Chervov, chief of the Board of the General Staff of the USSR Armed Forces, admitted that the disarmament problem was complex but not so complex that it was impossible to see what it involved. "Whichever way you look at the problem," he said, "there is only one choice—it is necessary to stop the arms race and to look for a way out of confrontation." Reagan, Chervov argued, held that if it can be successfully developed, the SDI would bring new stability to a superpower relationship now based on each other's fear of the other's offensive capability. That position was naive. Reagan's goal was actually to achieve decisive military superiority over the Soviet Union. If the United States sought to deploy the system, the Soviet Union would respond in kind with new offensive weapons and with a strategic defense program of its own.

At the afternoon session, questions from the audience elicited these replies from Chervov:

QUESTION: Does the Soviet Union have sufficient resources to develop and build a Star Wars defense of its own?

CHERVOV: Of course, fundamental research—I repeat, *fundamental research,* is being carried out in the Soviet Union to look for possible retaliatory measures to the American "Star Wars." As for developing space-strike weapons and "Star Wars" programs, there are no such plans or programs in the Soviet Union. We do not intend to take weapons into outer space and to threaten the United States or other countries from there.

QUESTION: The general stated that the Soviet Union has banned the use of chemical weapons. What about the chemical warfare the Soviets are using now in Afghanistan? If you had an opportunity to go back to that point in time, would the Soviet Union reconsider its decision to invade Afghanistan?

CHERVOV: Concerning the use of chemical weapons in Afghanistan on the part of the Soviet Union, I must say with full responsibility that this is a concoction. There have been many commissions, including from the United Nations, which have confirmed that there have been no instances of the Soviet forces using chemical weapons. On the contrary, all chemical ammunition—and such ammunition was indeed discovered—bore the trademark, "Made in the USA."

According to *Time,* the Riga meeting was dominated by tough talk on both sides rather than toasts to *mir i druzhba* (peace and friendship). The Soviet spokesman on arms control, Chervov, according to *Time,* delivered an attack on the United States that had all the subtlety of a twenty-megaton warhead. He accused the Reagan administration of holding "murderous positions" and of conducting "dishonest negotiations." Largely because of the Daniloff affair, the report continued, Chautauquans were given a crash course in old-fashioned Soviet stonewalling. After a particularly harsh counterattack on Daniloff by Petrovsky, one of the members of the audience commented, "It's like watching the machinery of the big lie in action—from the inside." One of the American delegates recalled how it would continue almost without cease on the platform. "Nevertheless," she continued, "we Americans groaned with the Soviets many times. We commiserated over the possible folly of such hardline expressions." According to her, the Soviet audience did not understand; indeed, they laughed nervously at some statements made on the platform by U.S. diplomats, for example, the Daniloff incident.

In its own report of the proceedings of the day, *Pravda* was less enthusiastic about Talbott than most of the Americans present seemed to be. "To the disappointment of the audience," it stated, Talbott "limited himself to very banal discussions of the supposed 'military superiority' of the USSR over the United States, the Washington administration's 'love of peace,' and the 'vital necessity to develop the Star Wars program. Apparently the strict shadow of the Pentagon also hangs over several unofficial American representatives." The official representatives of the U.S. administration participating in the meeting were trying to hold negotiations in their accustomed manner—not at all constructively. "And what's more," the report continued, "to hear them tell it, the main issue of Soviet-American relations is anything and everything except the issues of security, stopping the nuclear arms race, and disarmament."[10]

Regional Conflicts: Central America and Afghanistan

The third major issue of the conference, regional conflicts, came quickly to the fore. Speaking for the American side, Sonnenfeldt, former counselor of the State Department, began by referring to the many crises over the previous forty years in which the United States and the Soviet Union had been involved. All of these, however, occurred at levels of weapons lower than the levels prevailing at present. "So," he said, "there is no magic in simply reducing weapons; the magic is in the wisdom and restraint with which

10. Quoted in the USSR-USA public representatives meeting journal, *Jurmala Diary* (Moscow: Novosti Press Agency, 1987).

interests are pursued and solutions looked for in places where we are in conflict, actual or potential."

The Soviet intrusion by military means into Central America represented a serious potential danger. The United States was aware of problems in its own relationship towards Central America. The transformation of Cuba into a Soviet military outpost with continuous naval, air force, and intelligence operations greatly complicated the situation in Central America and had in turn forced other conflicts, particularly in Nicaragua, to become an issue of Soviet-American relations. The United States had welcomed the end of the Somoza regime and placed great hopes on the advent of the Sandinistas. But these hopes were profoundly disappointing. "I can tell you," Sonnenfeldt assured his audience, "and I can tell our Soviet participants here in particular, that whatever are our controversies at home in regard to our policy toward Nicaragua today, the American people will support any administration of any political party that has to confront the Soviet-backed Cuban intervention in the internal affairs of that region, including in Nicaragua."

Sonnenfeldt then turned to the problem of Afghanistan. What was happening in Afghanistan was a bloody war against a massive popular resistance, against the present regime in Kabul. Millions of Afghanis, inside the country and outside the country, regarded the regime in Kabul as one imposed by Soviet arms. Afghanistan had become an international problem not only because it violated the United Nations charter and was condemned by the United Nations, but also because it created enormous dangers for adjacent countries, notably Pakistan. "The road to a solution," Sonnenfeldt continued, "requires that there be a broad-based government in Afghanistan that has the support and respect of the people and that allows the voluntary return of the refugees, the quarter of the population of Afghanistan that now lives in Pakistan and Iran. It also requires the total and rapid withdrawal of Soviet forces."

Nikolai Shishlin, a ranking official of the Communist Party of the Soviet Union, rose quickly to respond to the accusation of imperialism. To the contrary, he replied, Sonnenfeldt's speech was an excellent example of the Sonnenfeldt doctrine of neoglobalism. The older idea of "zones of interest" was now developed to mean that the entire world community would have to deal with regional conflicts. But the problem of settling regional conflicts stood next to that of limiting and scaling down the race in arms, especially nuclear arms. The predominant American point of view was that regional conflicts were the result of "the Kremlin's intrigues" or "the hand of

Moscow." It was important to gain a more developed view and understand that regional conflicts arose against a particular historical background.

Regional conflicts, Shishlin continued, could be understood in terms of three levels. The first was the national level, as illustrated in the crisis of the apartheid regime in South Africa. The crisis of that regime was caused neither by the Soviet Union nor by the United States. It emerged within the country's national framework. There, as in almost every conflict, the national level developed into the second, the regional level. In Nicaragua, the emergence and strengthening of the Sandinista revolution would have remained a purely national task but for U.S. interference. The United States promised to help the victorious revolution, promising millions of dollars to the Sandinistas. But the dollars were never supplied. Officials of the United States had alleged that this tiny country was going to march two thousand kilometers and conquer Mexico, then lay claim to Texas and California. Who could possibly believe that? "Here," Shishlin said, "the conflict is already growing beyond the regional level to reach a global one."

This third level was very dangerous. The Twenty-seventh Congress of the Communist Party of the Soviet Union had put forward the idea of an all-embracing system of national security with these suggestions: strict respect for the right of each people to choose the ways and forms of its development independently; a just political settlement of international crises and regional conflicts; and elaboration of a set of measures aimed at building confidence between states and the creation of effective guarantees against attack from without and the inviolability of their frontiers.

"We are not simplifying the pictures of those conflicts at all," Shishlin insisted. "Who needs the war in Afghanistan? The Afghans? The Afghans need peace in their country. They want to get out of the sixteenth century and live a life worth living. Does the Soviet Union need the war in Afghanistan? We are losing our people there. Do you think we don't care? It is those who want the Soviet Union to have more difficulties that need the war in Afghanistan. It is those who send weapons there, who generously finance the counterrevolutionaries that need the war in Afghanistan."

Pravda, in its report of the day's proceedings, was critical again of the American side: "Apparently expressing the White House point of view on the issue, former U.S. National Security employee H. Sonnenfeldt (now retired) turned everything upside down. He attempted to whitewash the U.S. role in provocations against Cuba and Angola, its increasing aid to Afghan *dushmans* (enemies) and Nicaraguan 'contras,' and its occupation of tiny Granada. As far as present 'hot spots' in the world are concerned, he believes that these regional conflicts were created by the 'hand of Moscow.'"

The treatment of Shishlin was more positive: "N. S. Shishlin, who also spoke during the discussion, urged that a persistent search be made for ways to avert regional conflicts. Using a number of specific examples, he also showed the 'mechanism' of the dangerous increase in regional conflicts. This includes, in particular, American imperialism's open interference in Nicaraguan affairs, its undeclared war against Afghanistan, and attempts to assert U.S. military and economic domination in the Middle East."[11]

From the point of view of the Americans in the audience, two appreciative comments, one from a Russian and one from an American, indicated the generally positive response to the day's debates.

Yevgeny Fyodorov, a student from Riga and future construction engineer, said, "Like every other honest person I believe it is the duty and moral responsibility of the USSR and the United States to do everything possible so that peace reigns everywhere on our planet. I ask that the White House stop playing with people's lives as if they were pawns for the mercenary interests of the U.S. military-industrial complex. As a future builder, I would like to see the huge resources that kindle the military conflicts begun by imperialism throughout the world used for the benefit of humanity." Sarita Weeks, a retired foreign language teacher from Jamestown, New York, said, "All the men in our family have fought in wars far from our home. Should even one family have to endure this? I came here with an open heart to talk to Soviet people about how to make peace strong and eternal. I am seventy-seven years old, but I look to the future with hope." A Soviet member of the audience then asked why so many Americans carried handguns. The reply from a Chautauquan, "Because we don't have as big a police force as you have," brought laughter and resounding applause.

Correcting Misinformation and Stereotypes

With the conference moving towards a close, delegates heard a discussion of the role of the mass media in forming public opinion. Vladimir Lomeiko, special ambassador with the USSR Ministry of Foreign Affairs, and Ben Wattenberg, editor of *Public Opinion,* spoke and answered questions.

Lomeiko made a speech suitable to a conference increasingly marked by the obvious desire of the Soviet and American participants to understand each other better. "Despite all the differences in our ideals and worldviews," he began, "all of us, whether we like it or not, are neighbors in our common home, the planet Earth." One of the reasons for distrust, suspicion, and fear

11. Ibid.

was that Americans did not know the Soviet Union. Could there be, he inquired, new thinking not only in politics, but also in the field of information? "The new reality of the nuclear age demands that all of us give up the philosophy of the pre-nuclear era, the old stereotypes when we saw each other only as enemies. We in the Soviet Union have put an end to this tendency. We want to see in Americans not only people holding different views, but also partners in building the edifice of peace."

Lomeiko illustrated his comment by noting that at the beginning of the 1950s the Soviet Union adopted a law making the propaganda of war, hatred of other people, and hostility among nations punishable as a criminal offense. "We do not see this as a restriction on the freedom of speech. We see this as a restriction on the freedom of hatred." In the Soviet Union the mass media exerted enormous influence in the forming of public opinion. The Soviet Union wanted the press, radio, and television to contribute to the strengthening of peace. One of the reasons for the distrust that existed between the United States and the Soviet Union was that Americans knew very little about the Soviet Union and its policy. "When visiting the United States," Lomeiko reported, "my colleagues and I became convinced that, regrettably, many members of the American mass media, many journalists, are guided by the same principle: Bad news about the Soviet Union is good news for America. This is a dangerous principle."

Following Lomeiko, Wattenberg said that he proposed to speak candidly about people's attitudes to governments. He cited the results of a cross-national polling taken in 1985 in Great Britain, France, West Germany, and Italy, four nations comprising well over two hundred million people. To the question, "Which nation will be most likely to use military force to attain its goals?" roughly speaking eight in ten in Western Europe thought the Soviet Union used force to attain its goals. Public research institutes in six different West European countries interviewed East European tourists. Only an average of 5 percent said they would vote Communist in a free election. In the United States, a solid majority thought that the Soviets were seeking global domination.

If this was a misperception, Wattenberg went on, it could be cleared up. How? "Think about releasing the Jewish prisoners of conscience in jail now. Think about letting Soviet citizens travel or emigrate, if they want to, with or without their families. Let them come to us and tell us what it's really like here, in Russia." If Russia did that, it would not have to worry about public opinion. It would be perceived, quite properly, as one of the greatest and most beneficent nations in the world with a deep culture, with a profound literature, and a nation that could become the natural partner of the United States in defusing tensions around the globe.

The moderator of the day was Vladimir Pozner, who worked for the State Committee for Television and Radio Broadcasting of the USSR. His key position at the conference was regarded by members of the American media who were reporting the events as a tribute to the increasing skill in public relations then being exhibited by the Soviet regime. "To watch him at work," one observer commented, "is to watch a spider spinning on the Soviet Union's new-style propaganda net." The child of a Russian Jew and a Frenchwoman, Pozner was born in France and spent the first ten years of his childhood in Manhattan's East Tenth Street, where he learned to play baseball. The family—diehard Soviet sympathizers—left the United States at the height of McCarthyism. Settling first in East Germany, they returned to the Soviet Union after Stalin's death. On the platform at Jurmala, Pozner's pastel-colored shirt and brown jacket were admired for their color coordination—the other male speakers, Americans and Soviets, being decked out, it seemed, in the standard uniform of blue, black, and gray.

Pozner had the opportunity of summarizing the discussions of the day in his comments after the addresses by Lomeiko and Wattenberg. After some amusing comments about whether Russians smiled less than Americans, he went on to make a case by citing a content analysis that had been made by *Time* and *Newsweek* magazines. The words most used in regard to Russians were "savages," "adventurers," "barbarians," and "despots." The American study had nothing to do with politics. It revealed an attitude to Russians as people. The poll that Wattenberg had cited did regrettably correspond to reality. "The attitude towards us is bad both in Western Europe and in America." But if such a poll were to be conducted in the Soviet Union to see the attitudes of the Soviets towards America, the result would be positive, not negative. Why? It was because the Soviet mass media, despite all their shortcomings, did not teach the Russians to hate America in general.

The *Pravda* report of Friday's discussion was particularly negative towards the American editor:

> American B. Wattenberg, editor-in-chief of the far right *Public Opinion* magazine, spoke with open hatred toward the Soviet Union and social-ism. For example, he asserted that Soviet people, you see, are entirely devoid of objective information and lack basic freedoms. The speech by the American propagandists, permeated with the spirit of the dark-est days of the "Cold War," was amazingly reminiscent of provocative

broadcasts by subversive "radio voices." At the end of his speech,
Wattenberg bombastically stated that he was a board member of the
radio station Radio Free Europe. There was indignation in the audience when Wattenberg started to explain that he and his collaborators
in the United States did not consider Latvia to be a part of the Soviet
Union, and conducted radio broadcasts to our country in that spirit.
The moderator was called on to calm down the indignant audience
when this orator attempted to justify the atomic bombing of Hiroshima and Nagasaki by the American war machine.

According to *Pravda,* after Wattenberg's speech many Americans who were
in the audience came up to Soviet participants and asked them not to identify them with Wattenberg. "It turned out," the report continued, "that the
American representative's speech, permeated with such caveman mentality,
was fairly beneficial." *Pravda* continued, "One Latvian student, upon exit-
ing the hall, said, 'I never suspected that there are such low-class propagan-
dists in America, now I understand why some people in the United States
have the wildest ideas about us.'"

Beyond the Debates

For many and probably most of the participants, issues of communication,
collaboration, the settling of differences, and learning the truth about one
another's lands and policies were not simply matters of public debate by
diplomats and public officials. A major value of the Jurmala conference was
the opportunity for all participants to have meals, visits, and conversations
with one another in places beyond the debates. Lunches were served after
the morning sessions. One of the American participants, historian Alfreda
Irwin, recollected how welcome the break was after the morning's stress:
"Wonderful big cups of soup, usually very hot—and did we need it, for sitting outside all morning in the damp weather made us very cold! Vegetable,
borscht, cabbage, then the full main course, usually some kind of beef,
potatoes, vegetables, topped off with dessert." A New York elementary
school teacher also remembered the high quality of the food, the gracious
hosts, starched and ironed tablecloths on the tables, with flowers everywhere. In the afternoons the Americans had several choices. Some took the
opportunity of bus tours to a folk art museum in Riga, the university and its
medical school, artists' studios, a day care center, a secondary school, or a collective farm.

At the close of each day, buses took the American delegates back to the
hotel. A brief time was allotted for the evening meal, after which they

boarded the buses to attend the cultural programs that had been planned. Music again proved itself to be the universal language. At the first concert in the Philharmonia Concert Hall, for example, Fodor joined for a performance with the Latvian Symphony Orchestra. The feeling between the American musician and the Latvian players was clearly warm, and the warmth increased when the orchestra played music from Leonard Bernstein's *Candide,* obviously learned for the occasion.

Several evenings provided programs of popular music by Soviet and American performers. At one, an American member of the audience later recalled sitting beside a young man who told her in halting English that he was president of his jazz record club. He was enjoying particularly not only the playing of Grover Washington Jr., but also his warm-hearted openness with the other musicians and the audience. Another participant recalled how the audience and musicians were particularly moved by the beauty of Akers's voice and by the fact that she had taken the trouble to memorize, in Latvian and Russian, the introduction to each of her many songs. The concert had begun at eight in the evening, and many in the audience assumed it would be over by ten. The enthusiasm was such, however, and the applause so persistent that the evening went far beyond the appointed hour.

After the concert, Grover and Christine Washington, with some of the others who had played with him, went for a jam session to the Allegro Club in Riga, accompanied by a small crowd of Latvian jazz devotees. At first, the guards at the club refused to allow the party in if they were going to play. Washington was blunt: "If you guys don't let us in to play, we'll go over to that park and do the jam session there." The guards relented. It was, Mary-Therese Mennino reflected later, "a blow for freedom." The evening, according to Christine Washington, "turned into quite a musical and spiritual exchange as different musicians in the audience took turns joining Grover, Tommy [Cecil] and Henry [Black] on the stage." Later, Richardson joined the group on stage and sang a jazzed-up version of "What a Friend We Have in Jesus" and "You've Got a Friend." After her return to the United States, Christine reminisced upon her experience:

> The audience was completely enthralled. Two guests approached me during the evening and told me with tears in their eyes that what transpired was "magic" and that we were "magic." After the show was over, we were waiting outside in the van for everyone who was going back to the hotel. Our Latvian guests and several others, including the trumpet player who Grover had played with earlier that week with the Raymond Pauls Orchestra, and who had "sat in" with Grover at

the session, stood at the end of the driveway, looking down to our van. They lightly pounded their hearts with their right fists and then extended their arms to us while we blew kisses and waved. The trumpet player, who earlier in the week had been very distant and somber, walked back down to the van and placed his open palm against the glass, and we, on the inside, placed our open palm against the place where he was. No other words were necessary.

Closing Words and Comments

The keynote address on Friday was to have been given by Jeane J. Kirkpatrick, who had been prevented from coming by reason of the Daniloff case. In her place, Charles S. Robb, former governor of Virginia, offered closing words for the Americans. Many among the Americans complained later of Robb's negativity—perhaps the effect of his late arrival—and his superficiality. He began on a pessimistic note. He saw little chance of the two countries ever living in true harmony. Yet it was necessary to do everything to prevent the two countries from going to war. The fulcrum of East-West relations was mutual deterrence, keeping the military balance of power. In this, the crucial concerns of the two countries most clearly converged.

For the Americans it was left to Frederick Starr to work out what he called "a code of mutual communication, a code of mutual respect." Future conferences, he proposed, should work out such a code. It would include these five points: First, recognize the differences between the two systems. They existed in the past, even in the remote past, and they would exist in the future. Second, recognize that representatives from one side have the same number of brain cells and no less conscience than the representatives from the other. Third, recognize that none of us is perfect, that all of us have made mistakes and will continue to make them. Fourth, recognize that only compromises will help us coexist. Fifth and last, paraphrasing from the Bible, "treat others exactly as they would treat you."

Bratton began his closing comments by noting that on the journey from Riga to Jurmala that morning they had driven beneath a double rainbow. "I thought," he said, "how hopefully symbolic this is—two beautiful, intersecting rainbows over the place where Americans, Soviets, and Latvians consider the future of our common planet." He said, "Chautauqua is now a center and an idea with an international dimension. But now, here in Jurmala, Chautauqua has become more than a center where people come to learn and grow. It has become an agent of humankind's greatest agenda—

to know and understand each other better and to move towards achieving a condition of respect, dignity, and peace throughout the world."

The conference at Jurmala left an indelible imprint on the memories of those who traveled. One of the participants, Buffalo artist Rita Argen Auerbach, recalled later, "What was gnawing and aching inside of me was the concern I have for the people we met and left behind. Without words there was an expression of mutual caring and yearning for understanding. It seemed we weren't Americans, Latvians, or Russians, but citizens of one world during those brief encounters each day." Another of the Chautauqua delegates, Mace Levin, later wrote appreciatively of their hosts:

> They have a fierce sense of loyalty to their homeland, a conviction that their way of life is the right way of life, more concern for continued employment and a guaranteed source of income than for freedom of expression and of belief. They would like a more plentiful supply of material goods than what is presently available, and yet are disdainful of what they consider an obsession by us for the possession of things rather than what they think of as values. They seem unconcerned about standing in line, about the financial restraints which limit most to only one child, about the repressive rule by the KGB, their inability to travel abroad, read foreign books or newspapers, have a free press. On the other hand, they cannot understand why we tolerate and accept unemployment, homeless people, hungry people, crime, guns, discrimination against Blacks and so on. They are not pleased with their country's military involvement in Afghanistan, because of the average citizen's very deep dislike of war and fear of military losses.

Moscow and the Return

The American group left Riga on Friday afternoon by two charter flights for a few days' visit to Moscow. Moscow seemed to many of them more open than Riga. On Sunday, some expressed a desire to attend a service of the Russian Orthodox Church. In the end, fifty-seven of the delegates attended the service, which the Reverend Ralph Loew, one of the delegates, described in glowing terms, praising "the movement of so many people, kissing icons, buying candles and medals, milling about all the while as the divine liturgy was beautifully sung." That Sunday was the Feast of the Birth of the Virgin Mary, and dozens of parents had come with their babies to receive a blessing. In the midst, there were also mourners with an open casket, wrapped in pink, carrying the body of an elderly person. "It was the

meeting of youth, age, life and death," Loew recorded later, "the persever-
ance of a religious tradition, all wrapped into one experience."

Tours were also offered of the highlights of Moscow—the Kremlin, the
tomb of Lenin, the Armory Museum, the Gallery of Art, the New Maiden
Convent, the university, and the Pushkin Museum. A shopping tour on
Sunday afternoon gave a different impression of Moscow and its environs.
Sunday evening was the time for a visit to the Moscow Circus, which many
found the most enjoyable experience in Moscow. Some took the opportunity
of visiting the studio of Zurab Tsereteli, one of the most famous sculptors
in the USSR. Here they were regaled with a banquet of wines and food.
Arrangements had been made for the American musicians to play at one of
the museums and at the Blue Bird of Happiness Children's School. Many in
the group attended a concert given by the Paul Winter Consort, a guest of
the Chautauqua Institution from the previous year. Others attended a ballet performance in the Bolshoi Theater. Private visits were made and encouraged.

Several of the Chautauqua delegates took the opportunity while in Moscow to visit refusenik families, Jews who for years had been denied emigration requests. They expressed hope that the Gorbachev policy of glasnost
would give renewed hope. Many of the Jews spoke of loss of jobs, rejection
from university education, termination of pensions, and the need for proper
health care. The visits to the refuseniks left a deep impression on those who
experienced them. Usually arranged by a private telephone call, they would
begin with a walk through strange streets of the city to doors opened by
strangers. After some moments of discomfort, what one visitor called
"sparks of electricity" brought about an encounter that formed two groups
of strangers into a single family. Experiences were shared, photographs
exchanged—and most of all hugs and kisses were readily given and plenti-
ful tears shed.

Some of the refuseniks had been fired from jobs after requesting emigration. Their present jobs were low level, unsatisfying, and subject to termination. Families were divided. There was despair at the inability of children
to obtain university admittance simply because they were Jewish. Many felt
isolated from neighbors and coworkers who seemed to feel that anyone who
wanted to leave Russia was a traitor. Many of the Americans had brought
with them religious books and tape recordings as gifts, along with yar-
mulkes and prayer books, coffee, cocoa, clothing, and current issues of U.S.
magazines and newspapers.

Numbers of these visits produced significant results. For example,
Moscow-based refuseniks Boris and Elena Klotz and their four children left

for Israel later in the year as a direct result of the conference. Florence Ross, who had chided the official delegates for being like little boys, had written to Gorbachev, telling him how much the conference had meant to her and what a step forward she believed it was. "However," she recalled, "I told him that, in order to gain the trust and respect of Americans, the Soviets must perform more human acts that will go right to the hearts of the people, acts like allowing refuseniks to emigrate as a gesture of kindness." The following May, Ross received a phone call from an official at the Soviet embassy in Washington, notifying her that her letters did in fact reach Gorbachev. He wanted her to know that, as a gesture of thanks, the Klotz family, which had been refused visas to Israel since 1980, would be granted permission to leave the Soviet Union.

Monday, the last day in Moscow, gave opportunity for a visit to the GUM department store and also the American embassy. Once inside the embassy, Chautauqua delegate Rita Auerbach reflected, "We felt a magic transition to an American setting." Here the travelers met Acting Ambassador Richard Combs and Edward Djerejian and his wife, Frances, who invited a smaller number to meet with Nicholas Daniloff, now released to the embassy, and his wife, Ruth. Though released from prison, Daniloff was not free to leave the country. He wanted the group to know that he appreciated the decision of the delegates to withdraw from the conference if he continued to be imprisoned. He said he felt the conference was an important endeavor and was grateful that it had occurred. He did not wish to speak about his status, since it was delicate and tenuous at the time.

An hour and a half into the return flight to Washington, D.C., from Moscow on the chartered jet, the intercom was activated and a voice heard: "This is your captain speaking. We have just cleared Soviet airspace. Welcome to the Free World!" All on board burst into applause and cheered. According to Mary Frances Cram, "The relief we felt after just eleven days in the closed society of the Soviet Union erupted in a patriotic fervor most of us didn't know we possessed."

Subsequent comments by participants and those familiar with the conference were uniformly appreciative. Matlock called the conference "a notable first step towards exposing the Soviet people to the views of the American people. It broke new ground as the first such conference outside the United States where both sides could carry on a totally frank and uninhibited public dialogue." McFarlane wrote to Wallach and said, "The Chautauqua trip provides a vivid pledge of intent toward fostering a habit of U.S.-Soviet exchanges. The people of the Soviet Union have had tangible evidence of our good will."

By the end of the week in Jurmala, it had become clear that it was the right time for a third conference to pick up on the achievements of the first two in the series. This conference would again be held on the grounds of the institution. It was to be once more a collaborative effort on the part of the Union of Soviet Friendship Societies, the USSR-USA Society, and the institution itself. More than satisfied with the results of the previous two years, the three collaborators agreed to draw together an even larger number of representatives of the two countries.

In December, officials from the Chautauqua Institution met in Washington, D.C., with their opposite numbers from the USSR-USA Friendship Society. Touring the snow-covered grounds of the institution some days later, the Soviet officials, together with Stephen Rhinesmith and Gregory Guroff, set about shaping the format of the 1987 conference, the topics to be presented, and the scheduling of the evening performances. The following March, Daniel and Wanita Bratton visited Moscow along with Guroff for further discussions about the Soviet speakers and artists who were to have a part in the 1987 conference. The institution sought funding for the week through private and foundation gifts, including a grant of $150,000 from the W. Alton Jones Foundation. The Soviets, for their part, had made the decision to finance all costs for the citizen delegation—an indication, a State Department official noted, of how highly the Soviet Union valued the Chautauqua forum. The parties agreed that, within the framework of the agenda, the main question for delegates to consider would be the possible elimination of all nuclear weapons and the development of Soviet-American relations following the summit meeting held two months previously in Reykjavik.[12] Other issues to be discussed would include the historical and psychological aspects of Soviet-American relations; regional conflicts; human rights; the development of bilateral relations, economic contacts, and other forms of cooperation; public exchanges and contacts in the area of culture, the arts, and literature and their influence on the development of trust and mutual understanding. Under the agreed conditions, there was to be no censorship either in the speeches, unofficial presentations, or questions from the audience.

12. The discussion at the October 1986 meeting about eliminating all nuclear weapons was abortive. Some commentators portrayed Reagan as naive in comparison with Gorbachev. Shevardnadze regarded the summit as a time when both leaders disclosed their highest aspirations concerning the elimination of the weapons. See Eduard Shevardnadze, *The Future Belongs to Freedom* (New York: Free Press, 1991).

CHAPTER FIVE

1987: "Just an Enormous Event"

It is not yet clear whether this [conflict relationship] is still the dominant trend in American politics or whether the political pendulum has begun to swing in the opposite direction.

Marshall D. Shulman

SIBERIAN WEATHER, as one resident described it, descended on the Chautauqua Institution on Sunday, August 23, 1987. It was, she supposed, in anticipation of the arrival of the 240 Soviet visitors. Whatever the temperature, the will to offer a warm and enthusiastic welcome was already in the air. From eleven in the morning, Bestor Plaza had been filled with people coming and going like impatient children. Helium-filled balloons, tied to each lamppost on the plaza, danced in the wind, their colors, red, blue, yellow, and white, supplementing the flags that embellished the upper facade of the Colonnade building.

At two o'clock the Jamestown Municipal Band with its twenty-five players was ready to play a welcome of marches by John Phillip Sousa and Henry Fillmore for the arrival of the Soviet delegation. Nothing comparable had taken place in the United States during the years of the cold war. The clouds, which had threatened rain, were slowly scudding away; the sun was making intermittent appearances. The buses, however, were late. Finally at two thirty the first of the six appeared. The band began with a rousing march. The Russians were on the grounds at last; the cheers were loud and jubilant.

Earlier in the day most of the delegation had arrived at Buffalo International Airport from La Guardia, to be greeted there by H. David Faust, chairman of the Chautauqua Institution Board of Trustees, and by Tom Becker, vice president for development. Somewhat wearily the group made its way to collect the baggage. Members of the press, officials connected with the exchange, and passengers passing through Buffalo mingled with the Soviet visitors, making it hard for the welcoming party to tell who were

Russian until they spoke. "They look just like us," a woman commented to her husband as the Soviets filed along. A little girl, looking around at the visitors, addressed her father with an impatient query, "Which one is which?"

A People-to-People Understanding

Formal proceedings for the conference began at four o'clock in the Amphitheater. Thousands of quiet conversations created a roar like a strong wind. Faust, as chair of the board, invited the audience to stand for the playing of the national anthems of the Soviet Union and the United States. He then officially welcomed the Soviet guests and expressed thanks to the Chautauqua families for their generosity. As president, Bratton presented the chief Soviet delegate, Valentina Tereshkova, with a bouquet of gladioli, Chautauqua's symbolic summer flowers. Then, speaking with unconcealed joy, he offered his own welcome to the guests. Never before this time had such a large group of Soviet citizens come to the United States: "It is a wonderful, wonderful day for the welcome of such celebrities. No matter how you look at it, it's just an enormous event. Nobody else is doing it, and it's not just cultural exchange. It's not just people-to-people diplomacy. It's not just political debate. It's everything." Bratton then offered his appreciation to those who had had the imagination and courage to sponsor such an event. The success of the first two Chautauqua conferences had opened a way to a third. Chautauqua's own model of programming made it possible to employ many dimensions of diplomacy, whether by politicians, academics, artists, or citizens themselves. Further, Chautauqua's own rich historical heritage, which had contributed so much in the past to the improvement of the human condition, now found expression in this unprecedented enterprise.

Following Bratton, Stephen Rhinesmith was introduced to deliver greetings to the conference on behalf of President Reagan and Secretary Shultz. Chautauqua, he said, was a model of cooperation in the serious, open, and frank dialogue that was so much needed at this time between the USSR and the United States. The conference, as he saw it, had four objectives: first, to allow participants to talk together about policy issues separating or uniting the two nations; second, to stimulate the exchange of ideas through roundtable discussions; third, to give expression to the arts and cultural heritage of each nation; and fourth, to provide an opportunity for "an intensive, people-to-people dialogue" that would afford individuals the opportunity to ask questions and engage in issues of concern about their lives.

Valentina Tereshkova, honored as a hero of the Soviet Union as the first female in space and a member of the Presidium of the Supreme Soviet, then came to the podium. Speaking in Russian, she thanked Chautauqua for its welcome and expressed the hope that the discussions, seminars, and meetings would help all present to understand one another better. When she was in the capsule orbiting Earth, she said, Earth looked like a spaceship with all the peoples inhabitants of it. "We must," she said, "have teamwork to be able to navigate together." She turned to the two issues that would repeatedly come before the delegates during the week. One was the need for the Soviet Union and the United States to work together to preserve and use well each country's natural resources. The second was the ever-present danger of nuclear arms and the fact that even 1 percent of existing weapons had the power to harm all the earth. "Without mutual understanding and united by common goals," she asked, "how can we live on one planet?" She concluded her remarks, however, with a few words of optimism: "Between us there is no gap that cannot be bridged by good will and courage."

Two other platform guests brought the introductions to a close, each carefully choosing a figure known and respected in the other's country. Vladimir Petrovsky, who had spoken the previous year at Jurmala, cited Thomas Jefferson. "The course of America," Jefferson had said, "is the course of the whole of humanity." Petrovsky rephrased the quotation by stating, "the course of the whole of humanity is the course of the United States and the Soviet Union, the most powerful nations in the world." He believed deeply, he said, that this responsibility of seeking peace could be exercised only if the governments and people of the United States and the Soviet Union would act accordingly.

Rep. Amo Houghton Jr., greeting the Soviets present, said, "The hand that reaches out to you is the hand not of democracy but of brotherhood." He agreed with those who had already spoken that personal relationships were of the utmost importance to world peace. He and his own family had visited the Soviet Union at least ten times. Nothing, he emphasized, was more important than for members of the two nations to get to know one another well. He then cited the Russian playwright Anton Chekhov, who had written, "We struggle to change life, so that those who come after us will be happy, yet they will then say that the world was better before." Everything that Chautauqua stood for pointed to such a better life. So it was essential to realize that important things could happen even in small doses. Houghton ended his statement by using the analogy of the grandfather who taught his grandchild that if everyone carried a single pebble in an effort to move a hill, it would eventually be moved.

Members of the official Soviet and American delegations were housed in the Athenaeum Hotel. The citizen delegates, however, were to stay with

Chautauqua homeowners. Most of Soviets had come from across the western part of the USSR. Among their number were members of the intelligentsia, a scattering of workers, but, somewhat strangely, no collective or state farmers. Inevitably, host families raised many questions: It would involve a lot of work and presumably a lot of expense. Or the family did not speak Russian. One host asked how much the Russians would want to drink, since their own drinking habits were moderate by what they assumed were Soviet standards. "But in the end," one couple said, "the adventure was more than we could resist." A briefing session had been held shortly before the arrival of the guests, and the level of excitement had grown. Jokes were made about what was going to happen. Who would get representatives of the KGB? Had there been workmen around planting bugs in the houses? A question was raised about what should be done if one of the guests chose to defect. "Stay out of it completely," the answer was given. "The FBI will be on the grounds."

Host families were at liberty to take their guests outside the grounds at any time, but the government required that they report their destination if they wanted to go beyond a twenty-five-mile radius. It was assumed that many of the guests would want to see Niagara Falls, but they were not to go into Canada. Hints were given about how to make the guests feel welcome. Superstition, they learned, still had a prominent place in Soviet life. Hands should not be shaken through a doorway—a sign of bad luck. In the Soviet Union, one would always step inside first or risk offending not only the host but also the unlucky house spirit. A woman guest could be given flowers, the hosts were told, but in an uneven number. Even numbers had a negative meaning in Russian folklore and were given only for funerals. Hosts should not give knives or handkerchiefs as gifts. Salt should not be passed from hand to hand but placed on the table so that the guest could pick it up. With necessary questions of etiquette and superstition addressed, host families then received three sheets of paper with helpful Russian phrases printed phonetically. An enterprising group of women had earlier made up 245 baskets of gifts, one for each guest. The baskets contained crackers, cheese, candy, a Wrangler belt buckle, toothbrush, grape juice, and a small bottle of New York champagne.

Most of the Soviet guests spent some of their time during the conference week visiting places such as local stores, banks, auto showrooms, or places of interest such as an automated banking center. Many purchased gifts for their families. A Soviet physician was invited to visit a hospital in Pittsburgh by his host, himself chief of ophthalmology at the hospital. The physician, who was particularly interested in addiction, spent much time discussing his field with the American doctor in charge of the emergency wing.

Mario Cuomo, the governor of New York, was introduced to give a welcome to the delegates. In a speech interrupted frequently by applause, he said that the conference at Chautauqua offered many possibilities. "We can remain suspended in separate spheres," he argued, "or we can look beyond our differences to the whole range of shared needs. There is an interconnectedness of the human family which has become clear. There is no other rational choice than to recognize this." Cuomo then asked his audience to address a critical question. The two nations were driven by the icy logic of the cold war: neither side could ever use the arms they had created except at the risk of world holocaust. In the tranquil environment of Chautauqua, however, it might be possible to ponder the strangeness of the situation and remind one another of how utterly each nation depended on the other. Pounding on a theme that clearly evoked a lively response from the audience, Cuomo scorned the dilemma faced by both nations of having to spend millions on missiles that would go unfired, while people went unfed, uneducated, and uncared for. The time was at hand, he insisted, to end the cold war that the great powers had endured for so long. Where better to think such thoughts about lifting and energizing the whole world than in Chautauqua? "Wouldn't it be wonderful if, in the future, people looked back and recalled that a few of the first steps towards world peace were taken by the United States and the Soviets, who came together in a beautiful place called Chautauqua?"

The opening ceremonies ended with a group of local children singing a welcome song—in both English and Russian—encouraging understanding between nations. Alfreda Irwin, then historian-in-residence at the institution, offered her own reflection of the opening of the 1987 conference. "The coming of 240 citizens seems so logical and appropriate after Jurmala. There we viewed our fellow conferees from the Soviet Union as a sampling of people who, by just being there, contributed personal qualities to our idea of a mighty superpower. They in turn could look at us and add that impression to their impersonal image of the USA. We are eager to respond. We look forward to learning to know more Soviet citizens."

"We Belong to Two Different Societies"

From the first day, the atmosphere on the grounds was perceptibly different in tone and emphasis from the conference of 1985. Either by design or through the presence of hundreds of citizens of the "evil empire," the debates of 1987 began to reveal a determination to move to higher level of debate than attack and counterattack. The 1987 conference would not lead to any subversion of inherited frames of thinking on either side. Yet there was a larger willingness to recognize that the very differences of two such diverse peoples might prove in the end to be constructive of unity rather than threatening.

On the first day, Gregory Guroff, deputy coordinator of the President's Exchange Initiative, began his address speaking in Russian—to the delight of the Soviet delegates in the audience. From as early as the American Revolution, he noted, there had been a benign if distant relationship between the United States and the Russian empire that had lasted well into the twentieth century. The two powers on the edges of Europe found themselves united in opposition to the more established hegemonies. During the Civil War, Russia found itself in support of the Union against the Confederacy and in opposition to Britain. On the very eve of that war, Alexander II had signed a proclamation emancipating the serfs in Russia. This linking in a commonality of interests was typical up to the modern period.

Guroff then recounted how American historians within recent years had joined with their Soviet counterparts in reviewing textbooks for American and Soviet high school students. They were particularly shocked by the treatment of World War II in the textbooks of both countries and appalled when they read the American publications. It was as if the Soviet Union had not even existed during the war. They later found the same misreading of history was true also in Soviet textbooks. In this case, it was as if the United States and its allies had never existed. These misreadings of history, Guroff continued, were not simply myths of the past but continued into the present period. Most Americans even yet did not yet appreciate the enormity of Soviet suffering in World War II and especially in the Battle of Leningrad. The Soviets in turn belittled lend-lease, the invasion of Normandy, and the concurrent war fought by the United States in the Pacific. For these American and Soviet historians it was a shock to see how both sides had interpreted World War II because of their political hostilities in the postwar period.

According to Guroff, many examples could be given of the ways in which the two countries had depersonalized one another. Neither side gave a true or even reasonably close picture of the other. Yet each society comprised normal human beings who laugh, cry, and worry about their children's future. To illustrate his point, Guroff told a story about his Russian grandmother:

When I first went to Moscow, my grandmother was still alive. We became close very quickly. I had no doubt that we were open and honest with each other. One night over dinner she asked me innocently why I had returned to graduate school after working a couple of years in Washington. I explained simply how one applies for graduate school and the details about leaving a job, giving up a lease, moving and finding an apartment. She listened and nodded. Then she asked me quizzically, "But who gave you permission?" I said, "Babushka, no one gave me permission. I got into graduate school, and that's the way we do it." She said, "Well, fine." We went to get our coats a couple of hours later. She pulled me aside and winked at me and said, "You can tell me. After all, I am your grandmother. [Laughter] Who gave you permission?" This went on for a number of weeks. It wasn't that she didn't believe me, nor was she naive or foolish. Her whole conceptual framework of how a society ought to function was very different. For her, society was a series of institutions that kept order and avoided anarchy. You have to go through the bureaucracy to get permission to move from one town to another or to change jobs. It was a system she had grown up with and was used to.

Both peoples, Guroff continued, perceived the nature of society quite differently. For a Russian, society was a series of institutions that kept order and avoided anarchy. In the Russian way of thinking, one had to go through a bureaucracy to get permission to leave one place and go to another. Communication and understanding were not just a matter of providing more facts. One had to have a "feel" of how society functions. The concept of nationality was quite different in both countries. Americans did not recognize the right of the government to tell them where and when they could travel, for example. They had derived an entire system to protect the rights of individuals, and they held them as fundamental rights.

Guroff ended his speech with an appeal for mutual understanding. Viktor Malkov immediately picked up the theme, opening his own address by indicating that he found himself in much agreement with Guroff. "In recent years," he said, "the two countries have gone a long way to improve relationships and deal with issues such as nuclear disarmament. We can see the springs of new political thinking." Gorbachev's recent speeches in particular were an appeal to understand one another better. It was time now to ask difficult questions, but it was not necessary to abandon one's creed. "What is necessary," he said, "is free thinking. The barrier created by stereotypes has always been in the way of a clear understanding." Americans from the first had had a distorted picture of Soviet society. Earlier in the century it was national policy to regard Bolshevism as a threat to the United States. So the United States adopted a policy of nonrecognition. However, when Franklin Delano Roosevelt received his mandate in 1932, he tried to abandon stereotypes of the Soviet Union. The president was convinced that the two countries shared the same destiny.

Malkov went on to cite two major public occasions in its history when the Chautauqua Institution had affected national policy in a significant way. First, in his 1936 speech at Chautauqua, Roosevelt had warned that even the nation that most desired peace might still be drawn into war. In effect, he was making an appeal for dialogue between nations that were even then coming closer to war. Malkov then referred to a theme that had been widely discussed during the first Chautauqua conference on U.S.-Soviet relations, namely, the cooperation between the Soviet Union and the United States during World War II. What, then, stood in the way of collaboration at the present time?

One obstacle, according to Malkov, was the role of the press, especially the American press. He referred to a recent newspaper article that posed the question, "Is it conceivable that the big, bad Russian bear will become a cuddly teddy bear?" Was that to be the persistent American image of the Soviet Union—a big, bad bear? In contrast, it would be quite difficult in the Soviet Union to find a Soviet child who was frightened of Americans. Malkov related an incident in his travels when he had come across a young American boy who seemed to visualize every Russian as a heartless robot that was part of a system bent on destroying him. "I tried to tell him that I am a grandfather with two grandsons of my own his age," he said. "I wonder if he understood."

In the question-and-answer period that followed, both Guroff and Malkov took a lively part, at times contradicting one another's statements.

> QUESTION: Americans have images of the Soviets as not being quite human. Is the reason for this image the role played by the U.S. press, television, and textbooks?
>
> GUROFF: Yes. The American media have a role in the attitudes that we form of each other. On both sides serious inadequacies exist in textbooks and in our understanding of one another. But American attitudes to the Soviet Union often do have some relation to reality, so that activities the Soviet Union undertakes in its foreign affairs or domestic politics often have a major impact on American attitudes. In the area

of human rights, we do have to judge countries by the way they treat their citizens.

QUESTION: American mistrust for the last fifty or sixty years has been based on the thought that the Soviet Union wants to turn the world into a Soviet state. We understand that Marx and Lenin taught the doctrine of exporting communism. Is this true?

MALKOV: The Marxist conception is not one of exporting revolution. We are against that. Marx, Lenin, and Engels in their works or in public speeches taught this. They talk about the revolution that arises from a national situation. When we talk about the revolutions that took place in different parts of the world after World War II, that was the result of the internal development in different countries, for example, in China, Africa, or Latin America. Their revolutions for independence were all products of their domestic development. This is our position theoretically. We sympathize with the revolutions. We help them militarily and diplomatically, because the revolution must defend itself. But we are against exporting revolution. The reason for change in the political structures of East Europe was domestic. This was found by U.S. agencies such as the CIA.

GUROFF: This is silly. It is hard for anyone to believe that the change in social structures in East Europe was a spontaneous one. In those countries in which there were no Soviet troops, the seeds of socialist revolution did exist but nowhere succeeded. The revolutions succeeded because of Soviet troops, for example, in Hungary, Czechoslovakia, Poland, and even in East Germany. Soviet historiography of the movement of socialism is self-serving, unreal, and fraudulent. The question of whether the Soviet Union has supported revolutions and believes that they are domestic seems also to be beyond the point. The Soviet Union exports military advisors and weapons. If we recognize that, then we can discuss the use of force in the modern world. Until then, the discussions will be illusory.

Following this interaction between Guroff and Malkov, a question from the floor raised the issue of what was described as the inhumane treatment of refuseniks who were not allowed to leave the Soviet Union. Malkov responded that it was possible to deal only with concrete cases. As far as he knew, any who wanted to leave the Soviet Union could apply for a visa. There were, so far as he knew, problems only in isolated cases. The situation had changed markedly from what it was previously.

Guroff responded that there were two issues to be considered. Indeed, there had been changes in regard to the refuseniks in the Soviet Union, particularly those of long standing. There had been an increase in the numbers of those permitted to leave. But, he continued, Soviet law had become much more restrictive than it had been. The terms under which one could leave applied in cases only of a close family member. It was also true, however, that as the treatment of minority groups in the Soviet Union improved, there would be fewer who would apply for exit visas. Leaving a country, after all, was a wrenching experience.

Two of the major speeches of the week were given by Marshall D. Shulman and Vitaly Zhurkin. Shulman was senior lecturer in international relations at the W. Averell Harriman Institute for Advanced Study of the Soviet Union at Columbia University. Zhurkin was a deputy director of the Institute of US and Canada Studies in Moscow and a member of the Soviet Academy of Sciences.

Shulman began by examining what he called the external and the internal factors with which the two superpowers had been dealing historically. The cataclysmic changes wrought by World War II inevitably had effect on the international order that had dominated and stabilized international politics for most of the preceding century. Shulman methodically outlined what he regarded as the five major external factors in the relationship. First, the accelerating revolution in science and technology had transformed both the substance and the processes of international politics. In particular, the revolution in military technology, and notably the discovery of nuclear weapons and intercontinental missiles, had radically affected the character of the relationship between war and politics. Second, the rapid dissolution of colonial relations and the birth of more than a hundred new nations had created many sources of conflict, with border, tribal, and religious problems resulting in continuing worldwide turbulence. Third, the world economy was being transformed by the passage of the advanced industrial countries into a new stage of technological revolution, while the developing countries struggled with the basic problems of nation building. Fourth, the old balance-of-power system was being replaced by ambiguous configurations of power, with a bipolar distribution of nuclear military power and an undefined multipolar distribution of power and influence in various regions of the world. Fifth, a resurgence of nationalism, temporarily repressed during the immediate postwar years, began to manifest itself among many nations in response to the disorienting effect of the changes wrought by the effects of the revolution in science and technology in the way people lived.

Internal factors, Shulman continued, had also very much affected U.S.-Soviet relations: domestic politics, ideology, psychological factors, and the influence of military institutions within each country. All these, singly or in combination, had contributed to a process of interaction between the United States and the USSR that intensified their differences, making them more absolute and less tractable than the conflict of interest might otherwise have warranted. It was easy to see how the external and internal factors contributed to the development of the cold war. The cold war began more than forty years earlier in a massive turnaround in American policy. The years immediately following the war had been a time of collaboration with the Soviet Union, a "gallant ally" that had contributed heroically and with great loss of life to the defeat of the Nazi army. The relationship ended on the part of the United States in an alarmed and belated response to the problems of the postwar world, particularly the emerging Soviet dominance in Eastern Europe and the perceived Soviet threat to the Balkans and to Western Europe.

During the war, the United States had avoided involvement in discussions of postwar settlements, fearing that to do so would have detracted from the effective prosecution of the war. However, during the period from Churchill's March 1946 "iron curtain" speech at Fulton, Missouri, to the middle of 1947, a rapid succession of events marked a clear transformation in American policy—the delivery of U.S. aid to Greece and Turkey; a definite commitment on the part of the United States to resist Soviet expansionism anywhere; the Marshall Plan, announced in June of that year to restore economic vitality and political confidence in Western Europe; and the promulgation by George F. Kennan of the containment policy in July. The U.S. military demobilization came to a halt and began to be replaced by a renewal of military programs, including the development of strategic nuclear air power. The notion of containment became increasingly militarized and globalized. Anticommunism became the American ideology and the central principle of U.S. foreign policy. The primitive stereotypes of the Soviet Union laid down at that time continued to dominate American thinking and discussion of the Soviet Union down to the present day.

On the Soviet side, 1947 was the year of the establishment of the Cominform, the Communist Information Bureau (the successor to the Comintern). The Cominform preceded the Marshall Plan, which was part of the U.S. and British effort to undermine Soviet efforts to establish a cordon in Eastern Europe against a revival of a German threat. Stalin devised the Cominform as an instrument for tightening his control over that area and over the

Communist parties of France and Italy. He laid plans at that founding meeting for the coup in Czechoslovakia the following February. A tightening of controls to totalitarian levels followed, accompanied by a heightened militancy on the part of Communist parties the world over. The signal for this militancy was given in a speech by Andrei Zhdanov at the founding meeting of the Cominform, in which he laid down the proposition that the world was now divided into two hostile camps.

In retrospect, one could see how Stalin's harsh militancy, even if it might have been intended to protect Soviet security, had the counterproductive effect of mobilizing and antagonizing the West. It was also clear in retrospect that the response of the West and in particular the United States went beyond a measured reaction to Stalin's policies. In both the Soviet Union and the United States, psychological anxieties, ideological preconceptions, domestic politics, and the momentum of military organizations expanding into new military technology had all combined to heighten the sense of threat and hostility. But the most serious consequence was the militarization of both societies and the continued upward spiral of nuclear military competition.

Although there had been a range of views in the United States in regard to the Soviet Union, the persistently dominant view during most of recent years treated the relations between the two countries as a Manichaean struggle between good and evil. It was a struggle that maintained a fixation on Stalinism as the unchanging and unchangeable model of Soviet behavior, intractably hostile and unlimited in its aspirations for world dominance. The central core of this view was that Soviet expansionist activity was so inherently rooted in the nature of the Soviet system that such behavior could be modified only by bringing about fundamental changes in the Soviet system.

Several elements in Gorbachev's new thinking bore watching. One was his emphasis on the mutuality of security. As he had said at the party congress, "We can never be secure while the United States feels itself insecure." He had also observed that the Soviet Union had no need of an external enemy, breaking with Stalin's reliance on a capitalist encirclement to justify military programs. All of this suggested, Shulman continued, the possibility that the Soviet Union might have come a long way from the two camps doctrine of hostility towards a period when, if encouraged, it would be prepared to recognize its own self-interest in playing a more constrictive role in the international system and in international economic institutions. Gorbachev was, of course, working within the framework of Soviet politics and existing political institutions. He remained committed to centralized political control through a one-party system under socialism. But his approach was pragmatic rather than ideological. He seemed to evoke a new sense of participation in the population. And, while he advanced no blueprint, he sought to redefine what socialism meant that was different from the Stalinist model.

Coming towards the close of his address, Shulman then asked what these lessons of the past suggested about what needed to be done now to put the relationship on a more sensible footing. The point that required the greatest emphasis, he believed, was the necessity for both countries to broaden their perspective and to take account of the international context of which their relationship is a part. The Soviet Union and the United States, each acting upon its enlightened self-interest, must free themselves of the obsessive fears of and preoccupation with each other and therefore from the costly militarization of their societies. Only if they were able to cast off these constricting blinders would they be able to compete and cooperate on more constructive terms.

At the conclusion of his address, Shulman received sustained applause from the audience.

Vitaly Zhurkin followed Shulman at the podium. Zhurkin had credentials no less notable than those of Shulman, including three books, published in English, dealing with Soviet-American relations. He had been one of four experts invited by Gorbachev to accompany the general secretary to the Geneva and Reykjavik summit meetings with Reagan.

Zhurkin began by expressing his intent to speak in English since, he said to laughter from the audience, "Maybe bad English is better than a good translation." He agreed completely with Shulman that the record of postwar Soviet-American relations was bleak. But it would be wrong to forget one paramount fact. Both nations—and humanity itself—had survived. They survived at a time when the nuclear potential of the United States and of the Soviet Union could destroy both nations and the whole of humankind. This was happening at a time when a Soviet nuclear warhead might be targeted to the very building in which the audience was presently seated and when some American nuclear warhead was targeted at his own house where his wife, his children, and his grandchild were staying at that very moment.

At the same time, however, the present period—some forty years after the war—was one of unrealized expectations, chances, and possibilities. Who was to blame? "I would not be a Soviet historian," Zhurkin asserted slyly, "if I did not say that the blame lies with the Americans [Laughter]. And I think the blame that I put on the Americans is indeed justified." Zhurkin then asked what the Soviet Union had done or not done in making the most of the chances and possibilities that existed. Its position might not have been flexible enough on more than one occasion. One should take into consideration, however, that only after the Second World War did the Soviet Union enter the large international arena and begin to act as a major international actor. It did not have enough experience and at times was limited in its worldview and understanding.

Zhurkin then turned to deal with the Soviet position on control over arms limitations and reductions. With the growth and complexity of the existing weapons system, it was becoming more than ever necessary to accept international forms of control and on-site inspection in order to ensure that this control was valid and adequate. No doubt the forces of inertia would create delays in adjusting positions. Gorbachev had stated more than once that it was typical in international relations that it took time for a nation to adjust to quickly changing international realities, to understand them at depth, and to adjust policies accordingly. The Soviet position had already changed dramatically during the previous two years into different forms of international on-site inspection. This made the Soviet position in some areas of arms control and disarmament much more advanced in some ways than the American. So it was necessary to develop a mechanism and a mentality for quickly adjusting to these realities, because the shorter the period of adjustment, the better it was for international relations and for the nations that were willing to readjust.

It was clear, Zhurkin affirmed, that the differences between the two nations would continue. "We belong to two different societies," he said, "historically, socially, and economically different from one another."

> Americans do not agree with many elements of Soviet society. For us, many things seem strange in the United States. I was born, and my children were born, with a clear understanding that, for instance, the right to education is an inherent human right, and that every nation and state, with whatever meager resources, is obliged to provide free education for everyone. Education should be based on personal capabilities and not on money or other factors. We believe it strange that other approaches could exist, though I would respect these other approaches. From my point of view good health is also an inherent human right. And the state and the nation are obliged to provide me with free medical education. It is a right that everyone should enjoy.

It is strange to me that it is not so in other places. The right to work is also an inherent human right. We do not understand the phenomenon of unemployment, though economists no doubt could explain it. There are other things. I am saying this not just to balance American complaints against the Soviet Union but just to show that there could be different understandings about quite normal things.

Zhurkin then summarized what he took to be the Soviet view. For the first ten years after the Second World War, the Soviet Union believed that war between the United States and the Soviet Union was inevitable or at least probable. It prepared for this war and developed its military potential. It took ten years to understand by the mid-1950s that war was not inevitable and should not be recognized as such. It took another thirty years to understand that nuclear war was impossible and that every nation should do everything possible to avoid this nuclear apocalypse. Anyone in the Soviet Union who spoke of victory in a nuclear war or of surviving a nuclear war was, by any appearance, insane. Was the same, he inquired, true of the United States? On the one hand there were statements of political leaders in this country. The position of the American public was widely known. At the same time, Zhurkin insisted, the Soviet Union could not overlook voices heard from time to time that aimed at achieving superiority or even voices that suggested that victory in nuclear war was possible.

On the matter of international security, one of the latest developments in Soviet thinking was the understanding that security could not be based on military strength alone or on the accumulation of defensive weapons. Security was something much more than that. It involved political action in preventing or settling international conflict. It involved military collaboration in many new areas, for example, the prevention of international terrorism. Security also had economic dimensions but would not be possible unless other nations also enjoyed some kind of economic security. It would involve cooperation in dealing with the international narcotics trade and bilateral and multilateral collaboration in dealing with disease, including AIDS. Security also had humanitarian aspects. It involved human rights, and the strengthening of these rights would increase the security of the two nations. No doubt any security of this kind would be a huge task to achieve, but it was possible, Zhurkin insisted, by no means beyond the possibility of attainment. Strong applause broke out from the audience with this comment.

Zhurkin ended his address by appealing to both nations to undertake the necessary analysis of the situation that he had described. The Soviet Union accepted that necessity. He agreed completely with Shulman that history was giving the two sides another chance to challenge each other, not in the military field but in the fields of arms control, international security, and the settlement of other issues, including human rights. "May I assure you," he said—to rousing applause as the words were translated—"that the Soviet Union will try to prove that it stands for this."

Among the questions raised following the speeches, two in particular had a response from both speakers.

> Question: You, Dr. Zhurkin, said that security could not be based on military strength. Can you with Mr. Gorbachev work out a plan in cooperation with the United States to help withdraw the military presence in Eastern Europe, Southeast Asia, the Central American countries, and other places?
>
> Zhurkin: The Soviet Union is already positioned to withdraw Soviet troops from all other areas and states. It was not an easy decision. An international agreement is necessary, and it should be implemented in stages. It would help very much if the Soviet Union and the United States would reach an agreement about reducing or eliminating some of the nuclear armaments, which both of us have in great abundance.
>
> Shulman: The negative attitudes I spoke of are widely represented in the American public. What is absent today is a politically effective constituency that would support a more enlightened approach particularly to the management of nuclear weapons, but also to relations with the Soviet Union. That is where this conference comes in. It is a question of the gradual spread of information and understanding that gets translated into political action, which I hope will result in changes in American foreign policy [Applause].
>
> Question: It is a common belief in the American public that the Soviet Union is a threat with an expansionist foreign policy. Is it? And do Soviets see America as a threat to the Soviet Union?
>
> Zhurkin: There are such mirror-image conceptions on both sides. One of the most important things is through the actual policies of both nations to prove more and more that this conception is wrong. Dialogue not only between governments but also such as we have here in Chautauqua should help this process. I would call this mutual education.
>
> Shulman: Both countries perceive the other as expansionist and as having less than benign intentions towards the other. It is also true in

both countries that there is a difference between shadow and substance, between declaratory policy and actual policy. The United States prides itself on being non-imperialistic and non-military. In practice, if you look at what we are doing and at the weapons we are building, at where our troops are, at the effects of our policies, there are things that are difficult to reconcile with our declaratory policy [Applause].

Roundtables on Issues of Common Concern

Part of the week's design included the provision of a large number of round-tables at which issues of common concern were discussed by American and Soviet participants. The themes included future trends in museums, theater, film, education, music, regional issues, religion, the role of youth, cooperation in space, medicine, and law. Over fifty speakers participated in the many roundtables, which provided many opportunities for Soviets and Americans present to hear, debate and raise questions, and shift the focus from politics.

According to Palmer, the issue of human rights was paramount in the relations between the two countries, because it dealt with human beings as individuals. He began by making three general statements about the issue. First, the achievement of human rights was a lengthy historical process. Americans should not be self-righteous about it. It took a hundred years or more to free their slaves, longer for women to achieve the vote. America was a long way from achieving full civil and human rights, even late in the twentieth century. Second, an inherent human right was the ability on the part of all peoples to travel, to live free lives, to "kick the bums out of office" periodically, and to have a free press. Third, the crucial element was deeds and not words. Palmer acknowledged that in the last year or so there had indeed been much progress in the Soviet Union. But much remained to be done in both countries. It was important to redouble energies to achieve full human rights for everyone.

Taking his turn next, Alexander Sukharev, Soviet minister of justice in the Russian Federation, insisted that both countries needed to do away with suspicion and mistrust about one another. The problem of rights and freedoms was one that concerned them both and was a heavy burden in Soviet-American relations. Both sides, he agreed, had blame enough to carry, and certainly the heat generated in some of the discussions was intense. Sukharev went on to define the Soviet concept of human rights under his own three headings. First, the Soviets took a comprehensive approach to the implementation of human rights. All kinds of rights were important.

Economic, social, and political rights were indivisible. Second, Soviet constitutional rights were not just proclaimed but were also guaranteed by the state. Third, the respect for human dignity, human values, and international cooperation was central in dealing with rights. Soviets at present, he insisted, were not content with what had been going on in their country in the past: "We openly and frankly say this on the radio and in the press and television. No one prompts this. We just do it, because at the base of perestroika there is a human factor. We need democracy, we need glasnost, and we need freedoms. These are the areas in which the lawyers are working today."

The third of the panelists to make a formal presentation was Spencer Oliver, chief counsel of the U.S. House Foreign Affairs Committee. Oliver agreed with Sukharev on the need to speak honestly and forthrightly, to face facts and face the truth. But he was struck by the fact that Sukharev had never once mentioned the Helsinki Accords (1975), probably the most important human rights document to be signed by the United States and the Soviet Union. It was important because, despite the different cultures and histories of the two countries, the two sides agreed on definitions of human rights and fundamental freedoms. The leaders of both countries pledged to fulfill the promise of the accords, including the freedom of thought, conscience, religion, and belief. Also promised in the accords was freedom to move about, freedom of ideas, permission for families to be reunited, binational marriage, and equal rights in the self-determination of peoples.

Samuel Zivs, a member of the Institute for Government and Law and president of the USSR-USA Society, agreed strongly on the need to move from confrontation to cooperation. It was one thing to deal with obstacles to mutual understanding but more important to move towards agreement. He could illustrate in many ways the concern that the Soviet Union had for human rights. They were part of perestroika. They were an essential part also in the development of international relations.

Catherine Cosman, who had served on the Helsinki Commission, used her own five-minute statement as an opportunity for noting the difference in approach between the two nations when it came to defining human rights. "Human rights touch all of us," she began. "People around the world are concerned with the issue. But the different perceptions of what constitutes human rights goes to the heart of the difference between our two societies." Americans, she said, put great stress on individual liberties. Soviets, in contrast, saw economic needs as primary. The two societies also had different views on the relationship between government and the people. When it came to government, Cosman said, America's view was that "less is more," while in the Soviet Union the government, the people, and the party are a solid unit.

She then outlined some of the many positive steps already taken by the Soviets in the area of human rights. Over two hundred political prisoners had recently been released, and many had been allowed to emigrate. Glasnost had allowed many citizens to express their views on human rights. Demonstrations had been permitted in the Baltic States and on Red Square. Unofficial human rights publications had been tolerated. Glasnost had also allowed a flowering of Soviet culture, so that Soviet readers, listeners, and viewers could turn to their own culture for a discussion of human rights and other important issues. But many abuses still remained, she said.

A question came to Zivs from a member of the audience who had met him in Jurmala the previous year. Zivs had identified himself as head of the anti-Zionist organization of the Soviet Union. The questioner said that he had been informed at the Leningrad airport that he could not bring in materials written in Hebrew. Zivs admitted that there were such regulations, but they applied only to books in Hebrew written for propaganda or religious purposes. According to the questioner, Zivs had also said that it was forbidden to teach Hebrew in the Soviet Union and that there were no Hebrew teachers there. So, the questioner asked, "Who then teaches the inspectors so that they can distinguish propaganda from non-propaganda works? Will you now, with glasnost, permit people to learn Hebrew, to have teachers of Hebrew individually and in groups in the new open society?"

Zivs attempted to clarify what he thought was a misunderstanding. Religious literature, mainly in Hebrew, is imported in an organized way, synagogue to synagogue. Some weeks earlier, for example, the Moscow synagogue had received five thousand copies of the Hebrew scriptures donated by a congregation in New York City. A further ten thousand prayer books were on their way. Second, the teaching and learning of any language was expressly not forbidden. Hebrew was in fact taught in various universities —Moscow and Leningrad, for example. As one example of this freedom to teach, Zivs noted to the recent election of a Hebrew scholar as chancellor of Tbilisi University in Georgia.

Several members of the audience made impassioned pleas for the Soviets to allow Jews and others to emigrate. Mace Levin, a Chautauquan, called the Jewish refusenik problem a litmus test that would show the world whether the policy of glasnost was only words. There were hundreds of thousands who would like to emigrate but who were faced with severe difficulties even in applying for permission. Five thousand Jews had been given visas in 1987, but over fifty thousand visas had been given in previous years. Levin was greeted with prolonged applause when he said, "Let my people go."

Zivs challenged Levin's statistics on the number of Jews who wanted to leave the Soviet Union. There were, he said, 1.8 million Jews in the Soviet Union. At least 1.7 million of these regarded the Soviet Union as their home and as their mother country and had no intention to leave. He said that very few applications had been denied in recent years, that many indeed had been granted, and that those refused were turned down because of health restrictions or national security. "Mr. Levin," he said, "when we meet at the fourth U.S.-Soviet conference I hope we can find that our statistics coincide."

The self-determination of Afghanistan, Nicaragua, and the countries of Eastern Europe was the subject of several questions. When a former Soviet soldier who had fought in Afghanistan questioned the validity of the Soviet presence in that country, Igor Blischenko replied that the Soviets were doing their best to assure the Afghan people of their right to self-determination. In response to an accusation by an American member of the audience that the USSR had violated the Yalta accords by denying self-determination to the countries of Eastern Europe, Blischenko replied that the nations of Eastern Europe were indeed both free and sovereign. A Moscow lawyer asked Palmer why the United States did not respect a ruling by the International Court of Justice calling for the rights of Nicaraguans to choose their own system of government. Palmer answered that only a multiparty system with free elections and a free press could allow the Nicaraguans to choose their government. "When these political conditions are achieved," he said, "we will stop interfering." Several members of the audience referred to specific cases of human rights abuses. One asked Sukharev if the Soviet government was ready to open its labor camps to international inspection. Sukharev answered, "We don't have labor camps any longer. We have reforming centers." The audience, however, seemed unpersuaded.

A question came next from an American member of the audience. "Your constitution," he said, "gives each republic the right to separate from the Soviet Union. Yet in many cases involving Baltic dissidents, individuals have been found in violation of the USSR criminal code and guilty of anti-Soviet agitation for either possessing or circulating literature expressing such a desire on the part of the Baltic States to separate. You appear to have a right that is constitutionally guaranteed, yet the means by which to exercise this right is outlawed by your criminal code. Please explain."

Zivs responded by saying that there could be no question about the priority of the criminal code over the constitution. The guarantees of the constitution were clear, but, he insisted, the right to secede or advocate for separation had not been exercised. At this point a judge from the Supreme Court of Latvia, who was in the audience, came to the microphone to indicate his agreement with Zivs. In his two years as chairman of the court, he replied, there had not been a single case before the court in which petitioners had asked for the separation of Latvia from the Soviet Union. Those who were sentenced earlier for advocating such a separation were now free. Cosman, however, insisted that several thousand political prisoners were indeed still incarcerated, including many imprisoned for their religious beliefs. The laws under which they were imprisoned were still on the books. Thousands of Soviet citizens still wanted to emigrate, but the new exit and entry law did little to assist them. The more human rights became the concern of people and not of bureaucracy, the better things would be.

Palmer offered a summarizing statement in which he indicated what he took to be the unresolved issues in the matter of human rights. Whenever the Americans raised the question of human rights, fundamental freedoms, or binational marriage, he argued, a number of Soviet delegates would retaliate by constantly raising questions about unemployment in the United States and political prisoners. The meaning was obvious: Americans should not interfere in internal Soviet affairs and should look rather to their own problems. So between the Belgrade meeting in 1978 and the Madrid review in 1980, the United States did precisely that. They took all of the questions raised by the Soviet delegation, all the questions raised in their propaganda about the ills in American society—unemployment, American Indians, crime, prostitution, and drugs—and wrote a full report afterwards. There was no denial that there were problems, nor that American society needed to address some of its weaknesses. The Americans asked nothing more than that the Soviets do the same about the questions that they raised. The report was still being awaited.

A later Tuesday roundtable dealt with future trends in the theater in the USSR and the United States. Each of the nine panelists commented on the major changes that had occurred during the previous two years, and all agreed that theater reflects the soul of a people.

Edith Markson, president of Theater Exchange International, reported on the visit of the sixty members of her repertory theater in San Francisco for performances in the Soviet Union. They were, she said, "bowled over" to discover that theater people were the same there. Closeness came immediately, and before long an exchange was agreed upon. The Americans presented a Soviet play as a way of expressing thanks, with the playwright himself on hand. "It was," she said, "the most exciting experience she had had."

Mikhail Ulyanov, a Soviet actor, held that actors, anyway, are an international-minded group, more patient and understanding than some others. The roundtable, he said, meant one thing to him: How can we build bridges through the medium of the theater? He had come to the panel with some trepidation. "After hearing some of the other roundtables," he said, "I wondered, 'What are we going to argue about?'" But the climate was warming, he said. "We are still far to the shore, but"—and with this he drew loud applause—"we will get there." He went on to say that for citizens of the two countries to get to know one another better, they should look at the theater. The theater, he said, is the mirror of the people. "We are more free than politicians, even if we may be more naive."

Eugeni Lazaryev recounted a story that clearly affected the audience. He was fifty years of age, he said. He was a child of war who had been in the occupation of Byelorussia. He was the only man in his family alive after the war. After the reparation he lost his mother and for three years did not know if she was alive. She found him after the liberation. In July of 1944, Lazaryev continued, it was getting cold and he had no coat. Through American lend-lease he received a coat given by an American boy. The coat kept him warm for three years. "Now that I am here on American soil," he said, "I would like to express my gratitude to that boy, now perhaps fifty years old, and to his mother and father."

Ken Marsolays, an American producer, reported that in the previous eight months he had twice visited the Soviet Union. The theater in the Soviet Union, he found, was very different from that in the United States. Attendance was so great that people would line up for two or three blocks waiting for tickets—"like the seventh game of the World Series." He said that through the International Festival of the Arts in New York City he was arranging to bring a play from a repertory theater in Leningrad the following summer. Titled *Brothers and Sisters,* it was set in postwar Russia, had a cast of thirty-five, and ran for eight hours. In response to gasps from the audience, Marsolays explained that the play was in two acts, one each evening. The rest of the plan was to produce in the Soviet Union Eugene O'Neill's *Long Day's Journey into Night* and *Ah, Wilderness!* with Colleen Dewhurst and Jason Robards. Marsolays ended with the comment, "If I can do one thing in my life, I hope to raise the level of the artist in the country to match that in the Soviet Union, where they are national heroes."

Dewhurst, herself both actor and president of Actors Equity, was also present as a panelist. She recounted that from the previous December, when she went to the Soviet Union, until the present, she had never seen any barrier between performing artists. "The most important thing," she said, "is that we speak to each other from the stages of our countries." She had listened to several discussions in the course of the week at Chautauqua, she continued, and sometimes wanted to get up and say, "I am not sure I have truly understood or believe that either one is speaking from the heart or the truth." Then she added, "When my time and my life and my country are on the line, I would like to hear from artists, because they speak for us."

Music and Song, Concert and Art

Throughout the week and in a series of concerts and performances, Soviet and American performers achieved through the common language of music a full harmony that had so far eluded the morning platform speakers.

Early in the week, an organ concert by Talivaldis Desknis, assisted by Chautauqua organist Doris Eicher, began majestically with some of the organ works of J. S. Bach: the Fantasy in C Minor and the Chorale Prelude and Toccata and Fugue in D Minor. Following the playing of the Pachelbel Partita, Desknis won long applause from the audience with his playing of the Pastorales for a Summer Flute. The composition was an organ piece in six parts by a young Latvian composer, Imants Zemzaris. Some Chautauquans in the audience who had been in Latvia in 1986 would remember other works by the Latvian, who incorporated into his works simple material typical of his people's musical culture. Desknis ended with a presentation of the appropriately named concerto for organ *Cantus ad Pacem* (meaning, a plea for peace) by Peteris Vasks. The intonation, phrasing, and accents of the piece seemed to express the emotional and historical experience of his Latvian people.

Although the symphony concert that followed later in the week was not a part of its seasonal contract, sixty-five members of the Chautauqua Symphony Orchestra had made arrangements to stay and perform with the four Soviet soloists under the direction of Joseph Silverstein.[1] Interviewed before the performance, Silverstein called the program a musical and artistic

---

1. Silverstein himself had studied at the Curtis Institute of Music with Mischa Mischakoff, who had earlier taught violin at Chautauqua and had been the concertmaster of the Chautauqua Orchestra from 1929 to 1964.

adventure and said that the program would be a "very, very good vehicle" for the talents of the Soviet artists. The concert began with Glinka's overture to *Russlan and Ludmilla*. The opera, based on a poem by Pushkin, had become increasingly popular in Russia since its first performance in 1836 and remained a people's favorite in the Soviet era. Violinist Valdis Zarinish then performed Bach's Concerto for Two Violins, with Silverstein himself performing. Zarinish, a graduate of the Latvia Conservatory, was a recognized virtuoso in his own country and just prior to his visit to Chautauqua had toured in Sweden, Finland, Canada, and the United States. The choice of the concerto was a good symbol of the purposes of the week. In the first movement the two instruments share a bold, three-bar subject, followed by a second subject injected contrapuntally into the initial idea. As Zarinish and Silverstein joined in the second movement with its radiant melody, many in the audience were deeply affected by the symbolism: Soviet and American united in a shared communication that required no words. A critic present recorded: "The mathematical intricacies of the music were a healing balm to the disputes of the day."

Zarinish, in what a reviewer called "the highlight of the evening and the summer," then played the Introduction and Rondo Capriccioso by Camille Saint-Saens. "Its virtuoso passages," a Chautauqua reviewer wrote, "its lovely melody, touched with brilliant embellishments, had the large audience on its feet in a roaring ovation." Pianist Evgeny Ryvkin next gave what another reviewer called "a precise and exciting performance" of the Beethoven Piano Concerto no. 5, "Emperor." Ryvkin himself was a graduate of the Moscow State Conservatory.

Tenor Yanis Sprogis, a Merited Artist of Latvia, had also performed with the Latvia Philharmonia. This evening the Chautauqua audience heard him sing Lenski's aria from *Eugene Onegin* by Tchaikovsky. Tchaikovsky's transposition to the musical stage of Pushkin's much-loved poem "Yevgeny Onyegin" created a work that had established itself not only in the Soviet Union but also in the world's opera repertory. The melancholy prelude from act 2, anticipating Lenski's farewell to life and to all he had loved, introduced one of the most notable tenor scenes in Russian opera, an aria most in the audience found touching in its pathos.

Soprano Nelli Dovgaleva, a Merited People's Artist of the Russian Federation, followed with two selections, Lisa's aria from Tchaikovsky's opera *Pique Dame* (*Queen of Spades*), another opera based on Pushkin, and Rachmaninoff's "Floods of Spring." Her performance again won sustained applause from the audience.

One of the members of the audience, an American woman, commented later that she had sat beside a Soviet woman who was smartly dressed in a white suit with white gloves and a light blouse. The American asked if she was warm enough in the cool evening and offered her a blanket to wrap up in. "Thank you," replied the Soviet woman. "I am warm. I dress like this," she later explained, "out of respect for the artists."

Three special art exhibits had been set up in connection with the week. In the Colonnade, Don Kimes, director of Chautauqua's School of Art, exhibited pictures by Latvian students aged thirteen to seventeen. Kimes had selected the pictures during his visit to Jurmala, when he was a delegate to the 1986 conference. On that occasion, Kimes and artist Rita Auerbach had visited the Janis Rosentals Art Academy in Riga. During the visit Kimes had suggested an exchange of work with the Chautauqua School of Art. The head of the Latvian academy had been so enthusiastic in response that he had immediately opened up the storage area for Kimes to choose the works he wanted. "One of the things that impressed me most about the academy in Riga," Kimes said, "was the level of facility and discipline in these very young and talented students." Arrangements were being made to send works by Chautauqua students to the academy in Riga.

The second and third exhibits of the week were on display in the Chautauqua Art Association galleries. In the main gallery there were photographs, brought by the Soviet visitors, of Soviet productions of plays by American playwrights. In galleries two and three there were ninety photographs taken by Kimes during the 1986 trip to Jurmala and Moscow. The pictures showed many scenes of interest, such as the familiar domes of St. Basil's Cathedral, but mostly focused on the faces and postures of the people Kimes saw on the streets or had met informally. Kimes had been able to photograph the interiors of several artists' studios, including an officially organized dinner party in the studio of one artist.

"Stuck on the Same Spaceship"

President Reagan had invited the columnist Jack Anderson in 1984 to serve as chairman of the U.S. Young Astronauts program. Before accepting the position, however, Anderson had replied to the president that he would accept the position if he could establish ties also with the Young Cosmonauts program of the Soviet Union. Reagan encouraged the idea, which was also received positively in the Soviet Union. In time, a group of young astronauts was sent to meet their counterparts in the Soviet Union, fostering a collaboration that found expression in a later visit by young cosmonauts to the United States. On that occasion, on their arrival at Dulles Airport a young cosmonaut, Tanya, spied Amy, a young astronaut whom she had first met in the Soviet Union. She dashed across to greet her and embraced her warmly. The stiffness and the awkwardness of both American and Soviet officials evaporated. There were handshakes all around and smiles, Anderson recorded. "If we can do it at that level," he said, "there is hope that even the stubborn oldsters can come around."

At a special seminar on space during the week, Anderson spoke further of his experiences. "The more I get to know the people who have explored space," he said, "the more certain I am that we can have peace out there. If you get to know a young astronaut or cosmonaut who has been in space, when they talk about it, there is a hush in their voice. It was an enthralling experience for them." Astronauts told him, Anderson recounted, that when they left the earth and looked back to planet Earth, it was the most breathtaking sight they had ever seen. It seemed like a jewel of swirling blues and greens, whites and browns. There was another experience, too, that those who had been beyond the bounds of the earth had had. They felt closer than ever before to the people they had left behind. They recognized also how vulnerable it was, this fragile biosphere named planet Earth. Soviets and Americans were stuck on the same spaceship. It was in their mutual interest to keep it safe.

Anderson went on to report what he had learned from Anatoly Solovyev, who was the commander of a backup Soviet crew for an expedition that visited the Mir space station. He told Anderson what every cosmonaut took with him when he went into space—a tuft of grass, a piece of the earth. Those cosmonauts who went for an extended period in space were given an extra privilege. Their favorites were recordings—the sounds of the wind rustling through the leaves, the patter of raindrops on the roof, or the warbling of birds. Solovyev told Anderson that he had met Judith Resnick and Commander Dick Scobee of the doomed U.S. space shuttle *Challenger*[2] in Geneva. "After they died in the accident," he said to Anderson, "I got a photograph of the *Challenger* crew. I took the photograph into space with me.

---

2. The *Challenger* exploded one minute and thirteen seconds after liftoff on January 28, 1986. One of the two solid rocket boosters ruptured the large external tank igniting the fuel inside. There is speculation that the orbiter did not explode but broke apart and that the crew was not killed until its crew cabin smashed into the Atlantic Ocean. The *Challenger* mission was the first to have a civilian as part of its crew.

The space capsule joined the space station. I took the photograph and placed it on the wall of the space station." Then he smiled, according to Anderson, and pointed upward and said, "It is still up there, going round and round the earth." Anderson concluded with these words: "I believe peace is possible, and that our best years lie ahead" [Applause].

Trade and Business Relations

On the third day of the conference, two delegates addressed the question of trade and business relations between the Soviet Union and the United States. John Chrystal, the first speaker, was chairman of the board and chief executive officer of Bankers Trust in Des Moines, Iowa. Chrystal, who had been a farmer, had been invited to observe Soviet agriculture and offer constructive criticism every other year over a thirty-year period. He had seen profound changes in the Soviet economic structure and on the return from his most recent visit called what he found "astounding." Gorbachev obviously intended to inject some business realism to make it work. The USSR had not produced the results of Japan or Germany, which also suffered greatly in World War II. Gorbachev, Chrystal believed, had a chance to be a major figure in world history and would make profound changes in the Soviet economic system. "The Soviet economy is beginning to lead a life of its own," Chrystal said, "and needs sophisticated management and better organization. Gorbachev is an educated, wise and self-confident individual with a vision of a better future for his country."

The Soviet economy, he continued, had been operating according to administrative law from the top down through a formal organization. Now, however, the laws of economics would decentralize decisions and offer to all levels of management responsibility for economic growth. A program of production contracts had been introduced in agriculture, for example, the farm to provide the input and the machinery and the family to provide management and labor on a 70–30 split. The aim of this was to increase production, increase quality, and reduce loss. Thus workers' earnings were growing substantially. In the past, the government had taken most of the business profit for itself and distributed that in the form of capital goods and grants by its own decree. The new price system would keep a good deal of the profit in the farm or the factory. Two of the social contracts coming out of the original revolution were the protection of the worker's job and a promise that low prices for rent and basics like food would make these available to everyone. The new Soviet plan allowed for unemployment, retraining, and new jobs. There would also be a restructuring of prices. "What we are seeing in the Soviet Union," Chrystal asserted, "is a redefining of socialism as practiced for nearly seventy years, a peaceful revolution, I believe." He continued:

> Gorbachev and his associates do not think of war with the United States as a reasonable proposition. Soviet citizens demand a strong defense in the light of their history. I believe Gorbachev will convince his country that adequate defense can be smaller and cheaper and will work the savings into the civilian economy. I believe we are headed for a superpower war of economics and commerce instead of military might. We have to recognize what the competition is about if we are to win.

This competition was a foreign policy and an economic opportunity for the United States. "We can sell technology and products, and, I hope, stop spending some of the money we spend on arms" [Applause]. Would we not all feel safer, Chrystal asked, with 10,000 nuclear missiles instead of 20,000? With 5,000 instead of 10,000? These were the questions the general secretary was reputed to have asked his associates.

The Soviet speaker, Albert Melnikov, trade counsel of the Soviet Trade Representation in Washington, D.C., had worked in various aspects of Soviet-American trade for the previous twenty years. The task of his organization was to develop trade between the two countries. Melnikov began by listing the products the Soviet Union was selling to the United States: tractors, fertilizers, precious metals such as platinum, furs, plywood, chipboard, fish and marine products, and genuine vodka. "I needn't mention," he said to laughter, "that Russian vodka is the best vodka in the world."

Dealing with Soviet purchases from the United States, he stated that the Soviet Union was buying from five to ten times more from the United States than it was selling. Two-thirds of these exports were agricultural products, one fourth minerals and chemicals, and the rest semimanufactured products, mainly insulation materials for the oil and gas industry and equipment for mining and road building. In contrast, only 5 to 10 percent of Soviet exports to the United States were machinery and equipment. What the Soviet Union wanted was to even this imbalance and trade with the United States on an equal footing and on the same basis as other countries. Such trade was the pillar of peaceful cooperation. Trade could be the foundation of peaceful cooperation between the two countries.

As of that year, however, trade between the two countries was diminishing. In 1984 the volume of trade between the countries was approximately

$4 billion. In 1985 it diminished 10 percent. In 1986 it diminished a further 46 percent to $2.149 billion. In the present year it was likely to drop substantially. During the period of détente, many business people thought that there would be a substantial increase in trade between the two countries. On that basis, Melnikov said, the Soviet Union increased meat production and the development of oil and gas equipment. It anticipated that it could collaborate with the United States. But access to the American market became closed. The Soviet Union began to wonder if the United States was a reliable supplier of what it needed. So it took measures to diversify the sources of its supplies and to increase the production of oil and gas equipment and grain.

There had been many arguments against U.S. trade with the Soviet Union. First, it was argued that Soviets had no goods that Americans wanted to buy. But that, Melnikov said, was not true, and the Soviets would be able to increase their exports by 50 percent if all prohibitions were lifted. Second, it was argued that Soviets wanted to import only high technology. Again, this was not true. Ninety-five percent of current imports were agricultural products and raw materials. If American barriers to Soviet exports were lifted, that would affect whether the Soviet Union bought from Canada, Australia, or the Common Market rather than from the United States.

There had been positive developments in recent years. Reagan had said the United States was in favor of peaceful trade with the Soviet Union. The problem was to decide which tendency was the stronger—the positive or the negative. So trade relations were presently at a crossroads. The Soviet Union was ready to cooperate with any other countries in such trade. It was the second largest industrial power in the world, and its foreign trade was substantial. The threat of world war made the question livelier than ever. Trade relations were a counterbalance to this threat. If perestroika were to come to its fulfillment, it would create a need for huge resources. In the development of mutual trade, the United States and the Soviet Union would not be rivals in trade but cooperators.

President Reagan's Speech

The long-anticipated speech by President Ronald Reagan was set for four in the afternoon of Wednesday, the third day of the conference.

Speaking via satellite from the Town Hall of California luncheon meeting in Santa Barbara, California, the president began by saying that when his administration took office, the sense of America's longstanding foreign policy principles held firm. Yet they were aware that much needed to be done to restore vigor and vibrancy. "In short," he said, "we sought ways to dispel rather than live with the two darkening clouds of the postwar era: the danger of nuclear holocaust and the expansion of totalitarian rule."[3]

Reagan then spoke of the meaning of the decision to move forward with the Strategic Defense Initiative as a plan intended to render mutual assured destruction obsolete. The goal was to take the advantage out of building more and more offensive missiles and more and more warheads. Eventually it might even be possible to remove from the world the specter of military powers holding each other hostage to nuclear retaliation. The United States was simply seeking to establish the feasibility of a defensive shield that would render the use of ballistic missiles fruitless.

In reviewing his foreign policy, Reagan said that it had been an attempt to reassert the traditional elements of America's postwar strategy, while at the same time moving beyond the doctrines of mutual assured destruction or containment. "Our goal," he said, "has been to break the deadlock of the past, to seek a forward strategy for world peace and world freedom." He hoped that a parallel interest had been found with the Soviet Union in a political end to the Iran-Iraq war. "We see movement," he continued, "towards more openness, possibly even progress towards respect for human rights and economic reform."

While there was hope, there was also uncertainty. Reagan spoke of unsuccessful attempts to join with the Soviets in discussing a cooperative approach to defensive deterrence that threatened no one. He had proposed another step forward toward reducing the arms race, an agreement that could eliminate a whole class of missiles. "If that is signed," he said, "we shall rely not on trust, but on the evidence of our own eyes that it is being implemented." He called for more openness, a departure from the habits of secrecy that had so long applied to Soviet military affairs. Then, fully aware that the Soviets would be listening closely, Reagan said, "It is time to show glasnost in your military affairs."

In addition to verification, Reagan said, the United States was hopeful that the Soviet Union would demonstrate that there was substance behind the rhetoric they had repeated so often—that they genuinely wanted a stabilizing, intermediate-range nuclear forces agreement. He offered the reassurance that all parts of the four-part agenda, including human rights, arms

3. Speech received via satellite at Chautauqua, transcribed from the tape in the Chautauqua archives.

reductions, resolution of regional conflicts, and bilateral issues, had been pursued.

In typical Chautauqua fashion, not even a speech by a president of the United States would be immune from comment. Three Soviet panelists had been listening carefully, prepared to respond to the speech of President Reagan: academician Evgeny Primakov, one of the senior Soviet experts on the Middle East; Shishlin, a member of the staff of the Central Committee and one of the senior members of the Soviet delegation; and Vitaly Zhurkin of the international department of the Central Committee. Three U.S. panelists were also present to take questions from the audience: Fritz W. Ermarth, senior Soviet advisor to President Reagan at the National Security Council; Charles Thomas, senior deputy assistant secretary of state for European affairs; and R. Mark Palmer.

The response of the Soviet panelists was uniformly negative in expressing serious disappointment at the president's speech. They had expected constructive suggestions and a renunciation of rhetoric but had found none. To be sure, Primakov admitted, the president did not speak about the "evil empire," but he did refer to Soviet totalitarianism. "This offends me and my colleagues," he said. The president had been unclear and even offensive in his remarks. Primakov wanted to know more about what Reagan thought regarding the processes now taking place in the Soviet Union. After all, what was going on there could not but have a deep impact on history. The president had not addressed the truly important problems confronting humanity, especially the problems of disarmament. "I waited for constructive proposals," he said. "There weren't any. I waited for a constructive tone. There wasn't one." However, he added, there was a bright side. Reagan had said the Soviets were far from American standards of democracy. "I say, 'Thank God.'"

To the laughter of the audience, Shishlin began with a wry comment: "It was good," he said, "that President Reagan, while on vacation, had taken time to address the Chautauqua conference. This is the complimentary part of my statement." Then to the applause of the audience he went on: "I would like the U.S. administration and the American people to agree to one simple truth. The United States will not act as a teacher to the Soviet Union, just as the Soviet Union is not going to act as a teacher to the United States." All in the hall, he said, whether Soviets or Americans, had one and the same teacher—practical experience and the realities of life.

On the question of regional conflicts, it appeared that the president had found it necessary to speak not of the possibilities of moving towards peace but of old and unproved accusations against the Soviet Union. In regard to human rights, he said, the Soviet Union was prepared to discuss this issue at any forum. "I have been thinking a lot about what President Reagan has just said," Shishlin went on, "particularly as regards democracy. I would like to say that we, Soviet citizens, are more happy than you are in some ways. From the president's speech, it appears as if American democracy is perfect. We believe that our own democracy is not perfect, and we want to develop it from day to day, we want to develop freedom and glasnost. And this will be to the benefit of both your freedom and ours" [Applause]. It was necessary to remember the past and necessary also to have a sober-minded and realistic picture of the present. Actions and hopes must deal with the future, so that there would be a future for the Soviet Union and the United States and all the people of the world.

Zhurkin was no more complimentary than his colleagues. On the question of the military budget, sometimes in the process of Soviet negotiation with the United States it was a question of calling the American bluff. What if the Soviet Union did open its military budget? Would the United States then agree to proposals the Soviet Union had been making for many years in regard to reducing the military budgets? Could the two sides reach that agreement and use some of the money saved to help the developing countries? President Reagan had used the word "crusade" in speaking of the extension of democracy. But in the name of democracy Vietnam was subjected to many years of torture, defenseless Grenada was crushed, and at that very moment people were being killed in Nicaragua. The U.S. president had also said that the defeat of communism was the moral imperative of our time. The Soviet Union viewed things differently. "We think," Zhurkin said, "that the moral imperative of our time is our mutual survival and the prevention of nuclear war" [Applause]. Soviet policy was therefore one of negotiating, compromise, and accommodation. The policy of the United States, in contrast, was one of confrontation and eventual collision.

The audience responded positively to a suggestion by Palmer in response to Primakov's comment about democracy in the Soviet Union. Palmer said that he and his American colleagues on the panel would welcome the opportunity to receive in advance a copy of the text of a speech by Mikhail Gorbachev—as the panelists had received Reagan's—and be able before a large Soviet audience (and perhaps on Soviet television) to offer their own comments on Gorbachev's speech. "That," he said, "is the measure of our democracy." A Soviet member of the panel responded that that could be arranged. If Ambassador Palmer would come from his post in Hungary to the Soviet Union the following year, he would indeed have such an opportunity to respond to a speech by Gorbachev. *Pravda* already published articles, speeches, and statements with this kind of response to speeches of Soviet leadership. Pozner at this point intervened to record that the entire proceedings of the day would be on Soviet television and seen by the whole country.

The audience erupted into loud cheers when an American questioner said that she welcomed the fact that the Reagan speech would be heard in the Soviet Union. It would prove what democracy was all about. "I was not disappointed in President Reagan's speech," she said. "I would never have expected anything different. But I know that in 1988 there will be a profound change."

An American questioner regretted that in his speech the president had said nothing about the kind of citizen-to-citizen diplomacy that had characterized the Chautauqua conference to that point. Did the panel agree with him that it was unhelpful for the president to refer to Soviet totalitarianism, as if the Soviets had to come over to the American side of democracy before there could be peace? Palmer responded to the question by saying that in 1985 Reagan had given a speech about people-to-people diplomacy and had initiated much of what happened since then in the way of exchanges. One only had to read Soviet publications such as *Pravda* to find a cold war rhetoric of the old hair-raising style. Ermarth added that the issue of rhetoric could not simply be brushed away. President Reagan came into office talking about an evil empire. The question now to be asked was, does this president accept the legitimacy of the Soviet Union? Thomas picked up with the comment that political systems established their own legitimacy. America had its values and the vocabulary that went with them. These values and that vocabulary had their own history. Part of the purpose of the president's speech was to recapitulate that history. He had tried to put the present moment in a particular historical context. The past had been dangerous at times, trying and sometimes grim. The future, however, was promising and full of possibilities. But the possibilities could not be realized unless citizens of the United States faced the realities defined in the values and in the vocabulary. That was not just rhetoric on the president's part.

Dance, Music, Comment, and Film

At the first evening performance of the week the Soviets had invited ten dancers of the Krasnoyarsk Ensemble to demonstrated with the style of their dancing the spirit of their harsh, Siberian landscape. Dressed in vivid and colorful native costumes, and to the accompaniment of folk instruments, they immediately won the hearts of the packed Chautauqua audience. Their three dances, with spectacular leaps and turns, celebrated the wooing, proposal, and marriage of a shy boy, friendships, and the exuberance of youth in love with life.

For the Americans, actress and singer Karen Akers came to the Chautauqua stage with the reputation of being one of the most polished and arresting singers in the cabaret field. She herself, as many in the audience would remember, had performed at the Latvian conference the previous summer. The *New York Times* called her "the quintessential cabaret 'art' singer of the moment."[4] Slim, tall, and beautiful, Akers served, as she had at Jurmala, as her own interpreter and introduced her songs bilingually. Among the favorites with the audience were two, "Twentieth century Blues" and the signature song of Edith Piaf, "Non, Je Ne Regret Rien."

Broadway entertainer Ron Richardson had also been a member of the 1986 delegation to Jurmala, where he had sung spirituals with a Latvian choir in the Dom Cathedral in Riga. He began his share of the evening with "Sweet Holy Spirit, Sweet Heavenly God," moved to a jazz version of "One Night Only" from *Dreamgirls,* and then to the sentimental "Sunrise, Sunset" from *Fiddler on the Roof.*

The next evening, with over five thousand seated in the audience and a thousand more standing outside the Amphitheater, the rain fell in torrents as John Denver strode on to the stage. The crowd roared for the famous performer and peace advocate. Singing from his well-known repertoire, he joined Aiya Kukole with the backing of a Latvian jazz group. In the Soviet Union, Kukole had been a soloist also with the Latvian State Philharmonic Orchestra. Her Amphitheater appearance that evening, according to a resident critic, "electrified the audience" with two songs in Latvian. She ended her share of the evening with a rousing version of "Cabaret," again to a roar from the huge audience.

Denver then occupied the stage for the rest of the evening. Over a year earlier he had recorded in Moscow a special version of his song "Let Us Begin" (or, "What Are We Making Weapons For?") with Soviet superstar vocalist Alexandre Gradsky. That recording represented the first time that the Soviets had allowed one of their performers to be included on a record with a major American pop artist. Their song criticized the resources that both the Soviet Union and the United States were pouring into the arms

---

4. Stephen Holden, "Cabaret: Karen Akers," *New York Times,* April 2, 1987.

race. Commenting on his Moscow performance, Denver had said: "I thought that I might be able to do something to further the cause of East/West understanding. This seemed like a good time to see the face behind all the propaganda. The Russians say that the first swallow of spring won't make the weather for the whole season, but it can mark the turn toward a warmer climate. I tried to be that swallow." Backed by two guitarists and a string quartet, he continued with more of his best-known hits, such as "Take Me Home, Country Roads," "Back Home Again," "Sunshine on My Shoulders" and "Thank God I'm a Country Boy." In the background, films projected peaceful country and underwater scenes, vistas from outer space, and more threatening clippings from time of war and threat. Talking casually with his audience, he raised laughter, read poetry, paid tribute to Soviet cosmonaut Valentina Tereshkova, and, as a visitor recalled, "laid song upon song on us. It seemed as if he had used up his whole repertory."

Introduced at a seminar on the day following the concert as "an entertainer who is as committed to peace as any human being on this planet," Denver recounted his history in cultural exchanges, especially in the Soviet Union. He had long wanted to visit the Soviet Union, since through his music he had found there was no village in Africa, no commune in China, and no town or city in the world where he had walked where he had not been recognized. He had been called "the Voice of America," an honor that he valued, since so many of his songs had been about places he knew and loved in America. Music, he said, was the universal language and people throughout the world were the same. He had been able to arrange a visit to Moscow years before through the Union of Composers and had traveled as their guest through the country. It was a successful trip and something of an audition. In 1985, he was invited to return and gave nine concerts on that visit. When he came back to the United States, he met Secretary of State George Shultz, who queried him: "Young man, what are you up to?" Denver explained that he thought that there was nothing more important than to reestablish the cultural exchange agreement. Second, he said to Shultz, he thought that the president and the secretary of state should themselves go to the Soviet Union and meet the people, wonderful, warm and friendly as they were, a statement that drew his Chautauqua listeners' applause.[5]

By the time of the Chautauqua visit, Denver had already sent letters to Gorbachev, Reagan, and Pope John Paul II proposing a possible way to wind

5. Denver was the first Western artist that year to perform a benefit concert in the Soviet Union for the victims of the Chernobyl nuclear accident (1986).

down the arms race. Denver called his proposal " The One Percent Option." He asked that the United States and the Soviet Union each take 1 percent of their defense budget and begin to invest it at home to help create jobs, clean up the environment, and increase productivity. At the same time, the savings would support programs in Africa and elsewhere that were beginning to make a dent in the obscenity of hunger and starvation in the world. Denver's letter to the world leaders expressed the hope that "with the initiative of our two governments and the commitment of all people we can take direction in the history of human events. We are," he said, "the family of humankind. We must act like it."

Denver then spoke on what he regarded as the role of an artist. Art, he said, opens a window into oneself. "Through art you discover who you are. When you see a performance, a flood of emotions arises from the depths of the heart." When art is working, he said, it cannot be stopped. The role of the artists is to take human feelings and give voice or expression to them. Through his own gift of song he knew he was able to evoke the response from someone, "Now that's how I feel." He continued, "It is obvious that great changes are taking place in the world. Through cultural exchanges we have the opportunity to know one another's art and to know that we are the same as human beings. Each of us through a rich history and incredible heritage—and also through great difficulties and obstacles—each of us is a human being, as much as we separate ourselves in the world today."

Chautauquans of the nineteenth century were no doubt studious and sober-minded, even in their entertainments, but to the delight of the 1987 zestful audience, many young and old came from the benches to dance in the aisles or clap to the beat of the music. "The program," a reporter from the *Jamestown Post-Journal* recorded, "was a true mélange of forms and sounds and rhythms."

Three times during the week, Alexei Guerman's film *My Friend Ivan Lapshin* was shown at the Chautauqua movie theater. Many Russian critics of the time regarded it as one of the best of the pre–Gorbachev era cinema. Film critic Judith Lewis had described it as bringing a perspective that made for "thought-provoking film making." It was just the thing, she added, "to revive the Soviets' ailing cinematic climate. The film's release augurs well for the future Soviet cinema, and consequently for the entire international scene." Produced in 1983 and released in 1985, it is essentially an ambiguous love story, graphically evoking the ambience of the Soviet Union in the 1930s. Gherman based his work on his father Iurii Gherman's stories about members of the NKVD, the Soviet secret police. At times cruel and even absurd, the film centers on the exploits of an idealistic police investigator, Ivan Lipshin, intent on wiping out a band of criminals at all costs. It depicts in a devastating manner the brutality, lawlessness, and dreary rigor of life in a small provincial town with its overcrowded apartments, lack of privacy, and chronic shortages of goods and food, and more particularly the seamier aspects of Soviet society—petty criminals, prostitution, police raids, and interrogations. Soviet audiences in the period of glasnost reacted favorably to Gherman's unflinching accuracy in dealing with conditions of life in the 1930s and acclaimed it for its exposé of conditions under the NKVD. Others found it disturbing because it was not sufficiently subversive of inherited ways of thinking that came from the time of Brezhnev, who had banned the film. In the period of glasnost, however, the Soviet Cinema Workers' Union had fought for the film's release.

Present and Future Relations between
the Soviet Union and the United States

The theme of the morning sessions of the final two days was to be an examination of present and future Soviet-American relations. Evgeny Primakov, an elected member of the Supreme Soviet of the USSR, the Soviet equivalent of the United States Congress, gave the first of the four major addresses of the week. His American counterpart was Sen. William Bradley. Primakov began by laying out certain ideas that could help in developing relations between the USSR and the United States. The issue being dealt with, he declared, was nothing less than avoiding actions that would lead to the destruction of humanity. The Supreme Soviet had already taken steps to initiate the unilateral moratorium on nuclear tests but without any adequate response on the part of the United States.

Primakov then turned to the issue of regional conflicts. It was important for both countries to collaborate in achieving a peaceful resolution here. He then dealt openly with the conflict in Afghanistan. "I am convinced," he said to considerable applause, "that we will take our troops out of Afghanistan." But in return, he wanted some assurance that the United States would stop its undeclared war against Nicaragua and restrain itself from introducing troops into other countries such as Grenada. Further applause followed this remark.

Furthermore, he continued, both the Supreme Soviet and the U.S. Congress could do much more to cooperate in resolving problems that affected the world's population and that might well prove to be as destructive as the means of mass destruction. It was to these that the two governments should increasingly turn—the environment, for example, the barbaric attitude towards nature, the conditions of backward peoples, diseases that could be cured but that continued as a result of human indifference, and so on. "Let us unite our efforts," he said, "in resolving human problems such as these, problems of democratization that can be resolved in both countries."

Primakov ended his speech by listing what he regarded as rules of thinking and activity that could be followed to achieve a radical improvement in relations between the two countries.

First, the two countries should refuse forever to continue the zero-sum game in their relationship and instead look for areas of common interest.

Second, the two must relate to each other as equal partners and reject superiority or sovereignty. When the attitude was "Do this and that, and then we will accept you as a partner" or when there was an attempt to deal with the other from a position of strength, no good results came from such an approach. The language of request on the part of the United States was always acceptable, but the Soviet Union would always reject the language of demand.

Third, it was important to reject the language of patriotism as a synonym of nationalism and hegemony. "When I saw how Americans in this hall were singing their national anthem," Primakov continued, "turning their gaze towards the Stars and Stripes, I felt an enormous amount of respect for your patriotic feelings and towards you as a people. But when love for one's country grows into a desire to prove that it is higher than other countries, that debases patriotism. It interferes with our closeness to each other as human beings."

Fourth, Primakov said, "we need to reject double standards in evaluating our own actions and the actions of others. We should stop thinking in categories of 'good guys' and 'bad guys.' One does not play basketball by having different rules for each team. One rule applies to both."

Finally, it was necessary to be well informed and not continue to depend on the stereotypes that each nation held about the other, stereotypes created during the cold war. "Let us," he concluded, "be well informed and optimistically thinking people." Primakov ended with words of appreciation for the determination of Chautauqua's leadership and people in holding the 1987 conference. "Our meeting in Chautauqua has demonstrated convincingly the sincere desire of both the Soviets and the American people for mutual understanding and improvement of relations between the USSR and the United States and for peace on the earth." Lengthy applause from the audience indicated its own assent to the comments.

Bradley began his address by saying that he could reduce what he wanted to say in very simple terms. He had doubts and concerns about U.S.-Soviet relations, but above all he had hopes. The week at Chautauqua occurred at a time when doors, long closed, might be opening. Providentially, the Soviet Union and the United States held in their hands the destiny of half the world. There were those in both countries who saw in present relationships the seeds of a new cold war. They believed the world was too small for two superpowers. "I reject the destiny," Bradley stated with emphasis, "that dooms us to be perpetual enemies" [Applause]. Soviet and American arsenals loomed heavy over the future of the world. The two countries had a single, categorical imperative—they must never meet in war. Yet avoiding war was not the same as securing peace.

A common possession of both countries study was a love of the land. Both revered the land as the source of their strength and the root of their values. Both had a history of triumph and tragedy, often on a heroic scale. The beauty of the land inspired their songs. Its cruelty was a source of their sorrow. Both were energized by the vastness of their forests and lakes, the sweep of the plains and steppes, the mighty rivers, and the great wildernesses. Both had been challenged and yet restrained by the land, trusting its generosity, even if too often taking its replenishment for granted. For the land was vulnerable to abuse, and its potential for giving its people rebirth might be slipping away. Early Americans derived from their experience of the land a sense of independence tempered by a respect for life, liberty, and the pursuit of happiness. These inalienable rights lay at the core of the American character, defining their aspirations for democracy.

Both peoples also had had the massive experience of revolution and the satisfaction of nation building. Unusually for world powers, they had never declared war on one another. To the contrary, they were allies in a war won in large part as a result of the heroic struggle of the Soviets against the invasion of Hitler's army, Bradley noted to applause. Both countries shared a yearning for freedom. They fought a war to purge themselves of a colonial power. They valued not just freedom of the nations but the liberty of each individual man and woman. "Freedom is the essence of man," Bradley continued, "it can't be bargained away or yielded for any prize." Russia and the Soviet Union historically shared these convictions with the Americans. How many times had the Russian people themselves—peasants and poets, Cossacks and party members—risen to save their country from the invader?

What had happened? The countries had grown far apart from one another. Their institutions differed profoundly. And whatever they shared in a commitment to freedom, Americans were mystified by many Soviet denials of freedom of expression. "We are grateful to have many Soviet artists, writers, and musicians who have left their country," Bradley said sadly. "But why has their country been so inhospitable to them and to such talent?" Gorbachev had said that the Soviet people must know everything and consciously make judgments about everything. "Put simply," Bradley continued, "the Soviet Union must come to terms with its own history. If the Soviet Union wishes to be trusted by others, it must show that it believes its own people can be trusted with the truth."

The senator continued with a litany of questions that he addressed in particular to the Soviet delegates present: a stronger role for trade unions, freedom to read what one chose, freedom to travel, a truthful examination of Stalin's purges, democratization. Would the Soviet leadership, he inquired, allow the people of Eastern Europe to restructure their own systems and their relations with the outside world? Or would Soviet youth be permitted the freedom to repudiate the war in Afghanistan with the same decisive vehemence with which young Americans rejected Vietnam? How broad a swath did General Secretary Gorbachev want to cut through Soviet history? "Most Americans," Bradley said to applause, "are rooting for the reformers." Then, drawing his remarks to a close, and again to long applause, Bradley said, "It is within our power to create a different future. Meetings like this one at Chautauqua are drawing together politics, religion, and art. We need powerful voices that express direct human feelings in ways that politicians hear. We need a U.S. and Soviet competition that celebrates and preserves humanity and does not endanger it, one that enables us to solve our nation's domestic problems instead of threatening the world with destruction."

In a lead editorial two days later the *New York Times* commented on three of the speeches of the week, those of Cuomo, Reagan, and Bradley. The three had given the topic very different turns, yet the speeches had made one compelling point: "After dreary decades, it is time for hope. But not for illusions: neither those implied by Governor Cuomo, that the differences are really not so great, nor Reagan's presumption that the Russians will make themselves over in our image if properly instructed." The editorial concluded with these words: "The time is for dreams, yes, but practical ones. For that, Senator [Bradley] wrote the text of the week."

The first speaker on the last day of the conference, John Whitehead, U.S. deputy secretary of state, began by expressing his hope that many such conferences would be held in the future, bringing large numbers of Soviet and

American citizens together to discuss their common problems, air their differences, and get to know each other better.

Whitehead, the former president of the International Rescue Committee, recognized that the differences between the Soviet Union and the United States were deep and could not be overcome quickly. In regard to arms control, the outline for the future was already visible. "We can envision," he said, "a world in which thousands of warheads and delivery systems would be eliminated" [Applause]. The threat of nuclear destruction would be greatly reduced by reliance on defensive systems rather than on retaliatory forces. There would be a stable balance of conventional weapons at much lower levels in Europe. Chemical and biological weapons would be destroyed and an effective international mechanism would be put in place to prevent their manufacture. Both sides would have achieved continuous, effective verification of compliance with agreements.

In regard to regional issues, the United States and the Soviet Union again could collaborate in ending conflict and fostering an environment in which they found their place as productive members of the modern world. In places like Afghanistan, Angola, Ethiopia, Cambodia, Southern Africa, the Middle East, and Central America—nations that for too long had known war—democratic governments, freely elected by the people, would manage their own affairs without outside interference or swollen defense budgets.

In the bilateral agenda, areas of past contention would become areas for cooperation. The era of secrecy, suspicion, and surveillance would end. Trade and investment would expand. American companies would increase their imports of the seemingly endless natural resources of the Soviet Union. Part of that increased trade would come from the large number of travelers moving in both countries. Tourists would be able to enjoy the geographic and ethnic diversity in which both countries were so rich. Physicians and medical workers could collaborate in treating heart disease and cancer as well as childhood diseases all over the world. Scientists would continue to work out formulas to counter ozone depletion in the atmosphere and find ways to protect each country's endangered species. American and Soviet space scientists, having collaborated on unmanned missions to Mars, would begin manned space flights to that planet. With European and Japanese colleagues they would have made the question of nuclear reactor safety moot by solving the age-old energy problem by the creation of clean and safe fusion power.

In the area of cultural and citizen-to-citizen exchanges, U.S.-Soviet relations would really take off. Major universities would exchange thousands of students each year, both at the graduate and undergraduate levels. High schools would arrange yearlong exchange programs. Sister cities would have expanded beyond the big cities. Soviet soccer teams would tour the United States, and American baseball games would help make that sport popular in the Soviet Union. Performing arts groups would include American and Soviet artists. Both countries would have access to one another's media. Op-ed pieces would appear in one another's newspapers, and talk-show hosts would regularly have U.S.-Soviet debates on current issues. Radio station jamming and disinformation campaigns would be only a bad memory from the past.

Whitehead ended by offering two challenges. The first, he said, would be to double the number of high school and college students involved in exchanges. The second was to multiply the number of conferences such as the Chautauqua conference as a way of getting to know one another. These would be small steps, but they were reachable.

Petrovsky spoke last. At the time of the conference he held the rank of ambassador, had graduated from the Moscow Institute of International Relations with a doctorate in history, and was chief of the U.S. section of the Administration for Foreign Policy Planning in Moscow. Over and over he kept emphasizing the need for trust. It was a shortage of trust that Soviets felt in their relations to the United States. One thing was clear, however: trust and the liberation from fear were the keys in Soviet-American relations, he said to applause. Trust was the politics that permitted collaboration at all levels in Soviet-American relations. What mattered was to proceed together to construct the edifice of trust, to build it brick by brick and set aside fruitless discussions, propagandistic bickering, and cold war rhetoric, he said, drawing further applause.

Any country, Petrovsky continued, was to be judged first and foremost by its behavior. In its behavior both in foreign and domestic affairs there should be no room for doubting the sincerity and purity of intention of Soviet words and deeds. The best proof of this, he said, was perestroika. "We seek only one objective," Petrovsky continued, "an all-around acceleration of the social and economic development of our country and the improvement of the living conditions of other nations. If our perestroika is part of creating a condition of international trust, it is hardly necessary to prove any further the organic relations between domestic and foreign policy."

Petrovsky asked only that people understand that glasnost—the process of renewal and democratization—gave full expression to present Soviet foreign policy and diplomacy, including their approach to relations with the

United States. This, he said, was to be the new political thinking in the nuclear age. It was a vision of the world as a single, integral, and inter-dependent world. People everywhere had the right to live their own lives as they saw fit and without outside interference. But their destinies were increasingly vulnerable to the nuclear threat. Survival was therefore the main concern of earth's tenants. Survival stood far above national goals or ideological or other considerations, he said to applause.

It was, therefore, all the more important to establish trust in the major areas of Soviet-American relations. The new approach to security left no room for ideological crusades or for Machiavellian moves in advancing pseudoscientific postulates about the applicability of the zero-sum game rules to Soviet-American relations. The goal of saving humankind from the fear of a nuclear, chemical, or other annihilation should be the supreme goal. Disarmament, Petrovsky insisted to applause, was the only way to achieve this goal. "We believe," he said, "that it is realistic to achieve this in the near future, provided both sides have the political will."

There could be no approach to trust without concern also for human rights and the development of personal causes. The Soviet Union took it for granted that it was not only politicians but private citizens themselves who should talk with one another. "Let the Soviet and American people meet more often," Petrovsky said. "Let them form their own impressions of each other rather than get them from newspapers and television. [Applause] Let us together walk on new roads of trust. Chautauqua to Jurmala is one of those such roads."

Petrovsky pointedly indicated his regret that the themes of trust and tol-erance were absent from much in the U.S. relationship with the Soviet Union. He had just returned from a major disarmament conference in New York, where he led the Soviet delegation. The conference, convened on the initiative of the president of France, François Mitterand, brought together representatives of almost 150 countries, including NATO countries. At this first conference of its kind in history, only one country was absent: the United States. It was, of course, the sovereign decision of each country whether or not to participate. But not to be at the conference meant not to know what was going on.

Farewells and Questions

Warmth and goodwill abounded during the ceremony closing the confer-ence. The 240 Soviet guests who had spent the week at Chautauqua were bade farewell in the same manner as they were welcomed the previous

Sunday—with applause and the waving of hands. Tereshkova, who chaired the Soviet delegation, spoke cordially of the week, admitting that the discussions were at times difficult but often characterized by a spirit of cooperation. "When the talking got tough," she said, "we turned to the language of music." She continued, "Both the Soviets and the Americans showed we have an inexhaustible store of humor." The discussions and contacts between families and professionals of both nations provided further evidence that "humanity has come to the stage that we all depend on one another."

Tereshkova insisted the two nations maintain relations, not because the United States and the Soviet Union were the "most clever" countries, but because they were the most important military powers that determined the destiny of the world. "We are united in that this dialogue must go on. So," she added with a broad smile, "I will not say goodbye, but 'See you next year.'" After thanking Bratton, John Wallach, and members of the U.S. and Soviet delegations, she expressed thanks to the host families "who opened their homes and their hearts to us Soviet people."

Tereshkova then presented Bratton with a golden samovar, which she described as "the traditional Russian souvenir." In his response, Bratton noted with gratitude that the Soviet delegation had donated more than three hundred books to the Smith Memorial Library on the grounds. The conference, he said, was another facet of the institution's task of "improving the human condition." What Chautauqua was doing in the exchange, he said, was not a departure but a new expression for this remarkable place. The audiences had been part of a noble experiment. "You can make a difference," he said. "Hope is not a lost word from our vocabulary." To the Soviet delegation, Bratton presented a Steuben crystal bowl. With this, he and Tereshkova shook hands and embraced one another. All of the Soviet guests present were then invited to come to the platform and receive the applause and waves of the Chautauqua audience.

"I was really teary by the time the dear soul got on the bus." The words of one of the hosts of the week were repeated in similar ways as the families bade their farewells on the last day and waved to the buses pulling away from the grounds. One asked, "Will we ever see them again or even hear from them? But if we don't, I still know that we will never be quite the same." Thomas Becker, then vice president for development at the institution, had been deeply involved in all three of the conferences to date and had assumed the difficult task of raising the funds that made the conferences possible. Asked to comment on the third conference, just concluded, he summarized by saying that the 1987 conference was notable in two ways. First, there was less political posturing and more intent to solve problems. Second, the great contribution of 1987 was the opportunity of welcoming Soviet citizens into American homes.

His assessment was echoed frequently when the guests departed. That afternoon a debriefing session drew most of the host families for a review of their experience. Almost everyone rated the conference very highly. Guroff said, "You cannot possibly understand the full significance of what has happened here in the past week. This has been so unbelievable to these Soviets. They have never seen anything to prepare them for such an experience." A member of one of the host families observed, "As the week ended, all participants began to sense strongly that the two nations had many things in common, not the least of which was an overriding desire for peace. The differences at times became bitter as truths had to be spoken; but the conference exhibited a surprising desire for cooperation and for shared concerns and interests." Another family reported, "They arrived as guests and left as members of our family." Several said that they felt they had done at least something to contribute to world peace.

For one week in the 1987 summer season Chautauqua enjoyed the attention of many of the world's major media. Print media representatives at the week's conference included the three major news weeklies, *Time, Newsweek,* and *U.S. News and World Report.* Reporters and commentators from the *New York Times,* the *Wall Street Journal,* Associated Press, United Press International, and the *Christian Science Monitor* were also present, along with others from Buffalo, Cleveland, and Pittsburgh. Radio operations at the conference included the Voice of America, Radio Free Europe, and National Public Radio's *All Things Considered.* The Wednesday *MacNeil/Lehrer Report* on PBS carried thirteen minutes of a discussion between one of the Soviet delegates and Ermarth. With twenty-nine registered crew members present, *Good Morning America,* ABC's morning news television program, was telecast live Thursday morning from Chautauqua.

Chautauqua Institution had made the question of U.S.-Soviet relations an immediate one for the American public. Two Soviet journalists who had been on the grounds for the duration of the week reported that they had found Chautauqua beautiful, "like paradise," though they also recognized that Chautauqua was not true slice-of-life America. As in any paradise, however, harmony and peace may be merely phantasms. Chautauqua 1987 was no doubt a week of large discoveries and declarations of enduring friendship. Yet serious questions still lingered and would remain in the air about whether the unity of which Tereshkova had spoken would ever become the new political reality and an era of peaceful cooperation made firm.

Seventy years after its founding, the Soviet Union was clearly in transition, wary about its past and uncertain about its future. The Soviet visitors who came to Chautauqua in 1987 had learned about American concerns regarding the arms race, human rights, Jewish and non-Jewish dissidents, and the Soviet involvement in Afghanistan. But would the Soviets present be able to examine dispassionately their own history of repression, especially the brutality of the Stalinist regime and purges in the Ukraine? Soviet officials, the delegates had heard, had made dramatic statements about their intentions to remove the Berlin Wall, but were these affirmations merely hollow propaganda? It was becoming increasingly obvious that nationalism was on the rise, led by Poland. In the third world, communism had been losing its ideological appeal for some time. China had already moved in a different direction towards the market mechanisms it regarded as indispensable for its economic development. At home, the material impoverishment and unsustainable economic, environmental, and social ravages of communism were increasingly obvious to many of the Soviet leaders themselves. The Soviet economy seemed less and less able to address the demands of international markets. Though still intact in 1987, it had at best been stabilized the previous year at zero per capita growth, but according to one analysis, by 1990 the Soviet Union was about to face a per capita economic decline that inevitably would be translated into an absolute economic decline. What really were Soviet global aspirations and intentions?

Thus by the end of the 1987 conference it seemed that it was necessary for Chautauqua Institution to prepare for at least one more conversation—once more in the Soviet Union. It was more than a necessity. It was a declaration of hope and a will to seek peace.

CHAPTER SIX

1988: "A Balancing of Interests"

The time has come for direct participation in citizen diplomacy to address the most important question humanity is facing now. In U.S.-Soviet relations we have hundreds and thousands of such citizen contacts. The Chautauqua meetings are the most important.

Anatoly Dobrynin

T BILISI, THE CAPITAL OF SOVIET GEORGIA, is one of the oldest and most splendid cities of the Soviet Union.[1] Founded, according to tradition, in the year 458 C.E. by King Vakhtang I Gorgasali (the Lion of Georgia), the city served for centuries as the gate to the central parts of Georgia. Securely fortified above the Kura River, it profited richly from its favorable location on the old Silk Road, the fabled trade route to the East. The name Tbilisi itself means "the place of hot springs." In character it still retains much of the charm it had when, known as Tiflis, it was the capital of an independent kingdom. In art and architecture it constantly evokes—despite the featureless buildings of the Stalin era—reminders of its fabled Greek, Byzantine, and medieval past.

According to the ancient saga, Jason set out with the Argonauts on a journey to Colchis, just south of the blue mountains of the Caucasus, to steal the Golden Fleece. The myth may describe an actual event, namely, an early attempt by the Greeks to get to the southeastern coast of the Black Sea. The

---

1. The words above, spoken by Ambassador Dobrynin the evening before the delegation left the United States for Leningrad, are recorded on videotape. Regrettably—and in contrast to the other four Chautauqua conferences—none of the lectures at Tbilisi was recorded. This chapter therefore lacks the names of the lecturers and the substance of the lectures, other than what can be reconstructed from newspaper accounts. Some tapes contain part of the discussions, but the speakers are not identifiable.

Christian origins of Iberia, or Georgia, date at least to the fourth century, if not earlier. According to tradition, the preaching of a Christian slave woman, St. Nino, led around the year 350 to the adoption of the Christian faith by the royal Iberian house. Magnificent churches throughout the land soon gave expression to the new national faith. Between 586 and 604, for example, the church of Dzhvari was built on a lofty cliff above the river Kura, the first example of the gracious style that was to become the standard in later Georgian ecclesiastical architecture. Down in the valley lies Mtskheta, the former capital, where the cathedral of Sveti Tskhoveli was built early in the eleventh century. In the two centuries following, the golden age of Georgian medieval culture, a rich Christian art and literature developed, some of which is on display in the ground floor treasury of the Tbilisi museum.

Georgia became part of the Russian empire in 1801. Before that time, it fought for its independence against successive waves of conquerors, including Mongol invaders and the hordes of Timur. By the late eighteenth century, struggles with Turks and Persians catastrophically reduced the population to a fraction of what it had been in earlier centuries. Ruins of two large and powerful fortresses, built in the ages of conflict, still stand guard on the approach to Tbilisi from the southwest. Linked from 1801 in its destiny to the tsar of Russia, Georgia seemed to be freed from both internal feuding and external invasion. Conditions were ripe for social and economic development. The tsars, however, in league with Georgian princes and landowners, pursued a policy of exploitation, arousing protests among the masses. National discontent came to a head in numerous rebellions.

After the October revolution of 1917, in which Georgians had played their full part, external and internal forces helped bring about severe economic dislocation and famine. In February 1921, the Red Army, under orders from Stalin and another Georgian Bolshevik leader, entered Georgia and installed a Soviet regime.[2] With the red banner of the Soviets now flying over Tiflis, the city reverted to its Georgian name of Tbilisi. The new

2. Georgia is the birthplace of Joseph Stalin. One of the 1988 visitors to Tbilisi, author Olivier Bernier, noted that on one of the hills bordering the city, in the most spectacular location possible, is a vast stone plinth. But the statue it once supported and the lettering identifying the figure are gone. "Stalin," said Bernier, "has become a non-person." But this is not so in his native city of Gori, where he remains a hero. The main street of Gori is still named Stalin Street, and a statue, fifty feet high, stands above a local government building.

Georgia republic initiated a series of Stalinist reforms, such as the nationalization of industry, banks, and railroads and the collectivization of agriculture. During his rule (1928 to 1953) Stalin was brutal in his repression of any popular nationalist uprisings. He imposed his Georgian comrade and faithful follower Lavrenti Beria (later head of the secret police in Moscow) as Communist Party chief both in Georgia and over Transcaucasia itself. In 1956, more than a hundred died in a demonstration of nationalist discontent. Agitation increased in the 1970s and 1980s, and as late as 1989 Soviet troops again attacked a demonstration, killing twenty people and injuring hundreds.

During World War II—the "Great Patriotic War," in Soviet terminology —nearly seven hundred thousand Georgians, a fifth of the then population, fought in the Soviet army and took part also in the defense of Moscow and Leningrad. The Georgian losses were disastrous beyond measure: almost every other Georgian fell in battle. Before and after the war, Georgia changed from a predominantly rural economy to a relatively prosperous modern industrial state, and Tbilisi became a richly diverse community with a population of little more than a million in 1988—a quarter of the republic's total. The historical center is the old city, architecturally well preserved and the first choice of visitors who come to walk among the well-dressed crowds along Rustaveli Avenue or pass through the spider's web of narrow, winding streets to the new city with its spacious squares and broad streets. Modern Tbilisi is a major economic, educational, and cultural center of the Soviet Union, with its notable Academy of Sciences, the university, more than a hundred research institutes, theaters, libraries, and concert halls.[3]

A Sustainable U.S.-Soviet Relationship

Much had taken place in U.S.-Soviet relationships prior to the September 1988 Chautauqua conference. Reagan, who had well-grounded fears about conflict with the Soviet Union, did not want to end his presidency without achieving serious arms reduction. He and Gorbachev had met on October 11, 1986, in Reykjavik, capital of Iceland, to discuss substantial cuts in long-range intercontinental ballistic missiles. The Soviets, however, had linked any treaty on intermediate-range nuclear forces (INF) to constraints on the

3. The Republic of Georgia was engulfed by civil war in 1992 when President Zviad Gamsaxurdia was overthrown and Eduard Shevardnadze was elected. The war was fought between forces of the Georgian government and the Abxazian rebels who were supported by ethnic minorities in southern Russia.

Strategic Defense Initiative, constraints that Reagan refused to accept. Reagan had also introduced as part of his Reykjavik agenda a list of twelve hundred Soviet Jews who sought to emigrate from the Soviet Union. In February 1987, however, Gorbachev unlinked the INF treaty from the constraints. By September, Eduard Shevardnadze and Shultz reached an agreement on an INF treaty in principle and announced that Gorbachev would attend a summit meeting in Washington, D.C., at which he and Reagan would sign the treaty.

In the afternoon of December 8, 1987, sitting beside each other in the East Room of the White House at a table once used by Abraham Lincoln, President Ronald Reagan and General Secretary Mikhail Gorbachev signed the INF treaty, the first of any such to provide for the destruction of nuclear weapons. The treaty arranged for the verified elimination of an entire class of missiles. Caspar Weinberger, secretary of defense, suspected that there was a danger in Gorbachev's aptitude for a public relations approach, skeptical that it would obscure the unchanging nature of the Soviet system. He regarded the treaty, however, as a good example of achieving peace by negotiating from strength, since Gorbachev had given up all of the Soviet nonnegotiable demands.[4]

Later in the afternoon Gorbachev received a group of seventy-five Americans at the Soviet embassy. The Americans, invited as "intellectual leaders," included such notable figures as Henry Kissinger, Cyrus Vance, John Kenneth Galbraith, McGeorge Bundy, and George Kennan. Also present were Billy Graham, John Denver, and Paul Newman. Bratton, one of those invited, introduced himself to the general secretary. "When I told him I was from Chautauqua," Bratton commented later, "he launched into a very energetic, excited, and articulate statement about the quality of the Chautauqua conferences and the favorable reports that have come back to him from his colleagues." Bratton then indicated that there would be a further conference in the Soviet Union in 1988 and expressed the hope that the general secretary would be a participant. "I'll even wear my sweatshirt," Gorbachev replied, referring to the gift given to Tereshkova the previous summer at Chautauqua to be conveyed to Gorbachev.

Gorbachev himself, in his address to the assembly, reiterated his stress on the need for new thinking in the Soviet Union. He argued that political

---

4. See Caspar W. Weinberger, *Fighting for Peace* (New York: Warner Books, 1990), 331–49.

leadership in both countries was lagging behind the will and needs of the people. The intellectual leadership that usually preceded change, he said, was not being exerted either in the United States or the Soviet Union. He then indicated that to him the most important aspect of the newly signed treaty was the fact that it represented a psychological turning point in the relationship of the two countries. Gorbachev was particularly blunt in speaking about the serious domestic agenda of the Soviet Union.

In a later comment to Chautauquans, Bratton, reflecting on the December meeting, agreed that the Reykjavik summit and all the events surrounding it had had a psychological impact about them that was perhaps as important as the actual treaty that was signed. "The whole mood in Washington," he reported, "would seem to substantiate that Mr. Gorbachev is trying to place himself squarely as a prominent public person in the minds and thinking of Americans. He's trying to build a sense of personal acceptance and trust with Americans."

Henry Kissinger later expressed his support for the treaty but with what he called grave reservations about its effect on the balance of power. He expressed his concern about Americans being swept away in a mood of euphoria in response to Gorbachev as a man. Richard Perle, the assistant secretary of defense for national security, who had declined to attend the 1986 Jurmala conference, also offered conditional support but regarded the whole process as a diversion from the real task, part of which was to ensure that the SDI would be put into effect.

Early in January 1987, Mikhail Gorbachev had spoken on the theme of "Democratization—the Essence of Perestroika, the Essence of Socialism" at a meeting of the Central Committee of the Communist Party of the Soviet Union. With the heads of the mass media, ideological institutions, and artistic unions present to hear the speech, Gorbachev was positive about the effect of his proposed reforms: "A major accomplishment of the first stage of perestroika is the establishment of a new ideological and moral atmosphere, characterized by broad openness, criticism and self-criticism, by a deepening process of democratization and a growth of the working people's responsibility for the state of affairs in the country."[5] The following month, he announced that he would withdraw Soviet troops from Afghanistan if there could be agreement in the U.N.-sponsored peace talks between Afghanistan and Pakistan.

5. Speech at a plenum of the Communist Party of the Soviet Union, January 1987.

Speaking in Seattle, Washington, in February 1988, Shultz made the observation, "The case can be made that we are near a threshold of a sustainable U.S.-Soviet relationship." However, he continued, the Soviet Union had barely scratched the surface of structural political reform. There had not yet been the changes that suggested that the Soviet Union had altered its historical objective of altering the international system to its advantage. It would be mistaken and unrealistic to expect to replace, in the near future, the international security system. "Our security, freedom, and prosperity," Shultz insisted, "will continue to rest on nuclear deterrence, on our system of alliances, on our efforts to expand and strengthen democracy and a free international economy, and above all, on our own strength and will to defend our interests and values." Two months later he visited Tbilisi to discuss preparations for the forthcoming U.S.-Soviet summit meeting.

Reagan and Gorbachev again met in Moscow, May 29–June 2. Speaking at the Danilov Monastery on May 30, Reagan conveyed the message that the people of the Soviet Union had the prayers and support not only of the American people but also of people throughout the world. It was, Reagan said, a moment of hope. "I wanted to convey this support to you," he said, "that you might in turn convey it to others, so that all those working for human rights—from the Urals to Kamchatka, from the Laptev Sea to the Caspian—might be encouraged and take heart." Reagan went on to applaud the changes that had taken place in the Soviet Union and spoke of the main aims of the Moscow summit meeting: human rights, including freedom of religion, freedom of speech, and freedom of travel. "I've come to Moscow with this human rights agenda," he said, "because it is our belief that this is a moment of hope." Reagan concluded: "On the fundamental dignity of the human person there can be no relenting, for now we must work for more, always more."[6]

In a dinner toast at the Kremlin that evening, Gorbachev said, "On the issues of peace and progress, we believe in the primacy of universal human values and regard the preservation of peace as the top priority." The main task was to continue working out an agreement on 50 percent reductions in strategic offensive arms while observing the ABM treaty. "We are expected," he continued, "to open up new horizons in the Soviet-American dialogue. This is worth any effort and any amount of good will."[7]

6. *New York Times,* May 30, 1988.
7. Ibid.

In the United States, the ratification of the INF treaty in Congress was not promising to be an easy accomplishment. Despite a letter-writing campaign by right-wing groups and opposition from conservatives such as Paul Weyrich and in the Senate by Jesse Helms, the Senate finally approved the treaty by a ninety-three to five vote May 27, 1988, two days before the fourth Reagan-Gorbachev summit. The signing of the treaty was a major turning point in the relationship between the two countries. Gorbachev's visit to the United States had introduced the country to a new and impressive style of Soviet leadership from which further agreements might come. Despite the euphoric mood throughout the capital and the country, however, there was still caution about the future and serious issues that had to be dealt with in the relationship.

Reagan had made it clear that he intended to raise the issue of human rights in Moscow. In particular, he wanted to draw attention to the plight of Soviet Jews and the enlargement of human freedom and peace. By the time of the Moscow summit Gorbachev had already released more than three hundred on the list Reagan had given him in Reykjavik. After the summit, tens of thousands of Jews were to leave the Soviet Union as restrictions of emigration were increasingly relaxed. Freedom, for Reagan, was the right to question and change the established way of doing things and particularly, as he put it, "the right to put forth an idea, scoffed at by the experts, and watch it catch fire among the people."[8] With the language of "evil empire" now consigned to the past, Reagan seemed eager to negotiate as much as possible with Gorbachev to reduce strategic arsenals. Speaking later in London about the summit, Reagan called it a turning point in East-West relations and the beginning of an era of peace and freedom for all.

The nineteenth special conference of the Communist Party, held in Moscow late in June 1988, included sharp debates that animated the gathering of nearly five thousand and an open call for the dismissal of four top leaders, including Andrei A. Gromyko, the seventy-eight-year-old former foreign minister and current head of state. Gromyko and Politburo member Mikhail S. Solomentsev were among several named in stinging criticism as members of the old guard who should be removed. A stormy final session included arguments between Gorbachev and several delegates about the new course the country was to follow. For Gorbachev it was clear that the end of economic reconstruction and renewal could come only through

8. Speech at Moscow State University, May 31, 1988.

increased openness and—albeit one-party—democracy. An entrenched bureaucracy, reluctant to cede power, had been responsible for the failure to move to a market-based economy. "I will tell you outright," Gorbachev warned, "if we do not reform the political system, all our initiatives, the whole massive task we have undertaken, will grind to a halt."[9]

The Tbilisi Assembly

To prepare for the Fourth General Chautauqua Conference on U.S.-Soviet Relations, Bratton had earlier in the year traveled to Washington, D.C., and later to the Soviet Union, to sign for Chautauqua Institution a protocol agreement with the Union of Soviet Friendship Societies and the USSR-USA Friendship Society. It was agreed that the plenary sessions would include these themes: "The Current State of Soviet-American Relations after the Summit Meetings and the Earlier Chautauqua Conferences," "The Balance of Interests—An Alternative Framework for Soviet-American Relations?" "Limiting the Nuclear and Conventional Arms Race," "Trade and Economic Relations and the Means for Their Development," and "New Political Thinking: Toward the Creation of a New Culture of International Relations and the Future of Soviet-American Relations." The Friendship Society had already confirmed Tbilisi as the site of the conference and the dates of the proposed visit as September 19–24, with additional days prior to and following the conference for visits to Leningrad and Moscow. Final arrangements still had to be made about the plenary topics, the programs of the performing artists, and the possibility of hospitality in homes for the American visitors.

On September 9, Reagan wrote to Tereshkova, regretting that he would not attend the conference but deputizing Marvin Stone, deputy director of the United States Information Agency and head of the American delegation, to convey to her and to the participants in the conference his warmest regards and best wishes.

> The Chautauqua experience plays an important role in our expanded relationship. The conferences have provided a format for Soviet and American public figures to discuss our differences as well as our similarities. I am convinced that this type of public discourse will help us find constructive ways to resolve differences and to identify additional means of cooperation between our two countries. What you have begun has become an important tradition.

9. Speech at the 19th plenum of the Communist Party of the Soviet Union.

The official Soviet delegation, to be headed by Tereshkova, was an indication of the importance that the Soviets attached to the meeting. Yevgeny Velikhov, science advisor to Gorbachev, was to be present, in addition to foreign policy commentator Alexander Bovin (present in 1987) and Nikolai Chervov of the Soviet General Staff (present in 1986 and 1987).

The official American delegation included such government representatives as Arthur A. Hartman, former ambassador to the Soviet Union; Mark Palmer, U.S. ambassador to Hungary (1986–1990); Lawrence W. Lane, U.S. ambassador to Australia; Deputy Assistant Secretary of State Thomas W. Simons Jr.; Marvin Stone; Madeline Will, assistant secretary of education; Peter Rodman, special assistant to the president for national security affairs; Spencer Oliver, chief counsel to the House Committee on Foreign Affairs (1987); Hedrick Smith, a former *New York Times* Moscow bureau chief and author of *The Russians,* a book many Soviets regarded as controversial; and *Apollo 11* astronaut Michael Collins. Murray Feshbach, the U.S. Census Bureau's Soviet expert for nearly three decades, had originally been one of a group of four barred from attending the Tbilisi conference but had later received approval and was to join the group in Leningrad. Since 1988 was an election year in the United States, it meant that members of the official U.S. delegation knew that care and caution were in order in regard to the points of view they expressed. The Soviet delegation was aware that if a member of the official U.S. delegation made a statement of policy, that statement might not reflect American policy a year later. Also included in the official delegation were actors Jessica Tandy and Hume Cronyn, cellist Colin Carr, Broadway star Tommy Tune, cabaret singer Barbara Cook, and other jazz and classical musicians.

By early September it seemed as if, short of a thunderbolt like the Daniloff arrest in 1986, all was in good order. The delegation met in Washington, D.C., Thursday, September 15, to attend a full day of meetings by State Department officials headed by Undersecretary of State John Whitehead. Senator Bill Bradley, who had spoken the previous year at Chautauqua, spoke about the importance of citizen diplomacy. "The more you can talk with people like yourselves," he said, "the better it will be for all of you." In a relaxed and witty manner he described his last visit to the Soviet Union to talk with politicians like himself.

Later in the evening the American delegates were welcomed at a reception at the Soviet embassy to enjoy canapés, champagne, and conversation with the Soviet ambassadorial staff and officials present. Charles Wick, director of the United States Information Agency, spoke about the mutual desire to improve relationships and about how the impending Chautauqua conference might be part of a constructive dialogue. The sentiments were easily and warmly echoed by the Soviet ambassador, Anatoly Dobrynin. "We are living at a special time in international life," he said, emphasizing each word with care. "The time has come for direct participation in citizen diplomacy to address the most important questions humanity is facing now. In U.S.-Soviet relations we have hundreds and thousands of such citizen contacts. The Chautauqua meetings are the most important."

At a further briefing the next day, Deputy Assistant Secretary of State Thomas W. Simons explained the fourfold agenda of the conference: human rights, East-West relations, exchange programs, and disarmament. Chautauquans in the audience asked how they might best respond to the kinds of questions that they would be asked. Guroff explained certain cultural aspects of the Georgian people. Richard Schifter, assistant secretary for human rights and humanitarian affairs in the U.S. State Department, outlined the human rights policy of the United States. Ambassador Hartman shared some of his own diplomatic experiences and insights. Part of the strength of American citizens, he suggested, was their innate optimism. Soviets, because of their history, tended to look at history from a more pessimistic point of view.

With departure set for Friday the sixteenth, the delegation of 297 Americans—government officials, experts from the private sector, media representatives, entertainers, and citizens—left their hotels Thursday for Dulles airport. The Pan Am 747 charter plane left at 3:00 P.M. local time with some 300 passengers aboard, arriving at Leningrad early the next morning. Among the passengers were about 150 Chautauquans, 10 Chautauqua staff members and spouses, about 25 each Department of State and media representatives, together with translators, program speakers, travel agents, and performers.

On arrival at Pulkovo Airport in Leningrad Friday, the American passengers were advised to complete their declaration forms carefully and precisely, since the Soviets were sticklers, they were told, for detail and conformity. "Don't smile at the customs officials," they were advised, "or make any remarks. And don't take pictures in the customs area." A somber line of passengers proceeded through passport checking, waiting for baggage, and going through customs. An old State Department hand muttered, "Leningrad is a bad place to arrive. We always tell our people never to come here."

Leningrad, the soul of imperial Russia, the city immortalized by Pushkin, Dostoevsky, and Tolstoy, the cradle of the Russian Revolution, and the place of Lenin's return from exile, was grey and overcast with drizzling rain. The Intourist buses carrying passengers skirted the city to arrive at the Pribaltijskaya Hotel, a massive concrete structure overlooking the Gulf of Finland, in which, two years earlier, the delegates to the 1986 conference had stayed en route to Jurmala. After breakfast most of the visitors climbed into the Intourist buses for a guided tour of the city, with a special excursion to Petrodvorets, the summer palace of Peter the Great. In the evening the visitors attended the Kirov Theater for a performance of Rossini's opera *The Barber of Seville.*

On the following day, Saturday, the group—again as in 1986—visited Piskaryevskoye Memorial Cemetery, burial place of the victims of the nine hundred-day siege of Leningrad, which lasted from late 1941 to early 1944. After an honor guard high stepped forward in the chilly drizzle, Bratton presented a wreath at the base of the twenty-foot-tall statue of Mother Russia, symbolizing the nation's sorrow for those lost. "There is not a person you will meet in Leningrad," Guroff explained to members of the group, "who has not lost a family member or more during the war." Understanding the effect the war had on the psyche of the Soviet Union would help to understand its people better, he said, one of the aims of the Chautauqua visit.

On Sunday, September 18, 1988, the Chautauqua delegation arrived after a three-hour, 1,210-mile flight from Leningrad to find a welcome that many recalled as overwhelming. "We were literally showered with flowers by our new families," one visitor recorded. Children in uniform offered their guests bouquets of flowers in welcome. Tbilisi offered its own distinctively Mediterranean flavor as young women and girls, dressed in native costumes, performed typically Georgian dances. A corps of boys, aged about twelve and wearing traditional black Georgian jackets, danced, whirled, and jumped into the air, landing—with gasps from many in the audience— not on their feet but on their bended knees, only to spring up immediately and continue their dance. The official delegation and some others checked in at the Iveria Hotel. Over 120 of the Chautauqua group, however, were assigned for the week to live with Georgian families, repeating the home-stay pattern of the previous year on the grounds of the institution.

The Georgian hosts began their welcome ceremony in the city's large and elegant Philharmonic Concert Hall with several thousands present. Tereshkova, president of the Soviet Friendship Society and head of the Soviet delegation, gave a cordial welcome to the guests and invited them to join in the American national anthem. The Soviet national anthem followed. Officials of the Soviet government, Bratton, and Marvin Stone, deputy director of the United States Information Agency, each spoke briefly, offering encouragement to participants to hew to the spirit of dialogue. The Georgian Philharmonic Orchestra and Tbilisi dancers, singers, and musicians then presented the first concert of the week, a sign and reminder to the delegates that the beauty of music, song, and dance could transcend any separation caused by political speech. Later in the concert, and in honor of the American visitors, a troop of young girls in black skirts and kneesocks sang, in English and to warm applause, "Doe, a Deer" from the Rodgers and Hammerstein musical *The Sound of Music.* At the end of the concert, young dancers moved through the audience with flowers. Later in the evening the government of the Georgian Republic entertained the citizens' delegation at dinner. To the delight of the audience, the director of the Philharmonic Orchestra himself danced a solo to some Georgian folk music.

Under three flags, Soviet, Georgian, and American, the opening plenary on Monday, September 19, dealt with the current state of Soviet-American relations after the summit meetings and the previous conferences in Jurmala and at Chautauqua. Soviet and American speakers alike agreed that improving relations had not been an easy task. Such improvement called for trust and goodwill on both sides. Nikolai Chervov opened the plenary with the statement that it would be a mistake to try to disregard the realities. "The differences," he said, "are there. They will persist. They will not be eliminated. What are we going to do? Just go and jump in a lake? No. We believe that given the differences we must build on our relations and on principles other than confrontation." Chervov then reiterated his country's proposal—step-by-step elimination of nuclear weapons by the year 2000. "Disarmament," he said, "has a long way to go before it is effective. However, there is no other way. The way to peace lies through disarmament. Only disarmament can guarantee the human race genuine security."

In response, the American representative, Maynard Glitman, ambassador to Belgium, repeated the American position of stability through strength. While arms control could help restrain the spread and development of nuclear weapons, he said, it could not "disinvent" them. Arms control and defense policy must therefore be based on the premise that nuclear weapons would either continue to exist or at a minimum be reintroduced into national arsenals. Thus arms control and deterrent policy were not in opposition to one another but rather were inextricably intertwined.

In the usual Chautauqua fashion, written questions were received after the two statements. One question from a Georgian related to disarmament: "Don't you think that if, even with complete, total nuclear disarmament, there was then a rapid increase in the number and quality of conventional weapons, perhaps laser weapons and others, this would just help to create a huge, new frightful club?" Chervov replied that the USSR was in favor of the prohibition of such weapons and had proposed to the U.S. side not to develop such weapons. In order to have control or verification, the laboratories of both nations should be open to inspection. "Unfortunately," he said, "we have different positions on this. The United States continues to develop new weapons, and there is the arms race again." Glitman responded that not every development in technology was a bad thing. If it were possible to find ways of countering certain weapons that were in existence, he said, that would certainly add to stability. The weapons were where they were and ready for us for only one reason: underlying tensions.

As at all such conferences, the subject of the day's debates was the topic debated also in an informal setting over meals and in walks through the city streets. In one such street conversation later in the week, Palmer talked as he walked slowly with Chervov about military exchanges at the highest level. Chervov turned to what could be done beyond the present relationship between the two countries. He conceded readily to Palmer that the Americans were good professionals and negotiators. They knew their business well, stubbornly defended their interests, and at the same time were open to compromise. He paused for a moment, measuring his words. "We know each other by half words," he said at length. "We know each others' characters." Then, reflecting something of personal and not simply political alertness to what had slowly been coming to the surface on both sides for more than two years, he said to Palmer: "It is one thing if you are dealing with a stranger. It is quite another thing if you are dealing with someone you have worked with for several years." Palmer at once and warmly agreed. "Yes," he said. "A place like this is the kind of environment where you can do free association and talk absolutely off the record. That for me is very helpful. It allows us to come up with new ideas. This conference is different from the earlier ones. It is more serious, more constructive, less confrontational." When he recounted the story later to a group of friends, one commented: "Perhaps, just perhaps, we are at a turning point."

At one of the evening performances in the concert hall, the Tbilisi Philharmonic Orchestra and Choir presented Verdi's *Requiem Mass*. American performers then joined the Soviet orchestra with ease in playing the Brahms Concerto for Violin and Cello. Following the concert, the official delegates learned a great deal about what the Georgians meant by banqueting as they enjoyed a sumptuous dinner, with toast after toast offered for peace and friendship. Singers broke in continuously during the meal with popular and folk melodies, mournful and joyous. A large birthday cake, symbolizing the birth of a new relationship, was cut and shared with due solemnity, laughter, and loud applause.

Music and dance again played a large role in the program of the conference. At the concert of popular music one evening at the Philharmonic Concert Hall, American and Georgian musicians combined to present what a U.S. reporter called "more glitter than the audience had ever seen." Tommy Tune, a towering six feet six 6 inches and dressed in turquoise, quickly won over an audience when, with his Rhythm Kings, he sang and danced his way through music by Irving Berlin, George Gershwin, and others. The day before his performance, Tune had come down with a sore throat that he attributed to the automobile pollution and dry mountain air. "It is like breathing cement," he said, "but the show must go on." Tune had already won Tony Awards in four different categories, and the show did go on with much enthusiasm on the part of performers and audience alike. Opening his performance with some words in Georgian, he began to sing, "Dreams can come true again when everything old becomes new again." At the end, a rhythmic clapping, a symbol of approval, brought Tune back for two encores. "Music and dance transcend words," he later said about the performance. "They do things that words fail to do and go right to the heart of the people."

At the plenary session on Tuesday morning, Peter Rodman, special assistant to the president for national security affairs, spoke on the theme "The Framework for U.S.-Soviet Relations—A Balancing of Interests?" The goals and actions of the two countries, he began, often reflected opposing political philosophies. Yet a balancing of interests was not a bad model for living together on the planet. The question was whether the two countries could achieve it. As Reagan had said, the two did not mistrust each other because they were armed. They were armed because they distrusted each other. The present situation, however, was dominated by the exciting changes taking place in the Soviet Union. "For conservatives like me," Rodman continued, "it is a challenge to reexamine our earlier premises about this system's capacity for change." For liberals, it might be embarrassing for some of them in the West who had tended to excuse or minimize the problems the Soviet Union had come to grips with. All in the West, however, were intrigued by new Soviet writings on foreign policy that openly criticized mistakes of the past.

Rodman went on to offer his own criticisms of these mistakes. One of the dominant features of the early postwar period was the ending of colonial empires. Some of these nations sought close relations with their former colonial powers; others adopted radical policies of hostility to the former colonial powers and to the West in general. The Soviet Union, not surprisingly, found a natural bond with the latter group. And many in this latter group found Marxist and Leninist economic and political theories a useful basis for maintaining their internal authority and shaping their external relations. It was not wrong for the West, Rodman maintained, to see the Soviet Union as pursuing a potential strategic opportunity, and it was not wrong for the West to be concerned that even small shifts in the global geopolitical balance could add up to a major strategic shift against the basic interests of the West.

Reviewing briefly what this implied in the experience of the Indochina war, Angola, Cambodia, and Nicaragua, Rodman summarized by saying that even in these areas the USSR and the United States had made significant movement toward solutions. Afghanistan was the most dramatic example. Soviet leadership had made the bold decision to end that military engagement, which should allow the indigenous political forces to work themselves out. Withdrawal would improve the position of the USSR in the Arab world and in the world community generally. The Afghan people would gain a chance to determine their own destiny. Pakistan would no longer face the dangers of escalating war. In Angola also, the Soviet Union had played a constructive role in supporting efforts to remove all foreign forces—South African as well as Cuban and Soviet. The issue in Cambodia was complicated, but a solution had to be attainable that reflected the will of the Cambodian people and also balanced the interests of the Soviet Union, China, and the United States. In Nicaragua the prospects for diplomacy were more precarious, because the situation was not balanced. Military dominance by the Sandinistas, coupled with a military solution in Nicaragua, was not peace but a formula for continuing regional crisis.

In the Persian Gulf, cooperation between the two countries in the U.N. Security Council created Resolution 598,[10] which became a blueprint for an end to the Iran-Iraq war. "Peace in the Gulf," Rodman said, "would diminish the danger of conflagration in an area of strategic importance. It would also blunt the force of a violent Islamic ideology that has threatened the stability of the entire region." In the Arab-Israeli conflict, he continued, the

---

10. The resolution, adopted by the U.N. Security Council in July 1987, demanded as a first step that Iran and Iraq observe an immediate cease-fire.

American side was impressed by Soviet efforts to broaden their contacts in the region to include Israel and moderate Arabs. The United States had provided, since 1973, a framework for four successful Arab-Israeli negotiations, which produced Israeli withdrawal from all of Egyptian territory and a large portion of Syrian territory in exchange for security. Any solution would require Israel to face up to some hard decisions, but it would also require some of the Soviet Union's clients—Syria, the Palestinian Liberation Organization, and Libya—to abandon violence and rejectionist positions.

Rodman ended with a hopeful message about the future. Both governments had the wisdom to respond to the opportunities thus presented. A revived Western policy had restored a kind of equilibrium in the international system. A decisive Soviet leadership had responded in a clear-cut manner to the new conditions.

> Your leadership has made it clear that it would welcome a breathing space in the international arena in order to concentrate on internal reform. The West, too, would welcome a time of peace but knows that the most reliable basis for it is an acceptance of the basic structure of the international system. Certainly there will still be turmoil in the world and great change—political, economic, technological, and social change. But it is not an iron law of history that the major powers must exploit this for unilateral advantage. On the contrary, objective conditions now argue for new approaches. A "balancing of interests" is a good way to describe it.

On Tuesday afternoon, Gregory Guroff moderated what proved to be a tense and emotional roundtable dealing with human rights. Two Americans, familiar to many in the audience from their part in previous conferences, presented the American viewpoint—Spencer Oliver and Mark Palmer. Two Soviet professors gave expression to the Soviet position.

Palmer began by asking what each nation wanted to achieve in the way of human rights. His own vision was to see in both countries and throughout the world an adequate standard of living. No child anywhere would go to bed hungry at night. No one, completing school or university, would be unable to find an apartment or a house. One of the human rights would mean that anyone could travel to anywhere without limitations. Every four to six years there should be a right to elect political leaders in a meaningful choice. Workers in all countries could have their own associations or trade unions that defended their own rights. Newspapers should have the right to criticize the leaders of the country and publish what they chose. Such a vision was desirable in both material and spiritual terms. The countries in the world that were making most progress were those who had something like this vision of democracy. There was no contradiction between political freedom and economic justice but a necessary connection between the two.

For many years, according to one of the Soviet panel members, human rights were not a subject included on the agenda. Now the subject was always on every agenda and at every level. The speaker then turned to summarize the American approach to the question. Americans had often been blamed for seeming to interfere in other people's affairs or trying to teach people lessons in human rights—meaning, of course, the American version. One should understand that the United States was a young nation, founded by immigrants and refugees who came to America to find a new life, to practice their religion and to enjoy freedom. The American Constitution sought to protect that life, religion, and freedom. On the basis of this historical experience, Americans had then tried to project these ideals throughout the whole world. One of the achievements of the Helsinki Accords was to gain a measuring stick by which to assess the quality of freedom of conscience, movement, and thought. The Soviet Union was a willing partner to this emerging conversation. Foreign Minister Eduard Shevardnadze had said as recently as the past July that the Soviet Union could not be indifferent to how they were viewed by others. A government would be measured by its relationship to its citizens and its recognition of the sovereignty of each individual. In the Soviet Union there had been extraordinary improvements in recent months. Emigration figures had risen steeply, the Voice of America was no longer jammed, hundreds of political prisoners were being released, and the rights of the Orthodox Church augmented. Jewish emigration that year was to be around fifteen thousand, the previous year eight thousand.

In the discussion that followed the panel presentations, voices of criticism were thrown out to the audience, but the Soviet members of the panel were clearly the intended recipients. A Tbilisi citizen, Gurman Mamoulia, accused the Soviet army of destroying a twelve hundred-year-old Georgian monastery named David Garidze by setting up a firing range nearby. Vibrations from shells had damaged the structure's ancient frescoes. "Two of my comrades came here today," he said, "wanting to show fragments of the shells that are destroying the monastery. But they were barred from entering." The vice president of the Tbilisi State University voiced further complaints on behalf of Georgian members of the audience. "Why are Muslim Georgians denied their right of regaining citizenship? Why is there no

factory for Georgian-language typewriters?" Some other Georgian ques-
tioners in the audience challenged the delegates from Moscow who were
present about the persecution of Georgian Muslims and the clamping down
on the use of the Georgian language.

It was time for turning the fire also on the members of the American delegation who were present. A Soviet questioner agreed that human rights
must be observed everywhere. But, he argued, the criticisms addressed
against the Soviet Union were not justified. Consider rather how Americans deal with human rights for African and Native American citizens.
"American freedom," he said with obvious bitterness, "rests on the bones of
the American Indians." Changing the mood from one of hostility to hospitality, one of the Americans who had enjoyed her stay with a Tbilisi family
wondered if it would be possible for her to invite her hosts to come to the
United States for a visit. Would such be possible? The reply from one of the
Soviet members on the panel was that there were no hindrances at all to
such an invitation. All that was necessary was to follow procedures already
agreed to.

A Tbilisi woman in the audience asked why a friend was being illegally
evicted from her apartment because the state wanted it for someone else.
One of the Soviet participants responded that the case was not a serious
enough topic for a panel dealing with global issues. With this, and with some
irritation in his voice, Palmer jumped in, saying, "I don't think it's a waste
of time to worry when a woman is being thrown out of her apartment."

The meeting continued for some time with this exchange of retaliatory
complaints, but the atmosphere seemed to be less confrontational than a vigorous search for some kind of common mind on the matter of human
rights. One of the Chautauqua visitors present commented later, "You never
heard anything like that two years ago when we met in Riga." The fact, he
added, that such questions were being asked in a public way especially by
Georgians raised the eyebrows of many in the audience. Palmer himself
contrasted the tenor of the 1988 meeting with that of the first conference.
"In 1985," he said, "the Soviets did not want any discussion on human rights
and were very unhappy when we insisted. There was practically no real
debate back then. If you asked them about free elections, for example, they
refused to talk about it. Now they are willing to discuss the subject."

The most emotional exchanges in the week came during the discussions
of Soviet Jews who had been trying to leave the country. Oliver referred to
Jewish emigration from the Soviet Union. In 1988, he said, the figure was
around 15,000; in 1987, 8,000; and the year before that, 900. But in 1979, it

was 51,000. The Israeli government had sent around 350,000 visas to Jews in the Soviet Union. "One wonders," he commented, "what causes these great fluctuations." Were these people hostages to better times, better security, or better trade arrangements? American Jews in the audience broadened the criticism of the Soviets for denying Jews in the Soviet Union synagogues, rabbinical training, the publication of religious books, and the right to emigrate to Israel or the United States. In response, the Soviet speakers denied the charge, noting the flourishing synagogue in Moscow. Zivs, a member of the Institute for Government and Law, returned to Oliver's statistics, insisted that they were in error, and argued that, in contrast to 1986, when only 917 Jews were allowed out of the country, already in late 1988 more than 10,000 Jews had left the Soviet Union and that the number would reach 15,000 by the year's end.

Oliver, apparently unpersuaded, stated that the number of Jews allowed to emigrate was still far lower than the number of applications requested. He pointedly noted that one of the three members of the American delegation who had been declined a visa to attend the conference was Lenna Shival, who worked for the National Conference on Soviet Jewry. "Why so?" he commented. She had spent the previous ten or fifteen years of her life trying to help Soviet Jews emigrate or even teach Hebrew in the Soviet Union. All that she had sought to do when she was in the Soviet Union was to see that promises that had been made to Jews were observed.

It looked as if the dispute over the right of Jews to leave the Soviet Union would remain a cloud not only over the Tbilisi conference but also over the larger question of whether the United States and the Soviet Union were ever likely to reach an agreement on human rights, at least those affecting Jews. Then, in an unexpected turn, the cloud evaporated. Several of the Soviet speakers present astonished the audience with their admission of past mistakes. A representative from the Soviet State Law Institute admitted that the criticisms he had heard against the Soviet Union were quite justified. It was senseless to deny them, even unnecessary. The most important thing was that the Soviets themselves and on their own initiative had decided to correct the situation.

Significantly, Tuesday, the day of the dispute, was also the beginning of Yom Kippur. In the evening, about fifty members of the Chautauqua group, Jews and non-Jews alike, made the journey to an old section of Tbilisi to celebrate the holy day in the Sephardic synagogue, one of only two synagogues in the city. Passing through a rubble-filled street, to their surprise they found a Soviet film crew shooting their arrival at the synagogue and later their departure. It simply meant that their presence would be noted far beyond the synagogue. How far? They were not informed. Certainly it would be known locally, perhaps nationally. A counselor from Amherst, New York, Iris Rosenberg, commented on how thrilled she was when she walked in to join Jews whose language she did not know but whose heritage she shared. She was deeply moved, she said, hearing the Yom Kippur service in Hebrew from an Orthodox rabbi: "It makes me realize it's universal, that service, it's said all over the world."

A Cleveland couple, Alan and Kitty Greenberg, stayed for the week with Simon and Eferi Tetrashveli, both in their mid-sixties. With the Tetrashvelis they witnessed the life of a religious Georgian Jew. Simon, a distinguished portrait painter, rose in the morning, put on a yarmulke, and recited his morning prayers while touching the mezuzah fastened to his doorpost. The hosts and guests had lit candles together on Erev Yom Kippur. Simon invited the Greenbergs to join his family on that Yom Kippur day at the Sephardic synagogue.

Early the next morning another large number of the American visitors took a guided tour of the Sveti Tskhoveli cathedral in the walled city of Mtskheta, the ancient capital and seat of the royal Iberian house since 1700. As the Yom Kippur service the previous day had stirred deeply those who took part, the singing of the divine liturgy in the cathedral touched those who attended with its strong and distinctively Georgian style. One of the visitors commented on the number of younger women and men among the worshipers—a contrast to what she had found in an Orthodox church in Leningrad, where the vast majority of worshipers were older women, crossing themselves repeatedly and bowing their scarf-covered heads in prayer. Since being a believer seemed to be more acceptable in Georgia than in other parts of the Soviet Union, religious worship was apparently less of a threat to one's educational opportunities, career advancement, or even personal security than it was for Tbilisi's Jews.

Late in the afternoon of the visit, a session on women's issues dealt with sex education, abortion, prenatal care, and latchkey care. On the U.S. panel were Letty Cottin Pogrebin, editor of *Ms.* magazine, and Esther Coopersmith, former U.S. representative to the United Nations and the only woman other than Eleanor Roosevelt to receive the U.N. peace prize. The Soviet panel included Elena Ershova, a doctor of philosophy and senior researcher at the Academy of Science, and Alevtina Fedulova, first vice president of the Soviet Women's Committee.

Fedulova began by expressing her approval that a program on women's issues had been included in the conference. It was high time, she said, for these issues to come to the fore. Coopersmith agreed with her strongly and appealed for more women from both sides to be involved in any future conference and for more issues to be discussed that affect primarily women. Members of the audience quickly discovered how differently women were treated in the two countries. The Soviet panelists particularly wanted to know about child care centers and family planning and where Americans stood on equal rights and pay. They explained that in the Soviet Union the primary means of birth control in 1988 was still abortion. Partly this was due to the low level of medical education among young women. There needed to be a wider variety of contraceptive devices. The average Soviet woman—excluding Muslims—had at least four or five abortions during their childbearing years. Abortion clinics were free, but birth control was not generally available and men were unwilling to use condoms, so abortion was seen as the most practical way to limit the size of families. Most women, the Soviet panelists suggested, were ready for a change, since most doctors in the country were women.

The Soviets also wanted to know how American women dealt with the husband's "superiority" in family decisions. Pogrebin admitted to the Georgian women in the audience that their American sisters still had a long way to go to establish true equal rights. Middle-class and working women had children who were often placed on waiting lists for child care centers. So they had to place their children in unlicensed day care homes where the children were badly attended to and often propped up in front of a television set. It was a national disgrace. Pogrebin was asked how American men dealt with women in leadership positions. "We do not need to come to Georgia to see the attitude of Georgian men," she said. "We need only to go to Georgia in the United States, to the man in the next apartment or to our boss. We have the same problem as you do in trying desperately to get men to accept the basic humanity of women. Women are human beings. We want what men want: love and work in the same lifetime, and to realize ourselves fully, whoever we may be." Laughter of agreement came from Soviets and Americans alike, as did prolonged applause.

An American male in the audience asked if there was any one particular women's activist movement in the United States or in the Soviet Union. Pogrebin replied that there was no one movement, because the movement had grown and become diversified. Not all could be placed under one label nor described as "feminist." "We are targeted," she said, "to empowering the movement at the grass roots, to making the judicial system more responsive. The movement does not now express itself on the streets, or with slogans, or in a showy and melodramatic way." Addressing the situation in the Soviet

Union, Fedulova said that there were about 250,000 women's councils throughout the whole country. She said that it was important to emphasize the mass nature of the movement and its nongovernmental character. Many nonofficial organizations were also being formed of women in professional positions. An American delegate, expressing gratitude for what he had heard in the discussions, said that they revealed for him the huge gap—a sixty-year gap, he thought—in the present perceptions of women and men in the United States and in the Soviet Union about the place of women in society and their rights. For the rest of the evening, he was convinced, the issues raised would be the topic of conversation in the host homes.

Interviewed later, Wanita Bratton, herself a therapist in Jamestown, New York, said that American women were light years ahead of their Russian counterparts. Their refrigerators resembled those dating to the 1930s in the United States, she commented. That obviously meant waiting in long lines at the grocery store each day. The stores were crowded, did not have sufficient food for sale, and lacked the computerized technology that made egress easy. It seemed to her that almost everyone in Leningrad or Moscow carried a large shopping bag, ready to join a line at any moment for some hard-to-find item that was on sale. In her five visits there she had not seen a washing machine or dryer in any apartment. Most of the family clothing was washed by hand, and tourists were advised not to bring clothes that required dry cleaning. The women in the family worked but were still expected by their husbands to do the main household chores.

Several of the plenaries and discussions included a discussion of religion in the Soviet Union. One of the Soviets explained that to celebrate the millennium of Orthodoxy in Russia, the Russian Church, with official permission from the government, had hoped to provide every home in the country with a copy of the Bible—a goal, however, not yet achieved. Another Soviet delegate commented that even among members of the Central Committee there seemed to be a growing tolerance of religion. Shishlin, a ranking official of the Communist Party of the Soviet Union, said that the new thinking in the USSR included much more openness in regard to religious belief and practice. "Yes," he said, "some people in our country believe in God. Everyone has a right to choose for himself or for herself whether or not to believe in God and what religious faith to accept." Religion, he conceded, had some positive values for society, especially in moral issues.[11]

11. Two years after the Chautauqua conference, a multiparty election in Georgia in October 1990 brought to power a center-right nationalist government and

Primakov, who had been one of the Soviet delegates at Chautauqua in 1987, agreed with Shishlin that in the Soviet Union religious views were a matter of individual conscience, were not antithetical to communism, and should not be interfered with. Religion should be respected for its moral values. One of the American delegates found it surprising that both Shishlin and Primakov kept referring to God in their speeches in a way that suggested an underlying belief in God. Shishlin himself was asked if this were indeed the case. "As a member of the Communist Party," he replied, "I am an atheist. But I have read the Bible many times, especially the New Testament. I am well acquainted with God." The cognitive distance between the communist's atheism and his acquaintance with God was not lost on one member of the audience: "Perhaps," she said, "Gorbachev's glasnost is opening the door for Communist Party members who are private believers to be able to come out of the closet and allude to that belief publicly. Or perhaps the more open atmosphere is allowing party members the freedom to believe in God while continuing to mouth the party line of atheism."

Joan Chittister, of the Benedictine Sisters of Erie, Pennsylvania, discussed the role of religion in society and its place as a builder of values. Israel in the time of the prophets, she said, was constantly facing destruction. The prophets came to warn the people, but not about how to fight the war, or win the war, or even survive the war. They came to remind the people that calamity had come because the people had forgotten the widow and been unjust to the orphans. They spoke to their own people, not to the enemy. "'It is we who have done wrong,' they said. 'It is we who have lost our soul to profit, prejudice, or power.'" Chittister continued:

> We must, as religious people, unmask the feeble rationalization that
> the purpose of nuclear deterrent is peace. We have 99 percent more
> nuclear weapons than are necessary to ward off nuclear war and are
> threatening the entire planet with annihilation. No religious rationali-
> zation can defend this. We are using the best resources and the best
> minds on weapons of destruction. Nuclear superiority may be making

---

introduced a presidential system. In an April 1991 referendum, an overwhelming majority of the population voted in favor of independence from the Soviet Union. The following month a formal declaration of independence eventually led, after a brief authoritarian period of government, to the appointment of Eduard Shevardnadze, former foreign minister of the USSR, as chairman of the State Council of Georgia in January 1992. He was baptized in the same year.

us morally inferior in every other respect. We do not need religious justification for what is morally unacceptable. Religion must aim at the creation of a better world. The function of religion is to speak truth to power. So the state must not crush religion, for without vision the people perish.

The friendly and mostly peaceful atmosphere of the conference was shattered when news came that Soviet police and KGB agents had responded violently to street protests by Georgian nationalists in the capital. Thousands had gathered at Tbilisi University where appeals were made for a free and independent Georgia and the teaching of the Georgian language in school. As dozens of police and agents elbowed their way into the chanting crowd of protesters, fighting erupted, and the police hustled some of the protesters into waiting cars and police vans. "There were at least sixty police officers shoving me and everyone else," one of the Chautauqua delegates reported. "One man had his clothing all torn and another had a bloody face." Fifteen more protesters were arrested and scores more manhandled. As dusk fell, about 750 gathered outside the offices of Georgia's Supreme Soviet.

Later, one of the demonstrators, Georgi Chanturia, spoke candidly and with obvious pride about what had happened: "We were arrested several times. A pregnant woman was beaten. Her clothes were completely torn. A man was beaten until he was covered with blood. Then they were forced to let us go." Chanturia, a member of a Georgian nationalist movement, was asked if glasnost and perestroika were being effective in Tbilisi or in the republic. "I do not believe in them," he replied. "This is just a game, intended to deceive the West and to scare people into thinking that Gorbachev is good. We came out into the open not because we have glasnost but because we are strong." He went on to speak of the independence of Georgia and the breakup of the fifteen Soviet republics. "We Georgians will get freedom only if every nation gets freedom," he said. "Estonia, Latvia, Lithuania, the Ukraine, Georgia, Poland—and so on—or none of us will get freedom."

The protests in Tbilisi were part of a wave of nationalist unrest then sweeping across the Transcaucasian republics of Armenia, Azerbaijan, and Georgia. In Georgia, the unrest appeared to be mostly anti-Soviet. Guroff and Palmer, commenting later to the delegates on the demonstration, said that it was a sign for them that the society was actually becoming a more normal one. It was the essence of democracy. It clearly meant that citizens no longer felt terrified by the authorities. Pozner himself admitted that some of the students had been beaten up, but that, he said, happens in any demonstration anywhere in the world. In contrast, however, a member of the Communist Party who was present said that he was afraid that the demonstrations were playing into the hands of the forces opposed to glasnost and perestroika. They could use such violence in their battle against Gorbachev's policies.

In his closing remarks on Friday morning, Bratton listed the images that were beginning to form in his mind: the thoughtful and candid plenary sessions that had helped to give emphasis to what might be possible in the future; the fervor with which the two sides continued to disagree on regional issues, human rights, and arms control; the impact of some discussions, such as the role of women in society, in which shared feelings obliterated national boundaries; and, of course, the talent of the performing artists. Addressing the leader of the Soviet delegates, Bratton then said, "Madame Tereshkova, a wonderful custom in your country is the sharing of gifts—gifts of friendship. In that spirit I would like to make some presentations." With this, a number of American delegates stepped forward to present the Soviet delegation with two large Amish quilts. In keeping with the Russian tradition, and following a graceful speech by Tereshkova, the American delegation in turn received a painting by a well-known Georgian painter, Tsereteli. The two delegations stood for one another's national anthems.

According to one of the American visitors, "the daily plenary sessions and roundtable discussions were much less adversarial and more cooperative than the previous conference." Time and again, she explained, members of the audience heard the words "new thinking" when Soviet speakers presented their cases. The words glasnost and perestroika were commonly used both in public speeches and private discussions, but, she commented, "though the words seemed to be common among the intellectuals, the ordinary citizen still seems unconvinced." It was difficult, she said, to recognize the dramatic shift in leadership when the people have always lived in a controlled society and are still standing in line to buy shoes.

Home Stays and Coming Home

Important as the lectures and discussions of the fourth conference were, it was the experience of the city and of the people that left the deepest impression on the conference delegates. "The real artistry of Tbilisi," one of them said later, "is the artistry of their hospitality." Susan Eisenhower offered her own summary: "I don't know how to describe it. Georgian hospitality seems

to be family oriented. If you are a guest, you are drawn into the family circle." One of those who took part in the Tbilisi conference echoed what
probably most in the Tbilisi conference felt in one way or another. "This
trip to the USSR has changed my life. Never again will things be the same."

The idea of having guests stay with host families had been part of the
1987 experience at Chautauqua. By general verdict, the host families at
Chautauqua that year agreed at the time that the opportunity of having
Soviet guests in the homes of local families transformed their experience of
the week. The experience was the same and more in Tbilisi. "The first stiff
greeting on Sunday evening," one of the hosts reported, "changing to the
warm emotional farewell the following Saturday was amazing. The visit
was unstructured, personal, and another important step in people-to-people
diplomacy. We demonstrated, as citizens of the free world, that we all care
about the same values such as peace, freedom, and a clean environment."
Another reported, "The warmth, generosity, graciousness, and friendliness
of our Tbilisi host families will remain with us always as the highlights of
our trip." Yet another commented, "We were overwhelmed by the hospitality, overtired from not wanting to miss anything, and overfed by my host
family who would not take no for an answer."

Iris Rosenberg described the family life of her hosts:

> Nunu, the mother in the family, was sixty years of age and a lawyer.
> The father, whom we called Papa, was a professor at the University
> of Tbilisi. Sandro, the oldest son, was a theoretical mathematician,
> Rezo a clinical psychologist, Sandro's wife a biologist. They had a little
> boy a year old. This entire family lived in a one-bedroom apartment
> in a fifth-floor walk-up with no elevator. Nunu would be up at 6:30
> making a breakfast that sometimes consisted of fried cheese, cooked
> tongue, the most wonderful bread, homemade preserves, fried
> sausages, vodka, figs, and bowls of fruit. If you refused anything,
> she expressed disappointment with the saddest eyes. Nunu, like most
> Georgian women, has certainly not heard of the feminist movement.

A Georgian, Manana Ninidze, described her own response to the visit of an
American couple, Arnie and Jill Bellowe:

> I think that the Chautauqua conference had great political meaning,
> as it was for the first time that the politicians, military, scientists, and
> artists of both countries sat together with representatives of our "peo-
> ple's diplomacy" and spoke about the future relationships of the USSR

and the USA. We think that the most important thing was that the people got to know each other well, and after so much propaganda the people from both countries understood that they are very similar, that they need the same things in life, and that they had the same ideals. Nothing can be compared with the personal contacts, when people sit together and you can look into their eyes and see even more than the words can tell you.

Home stays in Tbilisi gave the Americans a close look at family life, domestic conditions, and the place of women in a Soviet republic. A chronic housing shortage meant that many host families had a cramped, one-bedroom apartment on an upper floor with no elevator or escalator. Most Soviet citizens rented their apartments from the state; very few had a whole house. The apartment could be purchased for from 15 percent to 35 percent of the monthly salary for ten years. Once the apartment was owned, however, it could be inherited by family members. Visitors found that prices were high in the stores but that goods were of poor quality and with only a limited selection on half-bare shelves. One out of four families had a car, the cost of which ranged from five thousand to ten thousand rubles. Visitors noticed long lines at state stores and at liquor stores where, they were told, to reduce drunkenness and resultant absenteeism from work, Gorbachev cut alcohol production, raised the price (a liter of vodka cost about $22), and limited sale hours.

Host families in Tbilisi went out of their way to make the Americans feel at home. Little was spared in making the guests welcome. Winemaking was one of the specialties of the region, and many local families were involved in the production of Georgian wine. Evening after evening, the hosts entertained their new friends with food, drink, and dancing. By the end of the week, one participant recorded, everyone knew how to dance, and if they did not, they tried anyway.

Hospitality extended even to home medical care. In the middle of the week, one of the group, Pati Piper, fell very ill. She and her husband, Steve, were guests of Lamara Margvelashvili, a school principal. Despite Pati's best efforts to conceal her discomfort, it became obvious. Lamara said, "Pati, you are sick. I will fix you!" She spooned goat grease from a jar and heated it over a flame on the stove. Pati removed her blouse, and Lamara rubbed the grease on Pati's neck and congested chest. She then applied a layer of thin paper and a piece of cotton over the area, tied a scarf around Pati's neck, and pinned it securely. A flannel nightgown completed the patient's clothing.

"Tomorrow," Lamara commanded, "you will not go out." Pati later recorded, "In the morning I was a new person thanks to the stomach fat of a Georgian goat and Lamara's nursing skill."

Some of the Tbilisi families had a small summer house or dacha, with fruit such as pears, peaches, and plums growing in the garden. One of the visitors recorded that she and her companion climbed ladders to pick the fruit, then sat down to a hearty meal that included many toasts. "We ate, drank, and sang," she said, "and I taught them a Jewish dance. The caring and sharing was electrifying." At another dacha party high above the city, plates overflowing with caviar, smoked fish, and stuffed roasted vegetables were a preliminary to an evening of feasting. By the time the evening ended, there had been multiple courses of grilled pork, chicken, and shish kebabs fueled by Georgian wine.

In spite of many advances in securing legal rights for women in the USSR, the American guests found that Soviet women still occupied a lower rung in society than men. While they were allowed equal educational opportunities, almost all the women who served as hosts in this week worked outside the home. It appeared as if the concepts of equality in marriage and shared household responsibilities were mostly unknown. Shopping, considered to be women's responsibility, involved standing in line for lengthy periods up to two hours. Returning home from work or shopping, women still had to do the housework, laundry, cooking, dishwashing, and child care, with little if any help from their husbands. One of the Intourist guides, a young, unmarried woman, admitted to an American visitor, "I want to be weak and have my husband strong. I don't want to be smarter than my husband or more clever. I want my husband to protect me and take care of me."

One of the citizen delegates, John K. Rogers III, a California banker, reported that he and some other Americans had been invited to visit a bedspread factory in a suburb of Tbilisi. The factory director, Dzemal Dzavahishvili, showed the Americans what they would have expected to see: men working at heavy steel machinery, women workers in boots. Behind a door, however, the director introduced his visitors to a second project—a private towel-making enterprise. With this, he hoped to make 100 percent profit on every towel made. Reporting on the visit, a journalist from the *Wall Street Journal* wrote: "This private business is of the kind allowed under the economic reforms of Mikhail Gorbachev. And it is practiced by a Communist Party member, Mr. Dzavahishvili. 'That's capitalism,' said Mr. Rogers, as he shared cognac and imported Belgian beer with the gentleman."

At this stage of development in Soviet society, there were many tens of thousands of Soviet citizens creating or working for what were essentially private companies. Though not universally approved, they offered entrepreneurial services—restaurants and clothing stores, for example—that were superior to state-run operations. As delegates to the Chautauqua conference in Tbilisi found, however, one of the twists in privatization was that it created even more shortages. The main car driven by taxi drivers was the squat, Soviet-made Lada. Until recently, it had cost nine thousand rubles—roughly twelve thousand dollars. But when the taxi cooperative was set up in 1987, taxi drivers bought so many of them that the price, officially still nine thousand rubles, doubled on the black market. By the time of the closing reception for the delegates, it was the common humanity that seemed more important than contemporary and political questions. "In Tbilisi," another said, "our differences seemed less distinct."

Reflecting on the fourth conference, Murray Feshbach commented later, "They have an enormous, complicated road ahead of them. But they don't know where the end of it is going to be, or when it is going to be." Guroff expressed his own cautious optimism. "With the people I know, if Gorbachev had to stand for public election, he'd be elected tomorrow." People were complaining that, despite all the openness, they have an even worse situation in regard to food and material goods than before Gorbachev. The working class, he said, was the crux of the issue. If they did not support it, ultimately glasnost and perestroika would crumble. "I think the Soviet leadership understands that. I am basically an optimist," he concluded, "but it will take many, many years." Susan Eisenhower reflected that there was a certain "edginess" in the Soviet Union with Gorbachev. "This country," she said, "was in an absolute state of euphoria for eighteen months after Gorbachev took over." But now that the euphoria had worn off, people wanted to know what came next. Perestroika was a long-term project. "It is not something that can be measured every day," she said. "It is going to take time."

Speaking at Jamestown (New York) Community College after his return from Tbilisi, Daniel Bratton began by saying, "When you've been doing this for several years, you are ready for an experience like this not to live up to the previous year's standards. But this year's journey to the Soviet Union was the best so far. With each succeeding year," he continued, "the language has become much less hostile, much less confrontational. There was very little table thumping and finger waving." He said that many of the sessions moved away from politics and helped both sides really understand each other's culture and needs as people. A few months later, in mid-December, Bratton met with Guroff at the University of Pittsburgh to discuss the thrust of his thinking about a proposed fifth Chautauqua conference on U.S. Soviet relations.

The proposal was that the conference be held at the University of Pittsburgh in the second week of October 1989, in cooperation with the university, the Pittsburgh World Affairs Council, and the Pittsburgh Council for International Visitors. Bratton wanted the conference to look particularly at the human, personal, and citizen-level dimensions of several U.S.-Soviet issues and how the two countries could address them. Guroff himself was to be in Moscow in late December to discuss with Tereshkova and representatives of the USSR-USA Friendship Society what he and Bratton had discussed in Pittsburgh. Conversations continued also with representatives of the United States Information Agency and the State Department. The following January, Bratton wrote to Tereshkova proposing that the Pittsburgh conference "include new dimensions and achieve new goals." The board of trustees met early in February 1989 and accepted the rationale for the choice of Pittsburgh: the location would have considerable logistical and financial benefits; it would be in one of Chautauqua's key constituent areas; it would be related to a major university, noted for its work in international studies; and it would be available for any who had time and resources to attend. In February he and Wanita Bratton, together with some others, made the journey again to Moscow to prepare more fully for the fall conference.

CHAPTER SEVEN

1989: "We Are Part of One Civilization"

Because we are living in a mutually interdependent world we are not allowed to become isolated. Self-isolation would be a criminal luxury. For this reason we must be able to know how to listen to each other, to hear each other, to learn from each other, and to understand each other. Then it would be possible that we could learn how to act together.

Nikolai Shishlin

F ROM THE FIRST DAY of the fifth General Conference on U.S.-Soviet Relations at Pittsburgh in 1989, it was clear how much the previous conferences had contributed to the creation of a new spirit and atmosphere. The four-year experiment in citizen diplomacy with its confrontation, struggle, and progress had prepared a ground on which those now assembled could approach one another in equality, enabling them to discuss in civil discourse even the most difficult questions. The choice of Pittsburgh—not Chautauqua—for the conference linked the institution with a major academic, medical, and cultural center. In the previous two conferences, U.S. and Soviet citizens had been able to live with one another in weeklong home stays. The near-unanimous verdict was that the experience had been one of the richest of the weeks. The Pittsburgh Council for International Visitors made it possible during the period of the conference for two hundred members of the Soviet citizen delegation to stay in private homes throughout the Pittsburgh area. Tours and site visits were arranged to acquaint Soviet visitors with the volunteer, cultural, business, government, and educational systems in the Pittsburgh region.

The Opening Ceremony: The New Agenda

At the opening ceremony, Bratton greeted the audience with an awareness of both the solemnity and the global importance of the occasion. "Few activities," he began, "few processes, few journeys have been more vital to this world than the nature and quality of relationships between the Soviet Union and the United States of America. The fate of humankind has depended on these. Few dimensions of recent history have been more profound and more dramatic than the rapidly changing nature of those relationships." Four years earlier the preoccupying issue before the first Chautauqua U.S.-Soviet conference had been sheer survival. But, as reflection on the content and character of the public speeches between 1985 and 1989 reveals, the rancorous debate of the early period gradually changed into a quest for a basic understanding and knowledge of one another's lives. The political agenda remained, Bratton continued, and it was vital to all people on the planet, but it now shared equal space with items of mutual human understanding. "Through its conferences," Bratton said, "the Chautauqua Institution has been at the center of this evolution. Since 1985 they have shaped it and reflected it." He then summarized what he regarded as the progress that had been made between 1985 and 1988.

In 1985, he began, the first of the Chautauqua conferences was held at the institution at the time when General Secretary Gorbachev had been only four months in office, the summits had not yet occurred, and a cultural exchange accord had not yet begun. In 1986, at one of the tensest times in Soviet-American relations, 250 Americans took part in the second conference in Latvia. It was a "no-holds barred" conference, and it continued in an open and uncensored fashion. In 1987, Chautauqua was again the site of the conference. The change was now perceptible as aspects of each other's culture began to appear on the agenda. That year more than 250 Soviets came to Chautauqua, the largest such group ever to come to this country. Two hundred of these stayed in private homes—another first. In 1988 nearly 300 Americans went to Tbilisi, Georgia, where the openness was astounding and the agenda again dealt with nonpolitical areas of understanding. "Now," he concluded, "with Chautauqua at Pitt, we bring these conferences to a truly great American university for another historic moment in U.S.-Soviet relations."

Bratton had perceived the development from 1985 to 1988 as a move from confrontation and caution to a sustained focus on issues that affected ordinary people. Questions of arms control, regional issues, and human rights were indeed on the Pittsburgh agenda, but these were to occupy a lesser place, not because they were unimportant, but because what could be said about them had already been mostly said in previous years. The themes that were to dominate the Pittsburgh conference were those of the bilateral agenda—alcohol and drugs, the environment, ethnicity and cultural pluralism, youth, religion, space, trade, the economy, and women and men in their changing social roles. In a private conversation after the conference Bratton summarized the achievements of the five years: "In 1985," he said, "we were talking *at* one another. In 1989, we were talking *with* one another."

The president of the University of Pittsburgh was Dr. Wesley W. Posvar, who had come to the campus in 1967. With bright red hair, thick eyebrows, a background that included fifty combat missions in Vietnam, and a reputation for having a "radically liberal" streak, he quickly gained the trust of campus dissenters and a faculty that came to respect his goals of quality and achievement. He first greeted the Soviet and Chautauqua delegates and introduced those at the center table, amongst whom were three who had played major roles in previous conferences: Tereshkova, Petrovsky, and Rhinesmith. He then recalled a striking memory of his own. Exactly thirty years previously, to the week, Chairman Nikita Khrushchev had led another Soviet delegation to the university campus. Khrushchev had said then that Pittsburgh reminded him of the days he had worked in the Donyets coalfields. Pittsburgh, Posvar continued, was then a city of steel and coal. It had since become a city of technology, ideas, and international linkages and networks. In a speech during the visit, Khrushchev addressed what most perceived to be the pressing issue of the day—namely, the competition between the United States and the Soviet Union. He tempered that comment, according to Posvar, with a call for the peoples of the United States and the Soviet Union to live together as good neighbors. "Today, three decades later," Posvar said, "we share a different world, a world of interdependence among nations, a world in which the Soviet Union and the United States bear profound responsibilities. Our search here, therefore, will be for consensus. What we do here will be a message to our governments and our leaders."

Shortly before the Chautauqua conference at Pittsburgh, George H. W. Bush had gained the Republican presidential nomination and was later elected president. He sent a letter to the conference in which he said:

> The conferences have played an important role in building understanding between the American and Soviet peoples, not only in matters of national concern but also on a personal level. The two countries have made significant progress in resolving differences and finding new paths of cooperation. The discussions at the Chautauqua conferences have been part of an ever-growing dialogue. It is my hope that this positive trend, marked by the free and open exchange of ideas, will continue.

Valentina Tereshkova then read a message that the general secretary, Mikhail Gorbachev, president of the Supreme Soviet, had asked her to convey:

> The five-year history of regular meetings between representatives of the USSR and the USA has reflected the long road traveled by the governments and peoples of both countries during this time. Perestroika and the new political thinking have made it possible to proceed from confrontation to mutual understanding and even interaction for the benefit of both nations and the entire world. Millions of Soviet and American citizens have become active participants in this beneficial process of mutual understanding, getting closer, forming proper ideas concerning policies and intentions, and restoring good feelings towards each other through their numerous organizations and direct contacts. I welcome their efforts, goodwill and contribution to renewed contacts between our great nations. I wish you a successful conference.

"We have traveled a long and difficult road since the first conference," Tereshkova continued. Yet over the years both sides had become convinced that they could work constructively in the spirit of mutual understanding. They could reassert their national interests and at the same time uphold universal human values. Soviet people, she asserted, valued kindness and kind words. They would never forget the navy convoys that went to Murmansk or the suffering for the sake of common victory. She had seen, she said, an old Latin proverb on the coat of arms of the United States, *e pluribus unum.* "The fact that we are different," she affirmed, "has stimulated a greater exchange, understanding, and cooperation between our nations. We are part of one civilization. We are one. We are interrelated through science, technology, and ecology and through the threat of imminent nuclear war and other major common threats." It was symbolic for her, she said, that the meeting was taking place at Pittsburgh, for in a way the delegates present were setting up there "a unique university which should teach us how to work and live together in this diverse world." The programs of such a university, she said, should include such items as enmity between nations and suspicion and lack of respect for other nations. "The university that we are opening this week is a university of friendship. It is a school of communication of a new type. It can be a good example for other nations to follow."

A further greeting from a Soviet diplomat came from Vladimir Petrovsky, who described himself as now a Chautauquan, since he had been a participant in many Chautauqua meetings. The improvement of Soviet-American relations, he said, had brought to light new patterns of behavior, an openness in dealing with military activity, an openness in the hearts of the people, and a transformation of traditional relations between the two nations. "For me," Petrovsky said, "the most important confidence-building measure is precisely these Chautauqua conferences that now represent an integral part of Soviet-American dialogue."

Bilateral Collaboration

The keynote speaker of the first day was U.S. Sen. John Heinz, whose address opened the way to a full discussion of the bilateral agenda. Heinz began by expressing his belief that what was happening at that time in the Soviet Union and in Eastern Europe would prove to be one of the turning points in modern history. He praised President Gorbachev for opening up the new possibility of perestroika and glasnost. Glasnost was not freedom of speech but permission to speak about political affairs freely. Perestroika was not capitalism but a program to decentralize the economy and provide incentives for better performance. Democratization was not about multiparty elections but about allowing Soviet people to choose from among more than one Communist candidate.

Heinz went on to propose specific steps that could be taken to advance this exchange. First, Soviet planners and managers could be trained in substantial numbers in U.S. management schools. Second, Soviet educational institutions could establish relationships with American business schools that could lead to management education schools in the Soviet Union itself. Third, Americans should prepare the ground for any significant investments they could foresee in the Soviet Union through exchange programs that placed Soviet and American firms here in the United States and American managers and Soviet enterprises in the USSR. All the United States could offer were a few tools and ways of thinking and analyzing that could help the Soviets find their own answers. With openness, the transfer of intellectual capital could make a tremendous difference in Soviet life, in Soviet-American relations, and in the world. Perestroika, democratization, and democracy demanded that people reassert their control over events and over society.

In amplification of the core of Heinz's speech, the plenary meeting on Monday afternoon dealt with one of many ways in which the two nations might cooperate—space. Former administrator of the National Air and Space Administration (NASA) and distinguished public service professor at the University of Pittsburgh James Fletcher opened the plenary by reviewing briefly the history of cooperation in space from 1972 and addressing the question of future cooperation in space. He recalled that the Soviet Union and the United States had already set up a large number of scientific exchanges and cooperative programs by that time, the best known of which was the Apollo-Soyuz program (1975) that linked Soviet and American spacecraft in space to conduct joint experiments. The official in charge of the American side of that program, George Jeffs, joined Fletcher in affirming that Apollo-Soyuz had shown that the two countries could indeed collaborate in space. Further, the two sides were working on developing a universal docking system, good rendezvous techniques, and rescue capability. It was important to understand how complex and difficult it was for the two nations to work together in space. As the nations increasingly probed the solar system (and perhaps beyond), he suggested, it would be important to weigh the pros and cons of using nuclear power in spacecraft.

Jeffs ended by looking at the possibilities of future collaboration. Space stations and Mir were examples of what could be built on present foundations. "I think we would be well advised," he said, "to lay the groundwork for a readiness plan when the situation presents itself. To do that, we would call on all the nations of the world to apply the best of their talent to help make it happen." If such collaboration were to happen, it would involve not just the United States and the USSR but probably also Japan, Germany, and other countries.

In opening the Tuesday afternoon plenary on the environment, Posvar noted gloomily that it might be possible to escape from the effect of our nuclear weapons only to succumb to toxic waste. The waters of the world were at extreme risk. One of the most serious problems was that the sources of drinking water were riddled with salt, heavy metals, and toxic and carcinogenic materials. Algae formation was worldwide. The health of future generations depended on safe drinking water. The world's oceans were steadily being polluted by hundreds of millions of tons of petroleum products. Fish production in recent years had dropped catastrophically. The entire flora and fauna of the oceans were threatened. Posvar's warning was endorsed by Boris N. Laskorin, a Soviet scientist in the hydrometallurgical field, who insisted that joint efforts were essential in order to prevent the progressive pollution of the oceans. He pointed to the degradation of soil, desertification, the destruction of tropical rain forests, and the reduction in the biological variety in many regions of the world. The soil of 50 million acres in the Soviet Union had been degraded in the previous decade, he added ominously, and creeping sands were consuming 120,000 acres per year.

Laskorin then drew the attention of the audience to power production. Traditional methods of obtaining energy by burning organic fuel as well as by nuclear and hydroelectric power led, he said, to an intensive depletion of nonreplaceable natural resources and to the thermal pollution of the biosphere. Nontraditional energy sources such as wind, wave motion, and solar power did not pollute. However, modern society demanded an expansion of power production. So for the near future it would be necessary to depend on nuclear and hydroelectric power. With the Three Mile Island and Chernobyl disasters,[1] nuclear energy had become compromised. But an objective comparison showed that more than four hundred nuclear power plants were efficient and operated successfully around the world. If these power plants had not been built, to get the equivalent amount of energy in the last fifteen or twenty years would have meant burning billions of tons of organic fuel. This would have had huge consequences in regard to the nature and temperature of the biosphere. The aim should be to create "super-reliable" power stations and use them until such time as nontraditional methods of creating energy were developed.

The American speaker on the environment was Alan Hecht, deputy assistant administrator in the Office of International Activities of the Environmental Protection Agency. He began with a personal anecdote. While attending college in Cleveland in the 1960s, the Cuyahoga River caught on fire. So did the Volga River in the 1970s. In response both governments introduced sweeping environmental legislation. These were not, he said, the best times politically. There were disputes over arms control, military superiority, and scientific and academic freedom. Nevertheless, concern about the environment was mutually advantageous.

Collaboration between the Soviet Union and the United States increased after this period. In more than fifteen years of work, this environmental agreement proved to be one of the most successful examples of U.S.-Soviet cooperation. Over three thousand Soviet and U.S. scientists were involved in this work.

Hecht ended his address by focusing on several problems, the resolution of which demanded cooperation between the Soviet Union and the United States: global warming, the increase of greenhouse gases in the atmosphere,

---

1. On March 28, 1979, the core of Unit 2 at Three Mile Island, Pennsylvania, released large amounts of reactive gasses. Contamination required a ten-year cleanup. On April 26, 1986, the Chernobyl reactor exploded. Over two thousand were killed.

the depletion of the ozone layer through the use of fluorocarbons, widespread marine and coastal pollution, urban air and water pollution, and deforestation. Many international groups were dealing with these problems. "Let's have a race," he suggested. "Let's see who can contribute the most to solving the environmental problems of the world. All other problems will pale in comparison. In the long run it will not matter who wins. All of humankind will be the beneficiaries."

Women, Work, Health, and Family Issues

In his welcoming address to the World Congress of Women, held in Moscow in June 1987, Gorbachev had quoted Lenin: "There is no real freedom, nor can there be, so long as women are handicapped by men's privileges." Gorbachev continued, "Women all over the world are justly demanding that their voice be heard and that their will be taken into account when priority state decisions are adopted. They want to see and feel that society values their labor and abilities and needs their practical wisdom, the warmth of their hearts, and their magnanimity."[2] When Raisa Gorbachev discovered that *Time* magazine was preparing a story on contemporary Soviet women, to be published in early June 1988, she sent an unsolicited message to the magazine:

> Today the Soviet woman is proud of her participation in perestroika, in the renewal of society. There are grounds for this. Perestroika is distinguished by a vigorous social policy. This is very important for improving people's everyday life and family life and for the upbringing of children. This policy provides women with greater opportunities to practice their chosen profession, to go about their favorite pursuits, and—not least important—to take good care of themselves in order to remain an equal and desired loved one, wife, and mother for many years to come.[3]

At one of the major plenaries of the week, former vice-presidential nominee Geraldine Ferraro and actress-activist Marlo Thomas enlarged from an American perspective on the themes of women, work, health, and family issues.

2. Welcoming address to the World Congress of Women, Moscow, June 23, 1987.

3. *Time,* June 6, 1988, 42.

In the United States, many changes had occurred in the work force in the previous two decades. Women now made up 44 percent of the workforce; 54 percent of women over the age of sixteen and 70 percent of women between the ages of twenty-five and forty-four were holding paying jobs. Having children did not inhibit their participation. Nearly a half of women with infants under the age of one year were working outside the home. Women were working because they needed to. In many cases they were the primary wage earners, because nearly two-thirds of all women in the work-force were single, divorced, or separated heads of households or they shared primary earning responsibility with husbands who earned less than fifteen thousand dollars annually. Economic necessity, however, was not the only reason for their working. According to a recent survey, American women felt positively about working. Eighty-three percent of wage-earning women surveyed would continue to work full- or part-time even if money were of no consequence.

Women were the ones holding the lower paying jobs. In the previous three decades they had been brought into the workforce but not all the way. Women still made up 65 percent of technical, sales, and administrative sup-port staff but only 43 percent of managerial and professional specialties. The result was a continuing wage gap. Too often women's wages remained too low for economic self-sufficiency. In 1989, 90 percent of single parents were women and 30 percent of those households lived below the poverty line. That, she said, was unacceptable in a nation that prided itself on equality and justice for all. The observation brought loud applause. "For those of us who have been part of the change," Ferraro continued, "it is easy to see how far we have come. But clearly we are only halfway there" [Lengthy applause].

Alevtina Fedulova, the first deputy chair of the Committee of Soviet Women, began by saying that the few steps she had walked from her chair to the podium had taken only a short time. It had taken nearly five years, however, for a discussion of the place of women in society to come before a Chautauqua U.S.-Soviet conference. The question was no longer a national problem. It transcended boundaries and had become an international prob-lem. Fedulova said she was in full agreement with much in Ferraro's ad-dress. The question of women's place in society was of importance because it reflected the particularities of the social and political organization of a state—its culture, development, and social consciousness.

"Progress and the development of society are impossible," Fedulova asserted, "without creating the proper conditions for the development of women as individuals. . . . Women have proved that they can be very successful and make great achievements in whatever they undertake whether on land, at sea, or in space—but unfortunately not for themselves or for their own families." The need at present was for a unified, integrated, and comprehensive state policy in regard to women. Women needed legislative assurance that such a policy was in place. Women in the Soviet Union had also begun to form professional and occupational societies in order to assert their equal rights. They had every intention of taking part in elections, asserting themselves, and being able to choose their life's path. Fedulova's address was met with a lengthy ovation.

Actress Marlo Thomas had received numerous awards for her work in drawing attention to the issues of women, children, and what she called "saving the planet." She had already discovered through two visits to the Soviet Union what it meant that the women of both nations had shared concerns. She had found that women who worked there typically had two jobs —the one in the office or factory and the other that started when the job ended, raising children, standing in line for the groceries, and keeping the home. The impetus for women in the Soviet Union and the United States was to create more options. The laws that had been passed to further women's rights in the United States had been great excuses to encourage people to change their behavior.

When she grew up, Thomas said, women were relegated to what was called "light work." Women were mothers and elementary teachers. At the university level, a professor was usually male. Television commercials aimed at women in those days focused on housecleaning, even if the women depicted did not look as if they were involved in housecleaning. They looked like what women were supposed to look like—fashionable, wearing a dress, jewelry, and high heels, and smiling even as they washed dishes. "'Ah, the good old days,' some Americans still sigh," Thomas said. "Unfortunately some of them are now in Congress and the cabinet." Laughter and applause quickly followed the comment.

The first speaker at a later workshop was Galina Semenova, a mother, a grandmother, and a people's deputy in the Soviet Union. She was also editor-in-chief of a woman's magazine that had a circulation of twenty million.

Perestroika, she said, had affirmed the priority of human values. It had forced society to deal with women and family. Women wanted the two roles to be linked in harmony with one another. Glasnost had revealed distortions in the understanding of what a woman was. First, she was not just a nursemaid who dressed and fed the children. Second, the fact that two-thirds of divorces in the Soviet Union were initiated by women was testimony to the anger and aggression that existed in many marriage relationships.

According to Semenova, glasnost had revealed a complex situation, but it also proposed ways of dealing with it and overcoming the existing contradictions. The first approach was to renounce any stereotypes that had lost their validity. One such was unique to Soviet society. Women who worked in the Soviet Union had achieved considerable prestige and praise for many reasons. They had become involved in productive work because so many Soviet men had been lost in the war. So they had achieved the heights in one sphere—work—only to lose in another—motherhood. An attempt to renounce this stereotype merely created another, namely, that the home and motherhood were to be regarded as having a lower value for women.

Alexis Herman, chief of staff of the Democratic National Committee, had served in the Carter administration as head of the women's bureau of the U.S. Department of Labor. She had served as a high school guidance counselor in the Deep South, working with young girls finishing high school and encouraging them to broaden their horizons and think new ideas, especially occupations in non-traditional fields. She herself was the child of a single-parent mother, a young, African American, teenage mother who awakened early in the mornings to prepare breakfast and dinner before departing for work. She worked in the evenings to finish her high school and college education. "It never occurred to me," Herman said, "that I would never not work. It was always a part of my mother's background and history as well as that of the women in the neighborhood."

Herman went on to list what she regarded as the significant items in work and family issues. First, in 1989, women occupied about 45 percent of the workforce—fifty-five million. In the past fifteen to twenty years, two-thirds of the expansion in labor was created by women coming into the workforce. The number was increasing, as was the trend. Second, women worked for essentially the same reasons as men—to take care of themselves and their families. Economic need was the pressing reason. More than 65 percent of women who were in the workplace were single, divorced, or widowed. Third, sadly the wage gap remained the same. The only change was the dollar figure around the wage gap. The median earnings for a male in the United States in 1988 was approximately twenty-six thousand dollars; for a woman it was seventeen thousand dollars. Fourth, 80 percent of all women who worked were concentrated in roughly twenty to thirty occupations. One of the reasons for the wage gap was that women had been historically, and continued to be, concentrated in low-paying, low-wage, low-status occupations. Lastly, women in the United States continued to be the primary nurturers of and providers for the family. They had the responsibility of creating the balance between home and work. Working women in the United States continued to be the ones primarily responsible for carrying the burden of single-parent family life and the increasing incidence of poverty. Two out of three women were on the poverty rolls. Of African American children, 75 percent lived in homes headed by women alone.

The United States, the Soviet Union, and Regional Conflicts

Regional conflicts, which had changed much during the previous four years —becoming enlarged in one area or diminished in another—came to the fore at another of the morning plenaries. The U.S. position was set forth by Paul D. Wolfowitz, who had served under three presidents—Carter, Reagan, and Bush. In the previous May, he had been appointed undersecretary of defense for policy. Prior to that, he had been ambassador to the Republic of Indonesia in 1989.

The record had shown, Wolfowitz said, that regional conflicts played a major part in the development of the cold war and, more recently, the downturn in relations between the Soviet Union and the United States in the mid-seventies. The demise of détente in this period was an effect of the use of Soviet military power directly in Afghanistan and indirectly in support of military interventions by Soviet allies in Angola, Ethiopia, Cambodia, El Salvador, and elsewhere. In Afghanistan, Soviet military aid was pouring in to the Najibullah regime at the rate of more than $250 million a month, dwarfing all the assistance received by the mujaheddin from all sources. New weapons systems had been transferred to that regime in what Wolfowitz called "the largest airlift of arms and materiel in Soviet history." In Nicaragua, while there was some assurance that direct Soviet military aid had stopped, East bloc and Cuban military aid continued at an annual rate of half a billion dollars a year, even though the United States had long ceased its much smaller military aid to the Nicaraguan resistance forces. With a total of $3 billion in Soviet bloc military aid since 1980, that country had become the most thoroughly militarized country in Central America.

North Korea was providing a less publicized but more dangerous story. It had demonstrated complete disregard for commonly accepted norms of international behavior. The provision of modern weaponry by the Soviet Union had only increased the military capabilities of an irresponsible regime. There had been disturbing signs also that North Korea might be in the process of developing a nuclear weapons capability. People should have the right to determine their own destinies, not to have them imposed by a super-power. Governments that enjoyed popular support were less likely in the long run to provide opportunities for outside military intervention, and governments that were genuinely open to popular criticism were less likely to engage in military aggression. It was no accident that two of the Soviet allies whose foreign behavior caused the most concern—North Korea and Cuba—had the most unreconstructed Stalinist regimes in the world today.

Wolfowitz brought his address to a close by making three proposals about how both countries could deal most effectively with regional conflicts in the future. First, both needed to recognize the common interest they shared in the solution of the conflicts by peaceful means. Regional conflicts should be resolved on the basis of self-determination, independence, and democracy. Second, all the industrialized nations should join together in taking precautions not to export materials or technology that would facilitate the proliferation of nuclear, chemical, or missile-delivered weapons. By the year 2000 over a dozen third-world countries could have the ability to deploy nuclear weapons. Many more nations could have chemical weapons, and at least a dozen nations could have a ballistic-missile-delivery capability. Finally, it should be understood that the superpowers were not the primary cause of regional conflicts. Such conflicts arose out of ethnic strife, historic animosities, poverty, famine, and uneven levels of political and economic development. To dampen regional conflicts it was necessary to deal with their causes.

The Soviet response to Wolfowitz was given by Nikolai Shishlin, a senior member of the Central Committee of the Communist Party. Shishlin took a few minutes to agree with many of the things that Wolfowitz had said. The Soviet Union was at that time in history in a more advantageous position than it had been. It did criticize itself. It did pay strict heed to its own history. Then, pausing as if the thought had just come to him, he announced to the audience that he had been ruminating the day before. Speaking in almost meditative tones, he said:

> Each person is alone, regardless of whether he has friends and family or not. Each person is solitary. Therefore one must value communion. Dialogue must be valued, as in the present conference, to lighten the burden of loneliness. Moreover, because we are living in a mutually interdependent world we are not allowed to become isolated. Self-isolation would be a criminal luxury. For this reason we must be able to know how to listen to each other, to hear each other, to learn from each other, and to understand each other. Then it would be possible that we could learn how to act together.

According to Shishlin there were three levels of regional conflict, each dangerous. The first was the national level, the source of the conflicts. Regional conflicts had their own national nature and character. The second level of conflicts, the regional, was never contained within national borders. The sparks of the fires were borne by the wind into distant regions, as in the Middle East, Central America, the south of Africa, and elsewhere. The third level of conflict was global, and this was precisely the one that touched the Soviet Union and the United States. With this, Shishlin turned to Wolfowitz and addressed him pointedly: "Paul, you addressed some questions to the Soviet Union. I will ask two of you. First, whose missiles are striking Kabul? Whose missiles are killing old men, women, and children without any discrimination? They are not made by the mujaheddin. One other question: Which country severed diplomatic relations with Cuba and does not maintain economic relations with Cuba? Not the Soviet Union."

Many questions came from the audience, some addressed to both speakers.

QUESTION: To what extent are the economies of our respective countries dependent on the export of military equipment to the third world? Is foreign policy related to economic dependence on the arms trade?

SHISHLIN: Speaking frankly, I do not think this is an easy thing to resolve. In the United States there are many industrial centers, companies, and corporations that are involved in the export of arms. The Soviet Union does the same, and much at the same level. But the questioner is correct. This problem must be resolved.

WOLFOWITZ: I do not believe there is any dependence of our economy on arms exports. [Loud shouts of "No."] The total level of arms exports, while it may be large in relation to the damage it can do in the Third World, is very small in an economy like ours. Our economy does not depend on the sales of arms. My own belief is that our arms sales have been declining over the last eight or ten years. The key to reducing arms sales is to resolve regional conflicts.

QUESTION: You were quick to cite Soviet instances of aggression, but you failed to mention our own involvement in Central America and elsewhere. How can you criticize the Soviets for their involvement while the United States is directly and indirectly supporting South Korea, South Africa, El Salvador, and Israel? We Americans are in no position to preach to the USSR the wisdom of applying domestic values to other regions of the world. Apart from hypocrisy, how would

you account for the U.S. support of repressive, undemocratic regimes
in South Korea, the Philippines, Chile, and elsewhere? [Long applause]

WOLFOWITZ: The temptation is to take on at least six factual mistakes in that recitation. The United States does not support a repressive
regime in the Philippines. The United States pushed the Marcos government to the kinds of reforms that eventually brought about its
demise. Similarly, we played a major role in South Korea in getting
President Chung to step down and to have his successor chosen by a
popular election, the fairness of which even the opposition affirmed.
We do not support South Africa, and we were one of the first countries
to impose a military embargo on that country. It was a misstatement
that I did not talk about U.S. policy in Nicaragua. We stopped almost
two years ago any level of support for the Nicaraguan resistance.
That support, during the few years in which we undertook it, totaled
around $200 million. That was less than what the Soviet Union and
its allies have been putting into Nicaragua in a single year, two years
after we stopped supporting the Nicaraguans. Our goal now is to see
a democratic process go on in that country. It is a fact that in the last
six months of the Somoza regime the United States imposed an arms
embargo on that government that helped to bring about its collapse.
When the Sandinista regime came into power the United States provided economic assistance to that country, fairly substantial assistance.
That assistance was conditioned on Nicaragua's minding its own business and not interfering in the internal affairs of its neighbors.

Ethnic, Religious, and Cultural Pluralism

Laurence Glasco, professor of history at the University of Pittsburgh, had
dealt professionally with factors involved in large-scale emigration. What
was remarkable about ethnicity in America, he began, was that for any particular group it was a relatively short-lived phenomenon. He raised the
question of what factors were at play in the persistence of ethnicity in other
lands and its ebb and flow in the United States. One explanation was the
absence of ethnic territorial hegemony in America—the fact that no ethnic
group had come to dominate a particular geographic area or even a neighborhood in an urban area for long. A second explanation was the lack of resi-
dential stability in America. Resident groups of immigrants had often been
displaced by other incoming immigrants.

Related to this was the fact that American immigrants had been remark-
ably successful in moving up the economic ladder from poverty and the

working class to the middle class. Those who moved up tended to move out both physically and psychologically from the world of their parents and grandparents. The first exception to this general scheme was Jewish Americans. They experienced enormous upward mobility and movement but still maintained considerable ethnic identity and consciousness. Prior to World War II, Glasco argued, Jews in the United States were following the same assimilation trajectory as other groups. Two things combined to reinvigorate their sense of ethnic identity: first, the Holocaust and the anguish, anger, and guilt felt by American Jews over the fate of their less fortunate coreligionists in Europe; and second, the establishment of the state of Israel and especially its perilous existence.

The second and more striking exception had been black Americans, whose sense of ethnic consciousness and identity at the present time far exceeded that of other groups. The historic experience of blacks stood in sharp contrast to that of white immigrants. They came to this country involuntarily, and they were systematically and legally excluded from the social and economic mainstream of the country. Blacks, especially in the South, who attempted to assimilate were criticized by racists for trying to be "white" or for not knowing their proper place. Those who did try to assimilate were, in fact, more disliked than those who did not try. Whereas upwardly mobile descendants of white immigrants were rewarded and accepted for their efforts to blend in, middle-class blacks who attempted to blend in were punished. As a result, black Americans developed an ethnic consciousness and culture that exceeded that of white ethnics.

Anatoly Sazonov, a senior staff member of the Central Committee of the Communist Party and an expert in the field of ethnic and cultural differences in the Soviet Union, expressed his appreciation that the problems of ethnicity in his own country were part of the week's agenda. It showed that the study of the subject now occupied a more important position in international conferences. In recent years, he said, much attention had been given to the interethnic relations and problems in the Soviet Union. He had often been asked why there were growing ethnic tensions and even open conflicts in different regions of the USSR. During the period of perestroika and glasnost, it had become necessary to create a new approach to the problem of nationalities. The challenge of new thinking was one for both official and nongovernmental groups; input from the experience of other nations was also important. Interethnic relations were closely related to the nation's economy, politics, demography, and ideology.

During the period of this renewed thinking, there had been much discussion about the need for a new national policy. One reason was that, in the decade before 1985, it had become clear that the national policy did not address the situation. During Stalin's time, Leninist principles concerning ethnic policy—the federative principles of the Soviet state—had been forgotten. The rights of various republics were being violated, and there was no consistency in carrying out local republican policies. In many cases the national and ethnic specifics of various regions were ignored. The Communist Party had therefore drawn up a new platform regarding the nationalities problem. This platform included two main points: first, the equality of nations, peoples, and individuals regardless of their nationality; and second, the principle of internationalism.

Sazonov then went on to indicate what he took to be the main directions the USSR was taking in regard to ethnic and cultural pluralism. The first aim was to preserve the Soviet federation but to fill it with a new content. The USSR consisted of fifteen union republics and a number of autonomous republics and regions. No fewer than 130 different languages were spoken. The second aim was to expand the rights of various autonomous republics and regions; the third, to establish all the necessary conditions for the free development of the various national cultures. What did it imply to give new meaning to the Soviet federation? It implied determining what the authority of Moscow was and what the competence of local governments was. The new changes would become part of the new constitutions of the USSR and of the national republics.

Sazonov raised the question of the effect of pluralism and decentralization on the durability of the frontiers of the USSR. In every region of the country, the Soviet Union had its own multitude of different ethnic groups and cultures. To preserve these, it was all the more necessary that the frontiers should not be changed. Every nationality of the USSR should have certain guarantees so that each could preserve its ethnic and cultural traditions, including its languages. The new concept in national policy was that of the absolute equality of all nationalities in the country. "It is our view," Sazonov concluded, "that during the years of Soviet power we have been able to make a valuable contribution to international culture and world civilization. At the same time we are fully aware that along with these positive experiences various problems and contradictions also emerged. I hope that the exchange of views that we have had during these days will help us to learn more about each other's experiences in the field of ethnic problems."

Relations between the Superpowers

Three sessions of the conference dealt from different perspectives with the current state of relations between the two superpowers, with the possible change of image from enemy to partner, and with what might be possible in their relationship in the decade of the 1990s.

The first plenary session to deal with the current state of U.S.-Soviet relations brought together as joint moderators U.S. journalist Hedrick Smith and Russian television commentator Vladimir Pozner. Both had been present at previous Chautauqua conferences, Pozner at Riga and Tbilisi and Smith at Tbilisi.

Smith opened by lamenting the absence of Soviet editor Vladislav Starkov, who had come under criticism for a poll he had published critical of President Gorbachev.[4] That apart, however, he said it was a fitting time for U.S. citizens to note carefully and with intense interest what was happening in the development of perestroika.

Smith then introduced Curtis Kamman, deputy assistant secretary of state . Kamman had spent most of his diplomatic career dealing with U.S.-Soviet affairs. Opening his remarks in Russian to express his thanks for sharing the platform with Petrovsky, Kamman continued in English by commenting on how closely the Pittsburgh agenda corresponded to the issues with which the U.S. government was then dealing in Washington, D.C. One of the effects of working on such a rich agenda was the discovery of new problems to work on. The expansion of the dialogue with the Soviet Union and the new emphasis on problem solving was a sure sign of progress and of a more mature relationship. After many years the two countries had moved beyond sterile ideological exchanges to seeking practical steps of benefit to both countries.

It was not enough, he continued, to address the top layer of issues between the two countries. That was what had happened in the 1970s, and it

---

4. *Argumenty i Fakty* (*Arguments and Facts*) began in 1978 as a bulletin for a scholarly society. Its editor, Vladislav Starkov, transformed it into a general weekly. The weekly grew at an astonishing rate to a circulation of 1.5 million in 1987, 10 million in 1988, and an overwhelming 33.4 million in 1990—a circulation figure that merited an entry in the *Guinness Book of World Records*. It was the first mass-circulation paper to break away from the stultifying style of most Soviet newspapers and the more orthodox line of the party chiefs. Publishing interviews with important members of the party leadership alongside its more provocative articles, *Argumenty i Fakty* survived by positioning itself beyond the control of the authorities. In the same month as the Pittsburgh conference, Gorbachev had tried to force editor Starkov to resign after *Argumenty i Fakty* published an opinion poll unfavorable to him. Starkov flatly refused.

ultimately proved futile. "We must go to the sources of the mistrust and suspicion," he insisted, "if we are to ensure continued progress in our relations." Reform, perestroika, and the move toward democracy were worldwide movements and would continue to affect international relations until the next century. Domestic and international affairs had become more intertwined, with the fate of one linked to that of the other. Technological innovations also had made ordinary citizens intensely aware of events throughout the world. Growth and competitiveness increasingly depended on the freedom with which a society could receive, absorb, share, and use knowledge and information. This was the awareness that lay at the root of perestroika.

What would it take, he asked, for the United States to be a partner with the Soviet Union in building mutual trust? First, time. "The key to genuine improvement in relations," he said, "is sustainability and longevity." Forty years of mistrust must yield now to years of positive efforts in meeting the legitimate concerns of both sides. Second, security. Security came from two sources: maintaining the armed forces necessary to deter aggression and concurrently making mutual efforts to reduce these very forces. Third, openness and transparency. "The great challenge of coming years," Kamman continued, "will be the removing of barriers that inhibit the exchange of ideas, goods, and human creativity." Openness was the way to remove misunderstanding—open cultures, skies, and communications. Fourth, human rights. It was essential to hear and respond to the concerns of the people. The United States had had two hundred years of building institutions that respected the will of the people. This explained why most Americans were genuinely excited by unfolding events in the Soviet Union. Fifth, cool nerves and steadiness of purpose. History did not always go smoothly, Kamman reflected, "So we must be ready to deal with both good and bad developments, never losing sight of our broader objectives."

Soviet moderator Pozner began by noting how significantly the tenor and content of the Chautauqua conferences had changed for the positive since his first involvement. As a journalist, he joined Smith in lamenting the absence of Vladislav Starkov from the Pittsburgh conference. Nevertheless, one of the achievements of perestroika was that, if the establishment was unhappy with a journalist, the journalist at least did not disappear but fought back and could fight back. With this comment he introduced the Soviet speaker of the day.

Petrovsky, speaking three years earlier at Jurmala, had lamented that, on both sides, the relationship between the Soviet Union and the United States was gloomy, even ominous. "The present state of our relations cannot be described as satisfactory," he had begun. In contrast, Petrovsky opened his 1989 speech at Pittsburgh by acclaiming the new political thinking that was going on not only in the Soviet Union and the United States but also throughout the world. The whole purpose of the Chautauqua conferences, he insisted, was not only to initiate dialogue but to encourage a drive towards people-to-people contacts and building trust among them. The present Pittsburgh conference showed how dramatically the entire atmosphere of Soviet-American relations and the overall situation in the world had changed. "Hope and optimism glow again," he affirmed. "Sweeping changes are taking the whole world into the post-confrontational era. When we look at the progress we have made in recent years, we have many reasons to be satisfied. New vistas have been opened that will be increasingly broadened in scale. We cherish the assets that we have gained in our expanding relations."

The Soviet Union was going through a hard time, yet it was also a time of optimism. The country was searching for the optimal forms of social organization within the framework of the socialist choice it had made earlier. All spheres of life were being restructured there. The democratic experience of the West over two centuries was one of the inspirations of that renewal. The Soviet Union itself had no intention of departing from its own unique identity, values, and ideals, nor did it seek uniformity with other countries. Socialism had not lost its historical perspective, he insisted. On the contrary, only now were the conditions being created to let it reveal its inherent creative and humanistic potential through cleansing it of what was deforming it. "As a result of perestroika," he said, "we shall remain a socialist but qualitatively new democratic state looking after human needs." Socialism, with a new human face and substance, would make a positive contribution toward universal progress and the establishment of a period of peace.

From "Enemy" to "Partner"?

One of the ideas that had been raised in earlier conferences was brought into prominence at one of the workshops in the form of a question: "How we view each other: Are the images changing from 'enemy' to 'partner'?" Petrovsky himself, speaking at Chautauqua at the 1987 conference, had used almost similar language: "Soviets," he had said, "would like to see the United States doing things to banish the image of the enemy and to replace it with the image of partner." Indeed, the language of partnership had been frequently heard in the public conversations of that week and obviously to the approval of the audiences.

Three speakers—one from the Soviet Union and two from the United States—offered their own comments on an observation made earlier by Pozner that "there were two governments with a vested interest in conflict" and that "they knew very well how to make us view each other as enemies."

"We are hostages of our own hatred." The sharp sentence, spoken by Leonid Dobrokhotov, an advisor to the Communist Party, was a painfully accurate summary of much that had happened in relationships between the Soviet Union and the United States in prior years. If only on the basis of the proverb that "a fault confessed is half redressed," it also opened up for the workshop one of the more productive conversations of the week. "War begins in people's minds." With this preface to his comments, Dobrokhotov, a member of the board of the USSR-USA Society, described the role that years of negative propaganda had played in shaping public opinion in the Soviet Union and the United States.

He asked how it might be possible to change the hostile image of enemy to the friendly image of partner. "Before we start a hot war," he continued, "we dehumanize the enemy. Then it is easier to kill. The propaganda of killing precedes the technology of killing." Through their information media, both countries had contributed to the spread of such propaganda. He himself, for example, had written many critical articles about the United States. However, when he first arrived in the United States in 1985, he was surprised at the discrepancy between what he had been writing about the country and what he found to be true about it. He also was surprised about the image of a communist in people's minds when he introduced himself to them as one. One person asked, "Are you married?" When he said that he was, the response came, "Look at him. He is a married man." He was then asked if he had children. When they learned that he had two daughters, they were again surprised. "Both sides were dehumanizing each other," he insisted. The process involved created antitheses—insiders and outsiders. Each side said that it was informing and the other misinforming. "*We* were telling the truth, *they* were telling lies."

It simply meant that neither side was understanding the other. Dobrokhotov reminded his audience of yet another way by which propaganda damaged both countries from within: "When we assign responsibility for our problems to our enemies, we give away our power to solve our own problems. If we believe our own propaganda, we will never be able to solve our own problems." To be sure, he said, there were many reports in the recent period about social and human difficulties in the Soviet Union, but these were written in a quite different way from previous years, without any vicious or hostile attitudes. There was greater empathy in the press, a feeling that both countries were alike in dealing with difficult problems, such as alcoholism in the Soviet Union and drug addiction in the United States. "I love America," Dobrokhotov confessed. And though America was not perfect, it was certainly not evil, as some of the Soviet reports had earlier argued. It was important to portray life as it really was in both countries without any malice.

Pozner opened the final plenary session by summing up in almost jubilant terms what he thought to be the main accomplishments of the five Chautauqua conferences:

> We have witnessed dramatic change. We began by speaking at each other, not to each other. We heard, but we refused to listen. We sought to score points. We played the game of one-upmanship. We have come a long way. Here we have addressed one another as newly found friends, working together for common solutions to our problems.
> We have experienced wonderful warmth and a surge of joy that we have overcome the barriers of mutual distrust and see the promise that this bears. With the scores of an old enmity still hurting, we have been careful in our efforts not to hurt each other's feelings. And that defines our goals for the future: to achieve a true, profound and solid friendship that allows for the most direct statements based on the understanding of our desire to come even closer and help each other understand.

A few days previously he had been given a slip of paper by someone who quickly walked away. It said, "Vladimir Pozner, defect now before it is too late" [Laughter]. "If that was an invitation to live in Pittsburgh," he continued, "I must decline, even if it is one of the most liveable cities in the United States. I decline because, as you all know, there is no place like home."

Smith expressed his own pleasure at having worked with Pozner during the course of the Chautauqua conferences. "If there is something striking about the conference this year," he said, "it is its *tone*. It is the ease with which people who have known one another for several years have come together to exchange ideas about a variety of subjects." He recalled the words of an American hostess the previous evening. "I didn't know Russians were going to be like that. I didn't know it could be so comfortable." The present meeting, he continued, was different from the others, because it dealt so often with issues that ordinary citizens had in their minds: women's issues, ecology, narcotics, and social issues that touched everyone.

Bradley and Primakov had shared the platform at the Chautauqua Institution in 1987. It seemed fitting that these two, each known and respected in the other's country, should bring the 1989 Pittsburgh conference to a conclusion.

Bradley spoke first, recalling the questions that he had raised two years earlier at Chautauqua. Would the party and state bureaucracy share more power with the Soviet people? The answer appeared to be yes. The long journey to democracy had begun. Would workers have a bigger voice and trade unions a stronger role? The answer again appeared to be yes. Would Soviet youth be allowed to repudiate Afghanistan as young Americans rejected Vietnam? The answer to that was yes. Shevardnadze himself had condemned that invasion as "the most serious violation of party and civic norms and the ethical standards of our time."

Two years ago, he reminded the audience, he had asked if Soviet history would be taught by people who cared about discovering the truth. Now archives were being opened and historical cover-ups exhumed. The process was slow, painful, and divisive, but it had advanced. Jewish emigration had gone from 681 in 1986 to 20,000 in 1988. Recent developments in Poland and East Germany would have been barely conceivable two years previously. The political geography of Europe was changing, and without tacit Soviet support, it would never have happened. The pace of change in the previous two years had been nothing short of astonishing.

If only the Soviet Union would combine with the United States in championing democracy, Bradley pleaded, it would not only serve their common interests, it would also inspire the world. Democracy was the best form of government, even if some voices in both the Soviet Union and the United States were warning about the dangers of moving too quickly towards democratic reform. Many of these people seemed to yearn for the repressive certainties of the cold war, unwilling to think through the meaning of the new reality. Yet a nation truly committed to democracy could panic in the face of some of democracy's manifestations: strikes, marches, protests, and criticism of government. But these were the seeds of healthy democracy. They should be nurtured. Economic reform thrived when combined with political pluralism. Open markets led inexorably to a more open society. Reform decided through public debate was more likely to last. "You cannot save perestroika," Bradley affirmed, "by abandoning democracy or by commanding economic conformity. You have to make a choice."

Primakov had ended his 1987 address at Chautauqua by speaking of the sincere desire of both the Soviets and the American people for mutual understanding, improved relations, and peace on the earth. He began his Pittsburgh address by noting that, since 1987, positive changes had been occurring not only in the Soviet Union but also all over the world, including the United States. With a gentle tilt at Senator Bradley's wide-ranging speech and with loud laughter from the audience, he said that, although he was in favor of perestroika, he would not restructure his own talk. He had decided he would stick to the subject that had been assigned to him, namely, U.S.-Soviet relations on the threshold of the 1990s.

He noted that only a few days earlier an unofficial summit had been announced for early December that would bring together the chairman of the Presidium of the Supreme Soviet, Mikhail Gorbachev, and the president of the United States, George Bush. This had become news item number one in the United States, and some of the comments made about it had caused the Soviets to smile. "Now that the time of confrontation has passed," he said, "it is not wicked laughter but a kind smile." Then, with wry humor that was obvious even in translation, he noted that there had been much talk in Washington about providing advice and expertise to the Soviet Union. But that would not be necessary, he continued: "I have become convinced of this by listening to Senator Bradley, because he has outlined in perfect detail what we should do. I think this is perfectly sufficient!"

Turning to the future, Primakov offered suggestions about what he thought would most likely be the political situation in the 1990s. First, the United States and the Soviet Union, already possessing over 90 percent of the world's nuclear arsenals, would remain the leading nuclear powers in the world. Second, with the removal of Soviet troops from Afghanistan, the normalization of relations between the two countries would determine the success of managing regional conflicts. Third, in the Warsaw Pact and NATO, the military aspect would weaken and their political relationship become more prominent. Both countries, however, would continue to be the key states in the 1990s in the military and political sense. Relations between them would continue to be the axis around which the whole international situation will revolve. Fourth, the cooperation between the United States and the Soviet Union could not but be the decisive factor in eliminating an ecological catastrophe. At the present time, the thermonuclear danger was becoming less, the ecological danger greater. "It is impossible to overestimate the potential significance of our cooperation in the 1990s in eliminating poverty, helping the third world to catch up and controlling diseases that are threatening to spread across the world," Primakov emphasized. He then quoted what President Franklin Roosevelt had once written: "Our progress is measured not by the growing prosperity of those who have much but by whether or not we can provide for those who have too little."

Primakov drew his remarks slowly to a conclusion by insisting that the Soviet Union had no desire at all to become the same kind of society as the United States:

> We have our own values, our own historical experience, our own tradi-
> tions, and the geographical conditions that dictate the course we choose
> to follow. We would like to have friendship and cooperation with the
> United States and draw from your experience in government or indus-
> try everything that is useful and applicable. But we will not deviate in
> doing so from the advantage we have in our own socialist values. We
> would like to renew socialism. We would like to see socialism open its
> democratic nature.

"I remain an optimist about the coming decade," Primakov affirmed in clos-ing. But, he insisted, the optimism must be based on agreed rules of behav-ior. Long and enthusiastic applause followed Primakov's speech.

Closing Ceremonies

After expressing his thanks to the Chautauqua Institution and the USSR-USA Society, the president of the University of Pittsburgh, Dr. Wesley Pos-var, made a presentation to the Soviet delegation of a print of Pittsburgh in 1880 by marine artist John Stobart (b. 1929), who was present for the occa-sion. He then introduced Bratton for a closing comment.

Bratton reflected on the process that had begun at the Chautauqua Insti-tution four years earlier. "The Chautauqua goals and mission of an im-proved, enlightened, and empowered citizenry took on international tones," he said. The first effort had been modest, but Chautauqua's mission proved to be congruent with the U.S.-Soviet agenda. The intervening years had not been easy. The atmosphere was initially and frighteningly contentious. The risks were high. It might have been prudent to stop, but Chautauqua chose not to give up the struggle. "Four years," he said slowly. "But a journey of incalculable distance has been traversed." As a gift to the USSR Friendship Society, Bratton then presented to Tereshkova a "century chest" by a James-town, New York, custom cabinetmaker, Michael Flaxman. It had one hun-dred drawers, a symbol of the fervent wish that there would be a century of peace and understanding ahead between the two countries. Each drawer contained a gift from an American citizen, including baseball cards from a boy, a Christmas tree ornament from a family, and a dove of peace from the Bratton family.

Tereshkova expressed her own gratitude, first to academician Primakov and then to Senator Bradley for their contributions to the conference. "Days of intense work are behind us," she said, "days of business-like and frank discussions. The exchange of opinions on major issues enabled us to get to know one another better. We have learned to ask questions in such a manner that we would not insult each other." The Soviets had seen enormous amounts of goodwill among the American people. "The same amount of goodwill, I can assure you," she continued, "is also to be found among Soviet people." She was gratified, she said, at the interest American citizens had shown in perestroika and just as much at the Soviet desire to get to know Americans better in their lives, joys, and sorrows. She congratulated Pittsburgh on its own perestroika—the restructuring of its economy, the social infrastructure, retraining of workers, and the protection of the environment. Trust, convergence, and cooperation had been evident throughout the week. "We have spoken in the language of simple human community, a language of hope," she concluded. With that she expressed her own gratitude to the Chautauqua Institution, the United States Information Agency, the president of the university, and the people of Pittsburgh. On behalf of the Soviet delegation she then presented two bells as a gift to the Chautauqua Institution and to President Posvar, modeled after the bell that had been rung at Chautauqua's first session in 1874.

CHAPTER EIGHT

"There Must Be More to Follow"

T HE PRECEDING CHAPTERS have been for the most part narrative and descriptive, with little in the way of interpretation. The evidence gathered from the conferences over a five-year period provides its own sufficient record. However, for any text, or summary of texts, there will always be a variety of meanings. In the sections that follow I shall try, first, to assess the "mind" particularly of the citizen delegates who attended the conferences. What did these "citizen diplomats" judge to be the central issues for them and for their nations? Second, I shall assess what seem to have been the most distinctive marks of each of the conferences and trace the movement of thought and attitude between 1985 and 1989.

Chautauqua's summer lecture programs, particularly since the end of World War II, have opened to its audiences a global perspective that is more prominent than it had been in the less threatening years before. Understanding, perspective, balanced interpretation, and fairness were the rubrics by which Chautauqua addressed the political, cultural, and economic issues of the times. In the five Chautauqua conferences, it became possible to see that behind the public appearance of Soviet communism or of American capitalism were human beings "just like us," to use the phrase of the woman who first met the Soviet visitors as they filed through Buffalo airport. More particularly, in private homes as well as public spaces at Chautauqua, in Juramala, and in Tbilisi, new relationships began between citizens who sought at the least to get to know one another as human beings and, they hoped, to open doors to new partnerships between their governments. "It was exhilarating," Joan Rosenthal later commented on the 1987 visit, "to know we had opened some doors." Her own experience of welcoming four Soviets to her house was, she said, the most powerful experience in her twenty-three years on the grounds.

Although the choice of Jurmala and Tbilisi was in some ways politically controversial, the choice of all four sites for the meetings created a safe political space for dialogue. Washington, D.C., or Moscow would have been out of the question. The pastoral character of Chautauqua and the easy urban settings of Jurmala, Riga, and Tbilisi offered settings in which the participants could speak with one another openly. The obvious enthusiasm at the end of the first conference to continue the dialogue meant not only that a whole range of issues and problems had still to be faced but also that the participants had only just come to gain a better understanding of how those on the other side thought, lived, and faced their common fears.

The "Mind" of the Delegates

Readers of the foregoing chapters 2 through 7 will have noted from time to time a reference to applause in the body of the text itself. The applause of a typical Chautauqua audience also indicates what it judges to be true, well spoken, or fair. No doubt some of the applause reported from the Chautauqua audiences was merely a courteous gesture. It may also have been an expression of gratitude, even of astonishment, that the conferences (against all likelihood) had actually taken place. So when Wallach opened the first conference at Chautauqua in 1985, stating that was rare to have high-ranking Soviet and American officials speak to and debate with each other publicly; that it was something of a feat to have Soviet and American performers on the same stage; and that it was an outstanding opportunity to show open democracy at its finest—and to do all these things with the support of both the United States and Soviet governments—the audience clearly agreed with what he said and indicated its agreement with "rousing applause." In the following year, "sustained applause" followed the announcement by Ambassador Dobrynin, at a peculiarly difficult time, that the group in Washington, D.C., frustrated by long delay, was finally going to Latvia. The audience welcomed the words with evident relief and enthusiasm.

Beyond these representative expressions of audience approval or enthusiasm, however, a reader of the preceding chapters can ascertain something of the "mind" of the Soviet and American citizens by noting the thoughts, sentiments, hopes, or beliefs that aroused members of the audience to interrupt speeches on occasion with a corporate vote of approval or, at times, dissent. Using this measure of audience response—applause—we can with reasonable fidelity identify four major convictions held by the citizen diplomats who were involved in the conferences.

1. The necessity to preserve peace and to struggle against the threat of war. Not surprisingly, the commitment to preserve peace and to struggle against the threat of war runs throughout all five conferences, beginning with the opening address by Sokolov in 1985. Sokolov asserted that cold-war think-ing belonged to a simple, two-dimensional world of black and white, of enemy and friend. In such a world, he said, the goal was crystal clear: to bring the enemy down. In face of the threat of war, then, let there instead be a competition. Let each system, he said, prove in the condition of peace which one was better able to ensure prosperity. Which one would produce a high quality of life and the satisfaction of the cultural needs and mate-rial well-being of the individual citizen.

For an audience that for years had known an unabashed ideology of enmity since the end of détente, words such as these opened a new possibil-ity and gave rise to a larger hope, however tenuous. The audience quickly indicated its assent to Sokolov's proposition with applause. A competition of ideas rather than of military forces might then, it seemed, be the pattern of a new age to which, in their different ways, Reagan and Gorbachev were pointing.

The theme of preserving peace and struggling against the threat of war was at the core of the two historical addresses given by Vitaly Zhurkin and Marshal Shulman, also in 1987. The notion of the impossibility of nuclear war, Zhurkin held, was a matter on which there could be no ambivalence, hesitation, or complexity. Only the fear of mutual annihilation could guar-antee that the acute differences made all too plain and painful in the cold war would not lead to a nuclear confrontation. With this sentiment Shul-man, too, was in cordial agreement. He argued that what was absent in cur-rent political thinking was a change in American foreign policy through a more enlightened approach to the management of nuclear weapons. With this the audience warmly agreed once again.

Similarly, in its own response to the militarization of space, the Chau-tauqua audience greeted with obvious approval Vitaly Zhurkin's strong plea that outer space should not be turned into a source of mortal danger and that the frontier of space should be instead a venue of peaceful collaboration. The overriding issue, it appeared, was whether the United States would con-tinue with the development of its Star Wars defense or commit itself rather to a moratorium on the development and deployment of space weapons.

For any citizen diplomat involved in the conferences, taking part even if only by listening to the speeches, and more particularly having the free-dom to ask questions or engage in private conversation, was at least one public way in which a single citizen could do something in favor of peace and in the struggle against the threat of war. Indeed, one of the participants in a Chautauqua U.S.-Soviet conference reported that her presence at the discussions and the freedom to ask a question was a part—"very small," she admitted, "but a part"—of being involved in a process that might well help in the struggle against a nuclear war and the emergence of peace between the two superpowers.

2. *The need for collaboration and trust.* Over and over, particularly in the 1987 conference held at Chautauqua, the theme of necessary collaboration was heard. For example, in a speech "interrupted frequently by applause," Cuomo said in his keynote speech that the Soviet Union and the United States had two choices: to remain suspended in their separate spheres or to look beyond their differences to the whole range of shared needs. For him there could only be one choice: to recognize the interconnectedness of the human family. Echoing the governor's conviction at the same conference, Petrovsky stated with emphasis, "If humankind is to survive, we need cooperation. We can only survive together through joint efforts." The Petrovsky speech at Chautauqua in 1987 was an intense appeal to overcome stereotypes inherited from the period of confrontation and replace them with the image of partner. The same theme recurred frequently at the Pittsburgh conference in 1989.

Acrimony and contention were only to be expected in any public discussion of relationships between the two superpowers in the second half of the 1980s. Both strongly colored the first three conferences and even part of the fourth. Only occasionally during these years did an American speaker, and less occasionally a Soviet, take a critical approach to some aspect of his or her country's national policy. At Chautauqua in 1987, Fritz Ermarth hewed closely to the position of the administration he served, arousing the response of Podlesny that his speech was "a catalogue of complaints against the Soviet Union." When Ermarth was asked in a question period how the situation in Afghanistan compared to the U.S. presence in Nicaragua, he answered that the United States was attempting to advance freedom, democracy, and self-determination in Nicaragua. The audience reaction was very strong, and comments were accorded an unusual number of boos besides some applause, particularly when he added that administration policy was that Nicaragua was "being subjected to a takeover by a Marxist-Leninist minority."

It is enlightening to compare this response—boos are both uncustomary and disliked in Chautauqua's normal civil discourse—with the obvious approval given to Shulman, one of the few official delegates to be critical of administration policy, when he said, "If you look at what we are doing and at the weapons we are building, at where our troops are, at the effects of our policies, there are things that are difficult to reconcile with our declaratory policy." Podlesny himself insisted that the conference in that year was not the time just for criticism by one side or the other. "We can accuse each other to the dawn," he said somewhat despairingly, "maybe even to the second coming of Christ." Did America really want normalization of relations? If so, it was time to face the new reality, of which glasnost and perestroika were examples, and not only think but also act in a new way.

The theme of trust recurs constantly in the public speeches. Two speeches during the 1987 conference took trust as their central appeal: Bradley's address and the remarkable speech a little later by Petrovsky, in which trust became almost the recurring theme. Related to the theme of trust, the appeal to reason is also constant. The Soviet Union and the United States together held in their hands the destiny of half the world, Bradley had affirmed. So it was time to create the conditions of a better future and to let rationality prevail. If, he argued forcibly, the two groups of participants reflected honestly on how to move American and Soviet relations out of stagnation, they will think about trust. He argued that both sides talked much of trust, but both had different understandings about what it meant. One thing, however, was absolutely clear: trust and the liberation from fear were the keys in Soviet-American relations.

Warm approval from the audience could be heard throughout the Amphitheater when Petrovsky enlarged on his own theme. Trust and disarmament were inextricably linked. Trust was the form of politics that permitted collaboration at all levels. What mattered was to construct the edifice of trust and put aside fruitless discussions and the rhetoric of the cold war. The Soviet Union was prepared to work on eliminating weapons in outer space, on ensuring a world without chemical weapons, and even on the complete and global elimination of weapons by the beginning of the twenty-first century, for the question was precisely, "What kind of world will there be in the twenty-first century?"

3. Human rights and the resolution of regional conflicts. Palmer, on the first day of the first conference, specifically named human rights as one of the key issues in any U.S. engagement with the Soviet Union. In the course of the 1987 conference, Zhurkin had insisted that there could be no mutual security between the two superpowers unless it involved human rights. The Soviet Union, he assured his audience, would try to prove that it stood for this. Primakov later, in his own remarks, echoed the same conviction. Unless major issues affecting the human family were dealt with—for example, the environment and ecological problems or the problems of developing nations, such as AIDS—these could be as much of a threat as the present means of mass destruction possessed by both sides. To be sure, the two countries had different understandings of what human rights meant. But "let us unite our efforts," Primakov pleaded, "in resolving human problems such as these, problems of democratization that can be resolved in both countries."

The inhumane treatment of the refuseniks and the refusal of the Soviet government to allow Jews to emigrate from the Soviet Union was an issue to which American delegates in particular referred constantly. The 1987 Chautauqua conference abounded in references to the question. Malkov, in addressing a question from the floor about the general situation, received a fairly negative response when he asserted that any who wanted to leave the Soviet Union could indeed apply for a visa and that, so far as he knew, there were problems only in isolated cases. In contrast, a striking personal defense of the rights of refuseniks came when Mace Levin, a Chautauquan, called the Jewish refusenik problem "a litmus test" that would show the world whether the policy of glasnost was little more than words.

The question of regional conflicts also brought much positive response from the audience when one speaker or another pointed a possible way ahead in resolving such conflicts. At the 1986 conference in Jurmala the subject was hotly debated. The audience response throughout the addresses of Sonnenfeldt and Shishlin, for example, turned from negative to positive only when the speakers addressed the possibility of resolving the regional conflicts.

4. The arts. If we use audience applause as one measure of the "mind" of those who attended the Chautauqua conferences, the performing arts should necessarily be included in any list. The previous chapters have summarized many of these performances. The summaries typically refer to the "long" or "sustained" applause that followed joint Soviet-American recitals in music, theater, and ballet. The musical component of both the Riga and Tbilisi conferences was of particular importance. The cultural events, special performances, and classical and jazz performances added what Guroff later called "an emotional kick" and brought an easy camaraderie to balance the events of the day. The evening performances of jazz and classical music uniformly involved collaboration between artists of the two nations. With Soviet and American officials in the audience, the hidden political message became quite clear: "If they can get their act together, why can't you?".

It is important to note that at the first Chautauqua conference in 1985 very few of the performers and none of the Chautauqua staff had had any experience of international artistic collaboration. Lists of who was expected to perform were regularly changed in advance of the conference. Initial attempts at simultaneous translation were frustratingly awkward. Some of the performers also proved that the prima donna temperament transcends national boundaries. Yet in the end, things came together well. It was a competition in which the participants sought only to do well together.

When Grover Washington Jr., Butler, and Cecil played with their Latvian counterparts in Riga, it was obvious from the look in the eyes of the Latvian players that there was, first, genuine gratitude for being introduced to the best in contemporary American jazz and, second, sheer pleasure in being part of a harmony they had not before experienced. A comment by Wallach deserves to be repeated. After attending the rehearsal of Fodor and Sarantseva, he noted that although they could not understand one another's language, they were conversing with each other in the universal language of music. Similarly, in looking back on these years, Mennino, then program director for the institution, turned aside from her usual manner of conversation to declare with feeling and solemnity, "We knew we were part of history."

From the first, then, a harmony was achieved in the arts—dance, opera, orchestral music, and jazz—that the public conversations seldom matched. Indeed, the various performers in some ways had their own separate conferences during the official ones. The artistic tasks—spending time in preparing for performances, going around theaters, setting up lights, doing sound checks, and rehearsing with the visiting Latvian or Georgian artists —separated the performers from most of the official conference activities but at the same time bound them together in a quite different way. As Mennino described the situation,

> Whenever the performers came through the door there was only one
> idea: We want to work together, and we want to find out about each
> other. Once you were behind the proscenium or in the theater, all the
> politics fell away. Everyone was there for the same purpose. They
> knew that, come six or eight o'clock, five hundred people or three
> thousand people were going to show up for a performance. And they
> expected a good performance. Everybody was there for the same thing.
> The only kind of conflict we had was how to do things better.

Certainly, unofficial political comments were made at such performances. In Latvia, just before the performance of *Swan Lake* with Susan Jaffe, Patrick Bissell, and Christian Holder, a Latvian stage manager pulled Mennino aside and said to her, "Go back and tell your people to remember us." On another occasion, another Latvian asked her if she would like to see how

Latvian musicians really lived. The two got in a car and, seeking to avoid the security police, were driven through the streets of Riga. They arrived at a large concrete apartment block, walked up five flights of stairs, and entered a small apartment. The occupants were a young musician and his wife who had not succeeded in having their names on the approved list. There was piano music, conversation, and tea, with Mennino wondering in the meantime how it had been possible to bring the upright piano up five flights of stairs.

The Five Conferences: An Assessment

Different as they were in style, content, and location, the five conferences had much in common. Each brought delegates together to discuss the four constant themes of arms control, regional issues, human rights, and the bilateral agenda. At Chautauqua in 1985, the Soviet government had only official delegates present, who presented for the most part the official Soviet line on the four issues. From the time of the 1986 Jurmala conference, citizens of both countries were present, far outnumbering the official delegates.

Since the three central conferences (Jurmala in 1986, Chautauqua in 1987, and Tbilisi in 1988) form a distinct unity and should be regarded as the dominant achievement of the Chaautauqua Institution during these years, it will be useful to deal with the first and the last in the series together.

The 1985 Conference at Chautauqua

The first conference was a courageous move on the part of the Chautauqua planners. It was a necessary preparation and a stimulus to venture further. It was also innovative, meaning that it brought invited Soviet and U.S. diplomats together to discuss international relations at a time when contacts between Soviet and U.S. officials were limited and strained. Many agreements between the two countries had been suspended because of the Soviet invasion of Afghanistan. The cultural exchange agreement had lapsed. There were no museum or performing arts exchanges. Academic exchanges continued but at a relatively low level.

The 1985 conference was significant also in that it assembled some of the best thinkers in the Soviet government and military. At the time, Primakov was not well known outside his own country, but he eventually became one of the most prominent Soviet leaders. Parastaeyev also rose to a position of high leadership. Chautauqua thus was an assembly from which Soviet political and military leaders like these could draw an enriched understanding of the values the United States espouses—freedom of speech, press, and religion, for example. However much they may have been influenced by the Chautauqua experience, it is clear that as they established their careers later, they did so in ways that were friendly to the United States and to their commitment to seek peace in the face of hostility.

However much it lacked by the absence of a Soviet citizens' delegation, the first conference at Chautauqua was essential, if only, first, for bringing into the open the aggressive confrontation then present in U.S.-Soviet relations and, second, for offering at least a glimmer of hope that these relations could move eventually to a level of cautious collaboration. From the beginning there was indeed confrontation. Nitze had insisted at Chautauqua in 1985 that the Soviet line was preposterous, predictable, and hypocritical. It was a speech so tough that moderator Wallach had felt compelled to remind the audience that Nitze was not really an "unreasoning zealot." Nitze's opposite number, Malkov, was no less uncompromising in his assault on the increase of American weaponry. "If one wants to make nuclear weapons obsolete," he asked ironically, "why does the United States want to increase the number of nuclear weapons? There is no logic here." Such confrontation was the recurring pattern of the 1985 conference.

Yet a note of hope was by no means absent. "We are in a period," Palmer had said, "when the overall relationship is bad. But I place hope on parts of the agenda where we can make headway." Furthermore, when the seven-member Soviet delegation from the Soviet Union appeared in the Amphitheater on the first day of the conference, a huge audience, mostly American citizens, would not only hear the official Kremlin line on disarmament and the American line on the Strategic Defense Initiative, they would also see Soviet officials in the unfamiliar role of taking part in a free and open atmosphere of dialogue and exchange with their American counterparts.

Finally, it is doubtful if any of the conferences that followed Chautauqua 1985 would have taken place had it not been for the courage, insight, and perhaps even at times bravado of the Chautauquans who planned it.

The 1989 Pittsburgh Conference

The concluding conference was substantial in its content, perhaps even too bounteous. The many programs covered a huge variety of themes. Confrontation was still present, as in the debate between Wolfowitz and Shishlin. Wolfowitz had accused the Soviet Union of engineering in Afghanistan "the largest airlift of arms and materiel in Soviet history," only to hear Shishlin in response say, "Paul, whose missiles are striking Kabul? Whose missiles are killing old men, women, and children without any discrimination?" In most of the discussions at Pittsburgh, however, we find ourselves in a new world of thinking—a new political and intellectual world—concerning relationships of friendship between the two powers.

To use the phrase of Bratton in a private conversation after the Pittsburgh conference: "In 1985, we were talking *at* one another. In 1989, we were talking *with* one another." Whatever it was, Pittsburgh was a *talking* conference. The following list covers only part of the bounty that was offered to the delegates: nuclear and conventional arms control, the changing roles of men and women, reproductive issues, abortion, family, drug and alcohol abuse, space, the environment, religious pluralism, and ethnicity and cultural pluralism. The list reveals that, for the first time in four years, women's issues were coming to the fore and in a necessary and appropriate manner.

Conceding that the Pittsburgh conference could not have taken place had it not been preceded by the four from 1985, it is probably fair to say that the conference was in a literal sense superfluous." By the time of Pittsburgh, all who took part had already discovered that they were very like each other, even if divided by language. They conversed for a week with one another of things they shared in common and of their day-to-day struggles and achievements. Yet the extraordinary character of the Pittsburgh conference lay in this very ordinariness. The times of confrontation were past, even if some doubts and fears still lingered concerning the future of U.S.-Soviet relations. Confidence and even optimism ran more strongly now in the blood than anxiety and disquiet.

By the time of Pittsburgh, however, the conferences had become a victim of their own success. Much of the debate had been heard before. To discuss in a single conference subjects as varied and far apart from one another as the Strategic Defense Initiative and religious pluralism inevitably left some issues little more than touched on in passing. The conference at Pittsburgh was probably too diverse, too extensive, and in some ways too repetitive, while the value of creating human contacts was less well perceived or even planned for.

The Second, Third, and Fourth Chautauqua Conferences
The three central conferences in the series should be regarded as the major contribution that Chautauqua Institution made to an amelioration of relationships between the United States and the Soviet Union in that period. They were a noble experiment and a constitutive part of a movement towards the peace and understanding that were crucial to the future of the world.

A year before the 1986 Jurmala conference, Gorbachev and Reagan had met in the Geneva summit. Reagan seems to have felt—with his sunny optimism—that if only people sat down and talked with one another, something might happen to improve their relationships. Guroff was soon afterwards appointed to direct the president's U.S.-Soviet Exchange Initiative, the agency intended to serve as a bridge between government-funded and privately-funded activities. Until the initiative was created, there had been considerable skepticism on the part of some government officials who preferred that the two spheres be kept apart. When Wallach and Bratton initially approached the exchange initiative to gain some official sanction for the Riga conference, one of their chief concerns was to ensure that nothing they did would fly in the face of government policy. At the same time they did not want to be too closely identified with government policy. The initiative became a willing partner in the operation from 1986 to 1988 and was responsible for securing the participation of U.S. government officials and prominent nongovernment people.

These three conferences began and ended with reminders that even the best-laid plans frequently go amiss and that the incubus of Soviet totalitarianism was still alive and threatening. The news of Daniloff's arrest had detained more than two hundred delegates in Washington and almost ended the conference before it began. It gave an occasion to several conservative figures in the U.S. government to withdraw their participation. That the Jurmala conference took place at all was a sign of what can happen at the intersection of opportunity and risk. This critical incident—or any other difficulty—could have stopped not only that conference dead but perhaps also any continuation of the series. Nevertheless, participants such as Sonnenfeldt, Wattenberg, Rhinesmith, Guroff, and Matlock were convinced that it was necessary to participate and by doing so gave high government visibility to the conference. Even as late as 1988 at Tbilisi, the violent response of the Soviet police and KGB agents when Georgian nationalists resorted to street protests in Jurmala reminded participants that the power of an older oppressive regime was still a force to be dealt with. The friendly and mostly peaceful tenor of the Tbilisi conference was shaken by an external event that might have seriously damaged the trust that had been slowly building in the days of the conference.

Despite continuing differences in rhetoric and confrontation—on both sides—the three-year period from Jurmala to Tbilisi was one in which reconciliation in present and potent form was realized against the background of long-standing hostility. Guroff had said in 1987 at Chautauqua that Soviets and Americans were really different people, but the difference did not arise out of an innate sense of hostility toward one another. They simply perceived the world around them in different ways.

According to Wallach, the five conferences were the first major test of glasnost and perestroika as a Soviet policy. The conference in Jurmala took place relatively soon after Gorbachev was inaugurated. By this time he had barely tested the concept of openness and restructuring. However, there appears little doubt that Gorbachev permitted (whether reluctantly or openly) the setting up of the Jurmala conference. It may be that he assumed that Chautauqua Institution was a left-wing organization and that it could be used to turn the American people against their government policies. In fact the opposite happened. Both sides ultimately accepted the bold experiment of the conferences because each thought it had particular advantages in doing so. The conferences offered an opportunity for collaboration at a time when there were literally no other conversations involving citizens of the two countries. Everything had been cut off. The conferences were an indication that something could indeed be done to bring people together.

The choice of Jurmala and Tbilisi was especially important as sites for the conferences. If they had taken place in Moscow, the likelihood would have been that invited speakers would have come in, delivered a prepared address, and then left. When Robb came at short notice to give an address in Jurmala, for example, the tone and tenor of his speech were more suitable to an American audience at home. The speech betrayed no awareness of the real achievements of the Tbilisi conference in the search for a language of mutual understanding. The separation made necessary by the geographical isolation of these two cities meant that the speakers for the most part stayed with the delegates for the days of the meetings. Citizens and officials got to know one another at a much closer level. In Riga and Tbilisi —and for the first time in the Soviet Union—Soviet citizens had been able to ask questions not only of the American delegates but also of their own. They could raise questions in uncensored debates of primary political importance. The debates were televised—in a limited fashion, to be sure— throughout the Soviet Union. Indeed, the word "Chautauqua" was adopted on Soviet television as a term for meetings to which the public had access. No doubt many in the audiences in Riga and Tbilisi were Communist Party functionaries, but the plenary sessions drew as many as three thousand at a time, most of whom were not subordinate officials but cultural and political leaders of some significance. Hundreds more were often unable to get into the place of meetings.

The 1986 Conference at Jurmala

In the words of Guroff, Jurmala was "a tough stretch" and the fact that it happened "nothing short of a miracle." The very holding of the conference contributed in at least some way to the development of the Latvian independence movement. The subject is large and complex and will be a subject to be assessed by Latvian historians. It gave public voice to what many Latvians had been thinking. While the independence movement began and would have continued without Chautauqua, the conference was a kind of catalyst to groups and organizations that perceived that they were otherwise on their own in their striving to achieve independence. Seven Latvians had been in the group that came from the United States. Had they not been part of the official delegation, it is unlikely they would have been granted visas to enter Latvia. In Riga they were able to establish contacts with many organizations. Guroff and his office proposed to assemble a much higher level of government officials in Riga than had come together in Latvia before this time. In this they had the support of Hartman, ambassador in Moscow, and of Matlock of the National Security Council. Despite the fact that several conservative figures took the Daniloff case as an excuse not to participate, participants such as Sonnenfeldt, Wattenberg, Rhinesmith, Guroff, and Matlock were convinced it was necessary to participate and thereby give high government visibility to the conference.[1]

There had been conflicts with the police about the admission of the public to the meetings, but the conflicts were mostly restrained. The Chautauqua response was simple: In the words of Daniel Bratton: "We are not selling tickets. These are public meetings." Many issues were raised in the plenary meetings and seminars that could never have been raised in public elsewhere. It was a week of constant coming and going: Americans, Latvians, and Russians walked with one another in the streets of the Riga, stayed in homes with one another, and visited strangers together.

The Jurmala conference was the first "town hall" meeting of its type held in the Soviet Union. As not least of its achievements, it proved that it was possible for an ordinary assembly to move governments in another direction. Governments in general do not regard citizen-to-citizen diplomacy as important. Interference in government policies and positions is not always welcomed, because government officials are often hostage to political and economic elites that basically set the policy. What Chautauqua did was to

---

1. In Chapter 2 there is a record of the vigorous disagreement between Becker and Wallach about whether the conference at Jurmala should be held in the face of Daniloff's arrest. In fact, whatever his initial response to the crisis, Wallach followed Shultz in his thinking about the better choice to take: the conference should go on.

insert ordinary people into a process in which they could have a position and influence. Pressure from the public can be discounted by officialdom or dismissed as inimical to prevailing policy. Chautauqua confirmed that the people-to-people track of diplomacy is a force to be reckoned with in political life.

If Gorbachev permitted or encouraged the conference, he deserves praise for taking the risk and for his courage in determining that the government and the nation were willing to face this kind of criticism. It may have been in his assessment of outcomes that since Jurmala was closest to Western Europe, it was one of the more liberal republics. So Jurmala would be the right place in which to test glasnost. The choice of Jurmala may also have been part of a deliberate design to force official U.S. recognition of the incorporation of Latvia into the Soviet Union. Bratton himself was later critical of Wallach's insistence on darting off the Aeroflot plane before any others after it had touched down at Riga airport. Wallach himself explained shortly before he died that he had done so deliberately, so that the first handshake by a Soviet official in Latvia should not be with a senior official of the U.S. government. He knew the Soviet government would use the occasion of the official U.S. party arriving in Latvia in an attempt to force a public recognition of Latvia by a simple shaking of hands. A gesture as simple as a handshake might have been a diplomatic incident.

Wallach was also convinced that the choice of Latvia as the site of the conference might or might not have been a Soviet ploy. Whether or not it was a ploy, and more to the point, it gave the United States, which had never recognized the incorporation of Latvia into the Soviet Union, an opportunity to reaffirm that position. It was for this reason that he sought to persuade some members of the Latvian community in the United States, a conservative community, not to oppose the conference but to become part of the official delegation. The visit to Latvia, he told them, would provide an opportunity to raise the flag of freedom in their homeland. As it turned out, the Soviet embassy was initially quite reluctant to issue visas to what they knew would be a right-wing Latvian delegation. Embassy officials assumed —correctly—that as soon as the Latvians arrived in their homeland they would begin to bring their message of support to the Latvian people in their occupied homeland.[2] Numbers of Latvians did indeed furtively give the

2. The American Latvian Association in the United States credits the Jurmala conference as one of the major motivators that led to the independence of Latvia in 1991.

Americans notes to take home to their families in the United States. As it turned out, one of the most moving moments of the week for the Latvians was when Richardson sang the spiritual "Free at Last" in the Dom Cathedral in Riga. To many Latvians in the audience it seemed like a call for revolution.

Jurmala 1986 was the first time in the history of the Soviet Union when a conference submitted Soviet policies to heavy criticism not only by U.S. officials but also by Soviet citizens. Moreover, it was televised from morning to evening throughout the nation. The majority of the audience in the first day or two was American citizens. Most of the Soviets present were Russians resident in Riga, some of whom had been handpicked by the government to participate and brought by train from Moscow. Very few Latvians were present. Every day outside the conference, however, there were hundreds and eventually thousands of Latvians who tried to gain access to the meetings. Soviet troops and police guarding the entrance prevented any access. Tension built up by midweek to such an extent that Wallach, as moderator, stopped the conference and declared that the American delegation would return home unless the Latvian citizens were given access and allowed to sit in the audience. Whatever else the gesture meant, and however risky the intervention, it was a blunt test of the limits of glasnost and a contribution of some kind to the Latvian struggle for freedom.

Prior to and during the course of the conference in Jurmala, a group under the name of Helsinki 86 had been exerting major efforts to achieve its goal of independence from the Soviet Union. The group had been secretly formed in the city of Liepaja, a port on the southwest of Latvia, earlier in the summer of 1986. Many of its members became involved in social and political activities to help free the republic from its "Sovietization." Others sought to revive the older Latvian folk culture, to repair old churches and monuments, or to address the problems of environmental degradation. On June 14 of that year the group held its first public demonstration at the Latvian Freedom Monument in Riga. Many political interpreters in Latvia regard this as the first step on the road to Latvian independence. Since the KGB did not bar the June 14 demonstration,[3] another and much larger demonstration took place in Riga on August 23, the anniversary of the Molotov-Ribbentrop Pact. Similar demonstrations took place in Tallinn in

---

3. Kalnins himself was informed that Gorbachev did not take the demonstration seriously and instructed the KGB to keep at a distance in the spirit of glasnost.

Estonia and Vilnius in Lithuania the same day, the first public protests in these countries. From that point, the avalanche could not be arrested. A group of the activists had learned about the September Chautauqua conference and had decided to go to Jurmala with a document demanding Latvia's independence. The KGB, however, prevented them from getting in to the conference.[4]

It is tempting to trace a line connecting the activists' petition with Matlock's opening statement in Jurmala reiterating official U.S. policy of non-recognition. A statement such as his, made on Soviet-occupied Latvian territory by a special assistant to the president of the United States, had a galvanizing effect on public opinion in Latvia, since to most Latvians at the time it seemed that the United States had given up on Latvia. Matlock's statement in itself, according to Kalnins,[5] gave the Latvian people courage and hope. Helsinki 86, Kalnins still believes, used that hope to instigate a mass movement that led to even larger organizations and eventual independence in 1991.

The 1987 Chautauqua Conference
The second conference to be held on the grounds of Chautauqua Institution was one characterized by the discovery and acceptance of different values and of the necessity for free thinking in political relationships. Guroff spoke in that summer about the difference between the Americans and Soviets, arguing that they were really different people but that the difference did not arise out of an innate sense of hostility towards one another. They simply perceived the world around them in different ways. These value differences affected the very way in which they approached each other in discussions. Malkov developed this idea of mutual understanding. "We can see the springs of new political thinking," he began. "What is necessary is free thinking. If we can project this new thinking on to present U.S.-Soviet relationships, we will begin to see an undistorted picture."

With Chautauqua 1987, we are in a different world from that of 1985, a different psychological and political world.

---

4. At the end of 1986, their statement was smuggled out of Latvia and made public by the American Latvian Association and the World Federation of Free Latvians. Helsinki 86 became even more active in 1987.

5. Kalnins, one of the U.S. delegation to the Jurmala conference, was born in a Latvian refugee camp in Munich, Germany. He lived in Chicago from 1951 to 1984 and was naturalized as a U.S. citizen in 1968. He gave up his citizenship in 1991 and in 1993 assumed duties as Latvian ambassador in Washington, D.C.

At the music roundtable held during the 1987 conference, Nathan Gottschalk, the head of Chautauqua Music School and conductor-director of the Music School Festival Orchestra, had extended his personal welcome to the Soviets. He said, "This is probably the only meeting where there is no reason for arguments." The statement was obviously appreciated by the audience and applauded by the panelists. "Music," Gottschalk continued, "gives us a pause for sisterly and brotherly love." His words have well summarized the form and content of the 1987 conference. The mood throughout was perceptibly different from the first at Chautauqua, held two years before. Controversy, dissent, and polemics were still on public display, and suspicions had by no means been allayed. Yet an underlying harmony was no less perceptible—or at least an intent to become closer as human beings and no longer as political adversaries. Chautauqua 1987 was a time of learning to trust more those whose culture, politics, and national experience had been so vastly different.

To what can we attribute the tangible change? Undoubtedly, for many who had participated, the week in Latvia the previous year had been momentous, even revelatory. Close up to one another and on a particular ground, American and Soviet citizens had come to know each other, not as enemies but as human beings whose primary needs—security, love, and nurture—were similar. The names and descriptions by which each had defined the other were no longer as divisive or even relevant.

On the concert stage, in conversations on Chautauqua's famous red brick path and in private homes, or on visits to farm, mall, or school away from the lecture platform, Chautauqua 1987 was a time of human discovery. The conference still centered on public speech—speeches about nuclear war, disarmament, regional conflicts, and human rights. For most who participated, however, it was the experiences outside the lecture halls that were to remain firmly embedded in their minds in later years—the arrival of the buses, homes stays, conversations on the plaza, and the making of new friendships.

The 1988 Conference at Tbilisi

The Georgia conference was the consummation of what the original planners of the series had hardly dared to hope for. Tbilisi and Georgia have always been different from the rest of the Soviet Union. The value of the Tbilisi conference is that it indicated the kind of impact that the Chautauqua process could have, namely, that of giving legitimacy to dissent. It provided a protective umbrella for people who wanted to speak out. And many did. Day by day, also, tempers could warm to explosion point. Many of the official delegates strongly held opinions, and inevitably there were many personal conflicts and severe differences of opinion. "We would wind up in hotels with people screaming at each other," Guroff later reflected. It may be, however, that anger is an emotion of attachment and controversy the ground of deeper knowledge and the way to fuller understanding. These Tbilisi had in abundance.

If an American government official had come to address a political issue in Tbilisi in 1982 or 1983, there is little question that the occasion would have been highly screened, and anything said would have been strictly edited. In 1988, things were quite different. The conference came at a time when there were the beginnings of a movement not so much for independence but for a kind of autonomy—the use of the Georgian language, for example, the practice of Georgian religion, and freedom from the Russian domination of policy. Questions had been raised by Georgians at some of the Tbilisi meetings: Why was it not possible to get typewriters with Georgian characters? Why was the Soviet army using a local shooting range that was next to a holy site? When the latter question was raised, Chervov replied that he had not known that such a thing was happening. The audience applauded his remarks. Following the meeting he was asked to call the chief of staff in Moscow and get a commitment to stop the shelling.

In Tbilisi there had been several street demonstrations, some by members of the Helsinki 86 group. Initially, the demonstrations had no connections with the conference nor any place in the agenda. As the week went on, however, they became linked to what was happening at the open meetings and even identified with some of the speeches. From the point of view of Soviet officials, the conferences meant that they had to be more responsive to the public. After the Tbilisi conference, there were some important changes in Soviet television programming. Pozner—who had been involved earlier in the Space Bridges program—was able to create public talk shows in which Soviets could express themselves on civic and political matters. He managed to convince some in the Soviet media that it was in their own interest to allow people to talk about such matters. While it was not a dam bursting, it involved a perceptible difference in the programming of Soviet television.

We may summarize the long-term importance of the Riga (1986), Chautauqua (1987), and Tbilisi (1988) conferences from the perspective, first, of the Chautauqua Institution and, second, of the citizen delegates. Finally we shall attempt to assess the part that the conferences played in the marked improvement in U.S.-Soviet relations between 1985 and 1989.

First, and from the perspective of the Chautauqua Institution, the impact of the conferences on those who took part was and remains extraordinarily powerful. They expanded the horizons of the institution beyond anything in the past and helped to shape its future directions. Unprecedented in the institution's history, they could be said to have worked out in a twentieth-century form the early credo of John Heyl Vincent: "Chautauqua has a message and a mission for the times." In this sense we may even affirm that the whole history of the institution—over a hundred years—was a preparation for the venture, not least because of Chautauqua's commitment to civil discourse and to the opening of the mind to new frames of thinking. Inexperienced in international politics though they were, Bratton and his staff neither flinched nor faltered. In the end, Bratton must be regarded as the institutional inspiration and Wallach the intellectual prime mover of the series. The process itself—bringing official and citizen delegates together, discussing issues in conversation with the audience, and creating a mix of speech and art—was no doubt open to being continued in other contexts. It was right, however, to end the series. The conferences began at the right time and ended at the right time. It was a responsible decision to recognize when the goal was achieved.

Second, the importance of the conferences was without question greater for the Soviet Union than for the United States. They were no doubt helpful to the American participants who took part, but Chautauquans had long been familiar with public debate and civil discourse about large political issues. For Soviet participants the experience was quite different. For years before the first conference in 1985, some of the best minds in the Soviet government and military had already been involved in discussing issues such as freedom and human rights. The Soviet government obviously placed a high value on what the conferences could represent and achieve. Having agreed to participate, Soviet officials of necessity had to sit down with their American counterparts and discuss political matters that, by the very fact of the discussion, were now open to public debate. The officials would discuss, but the public would eventually give the verdict by their applause or voiced rejection. The verdict would be given by citizens without regard to national identity or political loyalty.

One can see a kind of transfer of state sovereignty to popular sovereignty in the question-and-answer periods in the plenary sessions, the discussions in seminars and small groups, and the week's experience of strangers becoming friends. When Wattenberg referred controversially to the dropping of the bomb on Hiroshima and Nagasaki as a way of saving Soviet lives, there were hoots of derision. But the point was made at least to the Soviets: citizens had the right to freedom of speech in opposing a political interpretation from which they dissented.

The importance of citizen-to-citizen contact can hardly be exaggerated. During the 1987 conference on the grounds of the institution, two Chautauqua families, Marvin and Joan Rosenthal and John and Mary Ann McCabe, welcomed four Soviets as their guests. Two were interpreters (known to them only as Eugene and Alex) and two secretaries (Natasha and Nadia). The visit went well—initially. Evgeny Primakov paid a quick visit to the house, seemingly curious. Was all well? The hosts wondered. Joan decided to invite three refuseniks from Rochester, Helen and Boris Zapocechny and Vladimir Braave, to join the other four for dinner. She had helped to resettle the refuseniks in her city but had some apprehension about the visit. At dinner and the next day at breakfast all seven bonded well. Marvin later commented, "It's hard to be angry with people you've met and know."

The opportunity for home stays or home visits gave ordinary citizens an opportunity to get to know one another as human beings, first and to a small extent at Riga, in the next year and in a much larger way on the grounds of Chautauqua, and then fully at Tbilisi. It is harder to assess the part that the five conferences played in the marked improvement in U.S.-Soviet relations between 1985 and 1989. Without question, the critical second conference at Jurmala would never have taken place had it not been for President Gorbachev's interest and perhaps intervention. In the new thinking of glasnost Gorbachev had given primary emphasis to the need to avoid a nuclear catastrophe and to establish a dialogue with the United States intended to deepen mutual understanding. Chautauqua by this measurement provided for him the means, the locations, and the opportunity of working out, even in an early form, the implications of glasnost. According to Bratton, when he met Gorbachev at the Soviet embassy in December 1987 and introduced himself as the president of Chautauqua Institution, Gorbachev launched into "a very energetic, excited, and articulate statement about the quality of the Chautauqua conferences and the favorable reports that had come back to him from his colleagues."

In spite of his belligerent rhetoric, Reagan was genuinely dismayed by the policies of deterrence and mutually assured destruction and often spoke of the need to free the world of the peril of nuclear weapons. As early as September 1985 he had stated that there was no reason the two nations could not reach agreement on arms reduction. The Berlin wall, the most potent symbol since 1961 of the cold-war division of Europe, did fall in November 1989. In his welcome address to Gorbachev outside the White House in May 1990, Reagan's successor, President George H. W. Bush, pledged to help expand the new spirit of cooperation symbolized by glasnost not merely to resolve disputes between the two nations but also to build a solid foundation for peace, prosperity, and stability around the world. In his reply to Bush, Gorbachev paid tribute to "thousands of American and Soviet citizens" who had been involved in political contacts and humanitarian exchanges.[6]

Many thousands of Soviet and U.S. citizens had been involved in such exchanges even in the height of the cold-war years. So the Chautauqua conferences were five among many. Yet in several ways they were unlike any others. First, they were international, providing an opportunity for official delegates and citizens to see and gain a sense of what it meant to live in another land. Second, they were interfamilial—individuals and families welcomed foreigners as friends. To live, if only for a few days, with a host family was for the participants to discover that human beings may be divided by language but need not be by politics. Third, they involved what Chautauquans like to call "the mix." Chautauqua still describes itself as a center of the arts, education, religion, and recreation. The choice of the four nouns was not accidental. To spend a week or a month at Chautauqua is to be immersed in a series of academic courses, musical performances, leisure strolls, village square conversations, theological discussions, theater, seminars, instruction in the arts, gallery visits, opera, ballet, and services of worship with golf, boating, and sailing thrown in for good measure. The Chautauqua conviction is that learning is not an intellectual discipline alone; rather, "the whole of life is a school," to cite John Heyl Vincent once more. The five Chautauqua conferences on U.S.-Soviet relations were such a school of learning.

Several years after the last conference, Guroff himself raised the question of whether similar conferences may not be even more necessary in the present period but for different reasons. Since the formation of the Russian Federation, there has been an increasing feeling, he thought, particularly on the part of Russians, that the United States now regards and treats Russia no longer as a great power. Putin's decision to side with the United States in dealing with terrorism, the eastward move of NATO, the presence of American troops in Uzbekistan and Kurdistan, and the decision to let the ABM treaty lapse have all, Guroff suggests, contributed to an increasing distrust of Americans and their goals. It might well still be possible to have Chautauqua-like meetings across the Russian Federation and with enormous coverage in the media. It may be that some center—and which better than Chautauqua?—could plan and carry out a similar series of conferences on

6. *New York Times,* June 1, 1990.

U.S.-Iranian relations, or U.S.–Middle East relations, or even U.S.-Cuban relations. Any one would be hard to plan, harder to be approved, and harder still to accomplish. And yet—in the words of the memo that prepared the way for the first Chautauqua conference on U.S.-Soviet relations, "However great these risks, the possibilities are greater."

Selected Bibliography

Bialer, Seweryn and Michael Mandelbaum, eds. *Gorbachev's Russia and American Foreign Policy*. Boulder, Colo.: Westview Press, 1987.

Billington, James H. *Russia Transformed: Breakthrough to Hope*. New York: Free Press, 1992.

Bowles, Chester. *The New Dimensions of Peace*. New York: Harper & Brothers, 1955.

Gorbachev, Mikhail S. *Perestroika: New Thinking for Our Country and the World*. New York: Harper and Row, 1987.

———. *Toward a Better World*. New York: Richardson & Steirman, 1987.

Lippmann, Walter. *U.S. Foreign Policy: Shield of the Republic*. Boston: Little, Brown, 1943.

Richmond, Yale. *From Nyet to Da*. Yarmouth, Me.: Intercultural Press, 1992.

Shevardnadze, Eduard. *The Future Belongs to Freedom*. New York: Free Press, 1991.

Shultz, George P. *Turmoil and Triumph: My Years as Secretary of State*. New York: Charles Scribner's Sons, 1993.

Smith, Hedrick. *The New Russians*. New York: Avon Books, 1991.

Weinberger, Caspar W. *Fighting for Peace*. New York: Warner Books, 1990.

INDEX

ABOUT THE AUTHOR

ROSS MACKENZIE is historian emeritus of the Chautauqua Institution and the author of *Threads: A Book of Prayers and Stories*. Prior to coming to the institute, Mackenzie taught history at Union Theological Seminary in Virginia for twenty years.